THE COMMERCIALIZATION OF AMERICAN CULTURE

THE COMMERCIALIZATION OF AMERICAN CULTURE

NEW ADVERTISING, CONTROL AND DEMOCRACY

by Matthew P. McAllister

SAGE Publications
International Educational and Professional Publisher
Thousand Oaks   London   New Delhi

For information address:

SAGE Publications, Inc.
2455 Teller Road
Thousand Oaks, California 91320
E-mail: order@sagepub.com

SAGE Publications Ltd.
6 Bonhill Street
London EC2A 4PU
United Kingdom

SAGE Publications India Pvt. Ltd.
M-32 Market
Greater Kailash I
New Delhi 110 048 India

Printed in the United States of America

Library of Congress Cataloging-in-Publication Data

McAllister, Matthew P.
    The commercialization of American culture: New advertising, control and democracy / Matthew P. McAllister.
        p.   cm.
    Includes bibliographical references and index.
    ISBN 0-8039-5379-8 (c: alk. paper).—ISBN 0-8039-5380-1 (p: alk. paper)
        1. Advertising—Social aspects—United States. 2. Mass media—Social aspects—United States. 3. Advertising—United States—History—20th century. I. Title
    HF5813.U6M327   1995
    659.1'042—dc20   95-35569

This book is printed on acid-free paper.

96 97 98 99 10 9 8 7 6 5 4 3 2

Sage Production Editor: Astrid Virding
Sage Typesetter: Andrea D. Swanson

For My Mother
Marjorie F. McAllister

CONTENTS

ACKNOWLEDGMENTS

I am indebted to so many people who have helped focus this project, improve it and support it. I simply cannot name them all. Some deserve special recognition, however. The project was born during an advertising criticism seminar I taught at Denison University. In the Department of Communication there, Suzanne Condray, Laurel Kennedy and Lynn Lovdal provided a nurturing and enthusiastic environment for a young faculty member. My friends and colleagues in the Department of Communication Studies at Virginia Tech have also been fantastic. It is a great department to work in. Robert E. Denton, Jr., was instrumental in the early phases of this project, looking over initial conceptualizations. Other faculty such as Detine Bowers, Rebekah Bromley, Marshall Fishwick, Louis Gwin, Rachel Holloway, Gayle Noyes, Stephen Prince, Edd Sewell and Beth Waggenspack have likewise been very supportive and made helpful suggestions. Two departmental compadres have been especially dear. Scott Patterson has listened patiently to my gripes and offered insights about media studies in general and new media technologies in particular. Special thanks go to Mary Beth Oliver, who has read (very) rough drafts of the book, cogently discussed media issues and overall been a wonderful friend and colleague. Others have contributed as well. Valuable research anecdotes and poker lessons were provided by John Christman, a philosopher at Tech, and Rachel Parker-Gwin, a sociologist. My long-time pals Dan and Karen Davis, Kathy and Wayne Evans and David Walter provided places to escape to when the academic world became a bit too harried. The chapter on zapless ads benefited from comments by Carolyn Byerly, Sally Sevcik and Buddy Timberg. Ivy Glennon, Sharon Mazzarella, John Nerone and Anghy Valdivia helped keep my spirits up through book-writing problems. Catherine Warren contributed strength, good cheer and superb editing suggestions for two early chapters. Ross Wolin, as usual, offered observations about our world that astounded me with their depth. D. Charles Whitney gave me focus and confidence with his detailed review of an earlier draft. At Sage, Sophy Craze provided just the right combination of concrete suggestions and positive reinforcement.

Finally, I wish to thank the many students in my classes who have listened to different versions of these ideas, challenged them and helped me to justify my values and observations.

INTRODUCTION

W HEN politicians or social commentators evaluate the importance of different industries to society, they will often stress the economic weight of the industries. Different industries are important because of their contribution to the national economy. Media industries can be evaluated in this way, and by this criterion they are quite impressive. The communication industry as a whole generated around $137 billion in revenue in 1992 (U.S. Bureau of the Census, 1994). By this strictly economic measure, the media are socially important.

The economic clout of media industries is not their real social significance, however. Unlike the automobile industry or the fast-food industry, the media are important—if for no other reason—because of their potential contribution to democracy. Our entire philosophy of governance depends upon a functioning media system. The protection granted by the First Amendment, in fact, is an acknowledgment of the importance of media to democratic life. The media, then, serve the public interest and the public good beyond what economic benefits they provide. They are crucial not just to the people they employ, but also to every citizen. To use a definition from the field of public planning, a media organization serves the public interest when it "serves the ends of the whole society rather than those of some sectors of society" (cited in McQuail, 1991, p. 71).

Why are the media so important to the public good? Because a democracy—classically defined as government by, for and of the people—cannot work without as many of the "people" being informed as possible. A perfect system of representation, in which all people can expect and are granted full participation in the decisions affecting their lives, is useless if people are forced to make decisions in ignorance or with slanted information. Democracy assumes an informed populace. It assumes that all sectors and subgroups of the populace will be equally well informed. A well-developed media system, informing and teaching its citizens, helps democracy move toward its ideal state.

In order for a media system to function perfectly in a democracy, it must do several things. First, a democratic media must be accessible. One may define *accessibility,* though, in several ways. This ideally democratic media system must be *symbolically* accessible. That is, it has to be understandable to people. An advanced lecture on nuclear physics, although potentially chock full of useful information needed by us to make informed decisions about nuclear power, is useless if it is filled with technical jargon and assumes a Ph.D.-level of knowledge. The media must use images and language that people can access, whatever their educational level or knowledge of specialized topics.

Besides symbolic accessibility, a media system must also be *economically* accessible. If only the well-to-do have access to mediated information, then the media become antidemocratic because different sectors of society have different levels of information. Economic accessibility, though, does not just mean the media should be available to all regardless of ability to pay; if media content is written for and of interest to *only* the economic elites of society, then this specialization becomes a barrier as prohibitive as high cost.

Geographic accessibility is also a necessity for this ideal media system. All geographic locations in which citizens are found must have as much equal access to information as possible. Distinctions such as urban/suburban/rural or west coast/midwest/east coast should not bias the quality or quantity of media sources available. And as with economic accessibility, true geographic accessibility involves more than simple physical access to media, it also means having a media system that represents the interests of different geographic locations. A final aspect of accessibility involves access to the *industrial* process of media. Truly democratic media, for example, would cultivate strong feedback mechanisms to ensure that the media system does indeed fulfill, ideally, the needs of citizens. At the very least, this would ensure an authentic flow of communication not just from the media to the citizens, but also the reverse. Citizens would have access to media routinely and genuinely. This might even take the form of citizen-run media systems, in which different constituencies actually produce their own mediated messages.

But the complex nature of media access—symbolic, economic, geographic and industrial—is just one element of our perfect, democratic media. Besides accessibility, the *content* of media should be diverse. *Diversity* touches upon the issues discussed above: Media should have appeal for all economic ranges of society and all geographic sectors. The fullest sense of this concept, however, does not connote a "lowest common denominator" nor just an economic or geographic diversity. Diversity also includes the legitimate placement of different social and cultural voices in the media. As Curran (1991) argues, the democratic media system "should be organized in a way that enables diverse social groups and organizations to express alternative viewpoints" (p. 103). No one perspective would dominate. Different feminist positions, economic philosophies or ethnic groups, for instance, should have access to media in such a way that their voices and social perspectives are visible and easily available. One might also define diversity according to the purpose of the content. Different sources could exist for more straightforward, "objective" information, whereas others could clearly be analysts and interpreters of this information. Likewise, fiction or entertainment media would also contribute to the democratic diversity. By enhancing the identification and role taking of different social positions, fictional media would serve a valuable function in the spreading of diverse perspectives and social values (Curran, 1991, p. 102).

Relevancy to the democratic functioning of society is another criterion for judging the democratic value of media. Does the media provide not just accessible and diverse information, but is it also *relevant* to helping us make the decisions that affect our lives? Taking the issue of relevancy to its logical conclusion, do the media actively help people to participate democratically? Do they facilitate social and political organization? Do they help groups organize protests or meetings? The media may help turn the ideas of a democracy into the behavioral action of a democracy. In other words, the democratically oriented media should not just air or promote diverse perspectives, but also "create the conditions in which alternative viewpoints and perspectives are brought into play" (Curran, 1991, p. 102).

Finally, one last democratic characteristic of media is that content would be *engaging*. The content would not be dull and listless, but rather would grab the citizenry and excite them about the content. In this democratic utopia, content would draw in "media citizens," enticing them to learn more about their society and other perspectives. If the media are boring, so that people dread its accessibility, diversity and relevance, then such media are useless for political participation.

The ideal media system in a democracy, then, would be accessible at a variety of levels, diverse, relevant and engaging. Put another way, the media would serve as a prime vehicle for the creation of a truly functional *public sphere,* a term coined by the German philosopher Jürgen Habermas and later refined by such scholars as Nancy Fraser (Fraser, 1993; Habermas, 1989). The public sphere, as articulated by such scholars as Fraser, is a place where different social positions can gather to voice their positions, and no single voice dominates the discourse. Citizens hash out issues, and the notion of the public good becomes salient and central. The public sphere is not overwhelmingly influenced, especially by the powers of the government, nor of patriarchy, nor of commercialism. In fact, this is a social location where criticisms of such systems can thrive. Obviously, the mass media would be prime contributors to the vitality and usefulness of this public sphere. They would be a prime vehicle for the airing of perspectives and a place where dominant values and institutions would be explored, questioned and challenged. The media should provide public *spaces,* where public *discourse,* in the public *interest,* might help develop this ideal of the public *sphere.* With a perfect media system, true participatory democracy occurs in this vision of the public sphere.

Let us now leave the realm of the ideally democratized media and the ideal public sphere and move to reality. The current U.S. media system is not ideally suited to a democracy. In many ways it is abysmal, even antidemocratic. Economic barriers may prevent those with small incomes from affording access to cable television, for example, and thus effectively exclude them from such outlets as C-SPAN. Geographic barriers exist as well. One-cable-system towns might have a variety of home shopping channels on their system, but no Bravo. Towns dominated by mall theaters might have two screens that carry *Dumb and*

Dumber but none that carry *Quiz Show*. The one-newspaper town is now the overwhelming norm rather than the exception. Even when the media are physically pervasive, the creation of programming that appeals to such groups as the poor or the rural is shockingly scarce. The typical citizen's access to the industrial world of media is a joke. Beyond the Letters to the Editor page, the occasional phone call from Nielsen researchers or the marginalized public access cable station, the media's production process is blocked from the users of media. The behind-the-scenes world of media is a mysterious one for us.

Similarly, the diversity of media content is very limited. A 500-channel cable system that has been in the dreams of media decision makers is really a vision of more-of-the-same. The C-SPANs and Bravos are rare. The F/Xs of the world, with reruns of *Family Affair* and *The Ghost and Mrs. Muir,* dominate. When broadcasters do create new TV outlets, as in the 1994 launch of the Time Warner and Paramount networks, we are presented with such "innovative" shows as *Unhappily Ever After* (essentially, *Married . . . With Children* meets *Alf*) and *Platypus Man* (essentially, *Home Improvement* with a frying pan instead of a buzz saw). If one wants to see endless variations on the sitcom genre, of "reality-based" police in action or of scandal-based talk programs, then the media offer plenty. But if one wants to see capitalism critiqued from a socialist point of view, an exploration of social issues from a variety of feminist portrayals, a discussion of the homeless as produced by people who have been or currently are homeless or a wide-ranging discussion of the economy on prime time (when most people watch), then the media become a sea of sameness. Content, content, content everywhere, but not a democratic drop to drink.

How relevant is media content? The answer (at least for 1994-1995 media) can be summed up by two initials: O. J. The media's obsession with this celebrity/violence drama—from the hours devoted to the white Bronco to the hours devoted to lawyer strategy and bickering—reveals that something other than the democratically relevant dominates their agenda. And before O. J. there were Michael (now Michael and Lisa Marie), the Bobbitts, the Menendezes and Nancy and Tonya.

Do the media do anything well on the list of democratically desirable items? Of course. In general, the content of media is very understandable. Very rarely are sitcoms, or even the most prestigious PBS documentaries, confusing.

The media fare even better on another criterion; the media are profoundly engaging. They are designed to grab our eyeballs and glue them to the screen or page. That is why we have *The Brady Bunch* and O. J. and Michael so often on TV; that is why we have Ace Ventura at the movies; that is why we have colorful Lifestyle sections in the newspapers; that is why TV news often looks more like MTV than news. On this engaging criterion the media receive an A+. Of course, the criterion in and of itself is not destructive. What becomes destructive is when engaging content becomes the *main* thing that media offer. It is like a massive smorgasbord with nothing but different flavors of ice cream.

Why are the media like this? Why do the media, to which our government grants special First Amendment protection to encourage the democratic process, fail so badly in achieving the ideal? The answer is that the media have few incentives to serve democracy. That is not the primary purpose of media. The media are designed for another goal: to make money. Unfortunately, sometimes what is in the media's best economic interest is not in society's best democratic interest. If serving democracy is the cheapest, fastest or most efficient way to make money, then fine. If serving democracy gets in the way of making money, though, then the stronger, more direct incentive wins. The media in our country are economic and industrial entities. In this sense they *are* like other businesses. The *New York Times, Newsweek,* CBS and CNN all are overwhelming profit-driven organizations. The profit motive is the engine that drives decisions about the content we receive.

And for the majority of media, the fuel that powers this engine is advertising.

And even for media that appear to be non-advertising supported, advertising is often a crucial fuel additive.

This book is about the potential influence that new forms of advertising may be having on public ideas and on the media's role in a democratic society. With a few exceptions, I believe that industrialized media have not done a good job in serving a participatory citizenship. Unfortunately, unless things change, I also believe that the media will be even worse in serving this citizenship in the future. A major influence for this conclusion is the current direction of advertising.

In the 1980s, changes in society greatly affected advertising. These social forces included dynamics in the technological environment (like the popularization of cable television, remote controls and VCRs) and the political environment (the deregulatory policies of the Republican administrations during that decade). Because of these factors, advertising has initiated new venues and techniques for selling and promoting, with these new initiatives especially taking hold beginning in the late

1980s/early 1990s. This book discusses the pervasiveness and implications of advertising's new direction. The implications include not just the effect upon the ads themselves, but also upon the environment of the ads. The environment may be the media content that surrounds the ads (the television show, the magazine article). Or, increasingly, it may be the influence advertising has upon a more broadly defined environment: the supposedly "ad-free" motion picture, the auto race sponsored by Winston or the ad-supported Channel One found in school systems. Taken as a totality, the advertising context and promotional movement since the 1980s is pushing this industry toward one of two strategies: either exploring new social locations for its use, or tightening its control over established, already exploited, advertising locations. Such trends have profound implications for the thrust of American culture, including the forms that culture takes right now, as well as the direction that cultural phenomena are heading.

Although separate chapters of this book explore the different advertising trends, such as place-based media or cross promotion, one theme of the book is that these phenomena are related—sparked by the same trends and often designed to accomplish the same things. In fact, because of the common threads among newly developed advertising tactics, one occasionally finds examples that seem to illustrate *all* the advertising trends discussed. A good example is *Colors* magazine, the biannual publication by Benetton, the global fashion company ("Print," 1992, April 27). Because *Colors* is distributed at Benetton retailers, and because the magazine accepts advertisements for products other than those made by Benetton, it is an example of place-based advertising. Because many of the articles and the ads seem to blur together into Benetton's "hip" consumer environment, however, it is also an example of a camouflaged ad vehicle. And still, because the external advertisers are looking to plug into the preexisting company image of Benetton, the magazine has characteristics of cross promotion. Finally, because Benetton as a company was involved in the development and initial financial structure of the magazine, it is an example of sponsorship.

Despite such slippery examples, though, it is justifiable to separate the trends analytically. The advertising industry itself discusses these trends as distinct tactics. For instance, trade journals might have separate sections on Sponsorship or Place-Based Media. Also, the specific strategies and goals of the trends, as well as the reasons they developed, justify their autonomous discussion. Each trend illustrates different strategies and implications of advertising in the 1990s.

Chapter 1 discusses the context of advertising that has led to the increased popularization of new forms. The chapter explores the promotional environment that the 1980s created for advertising. During that time, the environment had a peculiar split personality. On the one hand, the industry was forced to change because of developments that it preferred not to have occurred, like the pervasiveness of advertising clutter. On the other hand, the environment empowered advertisers to change because of developments the industry eagerly welcomed, like deregulation. In other words, this chapter argues that the notions of advertising *control* began to change in the 1980s, with profound effects for our mediated lives now.

Chapter 2 explores what social critics have had to say about the degree of control over our lives traditional advertising has had, especially concentrating on some of advertising's antidemocratic effects. The chapter attempts to combine the work of economic critics of advertising (those who look at the effect of advertising upon media content) and symbolic critics of advertising (those who look at the messages of the advertisements themselves). The concept of control is a central one for understanding the promotional industry's new directions, as this chapter will argue. The first two chapters form a bond that binds the rest of the book together, and each of the following chapters will often refer back to the basic contextual and theoretical foundation laid out in the beginning of the book.

Place-based advertising, the systematic creation of advertising-supported media in different social locations (including doctors' offices and airports) is the focus of Chapter 3. After the widespread nature of place-based advertising is established—leaving practically no social place untouched—the chapter will explore the implications of the strategy, including what the strategy may do to these social places as well as to our "sense of place."

Chapter 4 turns its focus on traditional media, especially television. Many of the changes discussed in this book look at how advertising has explored alternatives to traditional spot ad placement. This chapter, though, examines the way advertising has tried to readjust spot advertising in the established media, especially television. Having as their goal the development of "zapless" ads, TV advertisers have cultivated techniques such as ads that exploit viewer expectations and anticipations (like the Energizer Bunny ads), ads with a liberal dose of written words and camouflaged ads (like infomercials).

Chapter 5 looks at the new cooperative attitude promoters have encouraged through cross promotion. Concentrating on specific contextual problems that have encouraged cross promotion as a major strategy in the 1990s, the chapter goes on to discuss the functions that cross promotion serves, stressing that trend's pervasive, multilayered and multi-placed nature.

Sponsorship, discussed in Chapter 6, has also increased since the 1980s. As the chapter discusses, sponsorship is a modern form of promotion that has been increasingly pushed closer to advertising than to philanthropy, its two philosophical, but dichotomous, touchstones. The chapter focuses on how sponsorship operates in modern life and its effects upon democratic spheres of society.

Chapter 7 focuses on advertising's use of computer technology. How has the computer allowed advertising to target its messages more specifically, through the use of "database marketing" techniques? Likewise, what are some implications for advertising control that are already apparent with the "information superhighway"? How has advertising used the Internet and commercial networking services to gain a foothold in this new communication technology?

Finally, Chapter 8 closes with a brief summary of many of the commonalities among the trends. The chapter reviews the antidemocratic effects of new advertising and discusses some avenues of resistance.

MATTHEW P. MCALLISTER

1

THE CHANGING NATURE OF
ADVERTISING AND CONTROL

IF you were an advertising executive in charge of a new advertising campaign for a new product—say a new hair spray product called "Stick 'EmUp"—you of course would want the advertising campaign to be as successful as possible. Your goal, after all, is to sell a lot of cans of Stick 'EmUp. But there are problems that get in your way of successful selling. If you do not get these problems under control, you might not achieve your sales quota. The biggest problem is that people are resistant to giving up money, and you ideally want to control their behavior so that they will reach into their wallets and plunk down the dough. Unfortunately for you, you do not have much direct control over that level of behavior. Yet there are other problems that you can correct, other things over which you have more control. Your hope is that you will have enough control over these other problems to help solve your biggest one. Some of these other problems revolve around the persuasive appeals in the ads themselves; others center on the mediated or viewing environment of the ads.

For example, one obvious factor that advertisers want to control is how potential consumers view their product. They know that advertising is a huge influence here. Thus, in your advertising strategy meeting for Stick 'EmUp, you might discuss how best to influence the buyer's perception of the hair spray. You might ask, "How can we best influence the meanings and associations that consumers have of our product?" "What are the images that are very desirable to our targeted market, and how can we link our product with these images in the ads?" "What anxieties about people's hair appearance can we exploit?" And once you resolve these issues, you then want to ensure that potential consumers interpret the ad in ways that agree with your goals. Advertisers want control over the audience interpretations of the symbols in the ad. So you might also ask, "How can we position the symbols in the ads to maximize acceptance of our intended meaning?" "How can we cut down on 'undesirable' interpretations?"

Advertisers also want control over the viewing behavior of the audience. You want to make sure that the audience actually notices the ad. You ask, "How do we grab their attention in this ad?" "Can we keep them from going to the bathroom during the commercial?" "Can we keep them from using the remote control?"

In addition, advertisers want to control things external to the ad that may influence how people view their product. This means, for example, that advertising tries to control not just the symbols in the ads, but even sometimes the meanings that the symbols represent. As the Stick 'EmUp advertiser, you might decide that you want to have a celebrity endorser, but you want only a celebrity who will maintain a certain image. If you decide to make Sheryl Crow your endorser, you might ask, "Should we put in an escape clause so we can drop her as an endorser if she is involved in a scandal?" "Should we demand that she not endorse other products that may not fit in with the image we want her to have for us?"

Advertisers want control over how and when the audience is exposed to the ad. "How do we best reach our desired market?" "What is the best media mix to blanket this audience?" "How frequently do we want to reach this market so that they'll remember our ads?" "How do we avoid paying for audiences we do not want to reach?" "Do we need to use other methods besides traditional media?" "What mix of traditional media, direct sales and sales promotion (like couponing) do we use?"

Another factor you want to control is the media environment that surrounds your ads for Stick 'EmUp. You want to make sure that the media content around your advertisements complements the messages and tones of your ads. Control over the media environment might be the focus of several questions during an advertising strategy meeting. You might throw out questions like, "Does the tone of *Rolling Stone* or of *Spin* better fit the tone of our print ads?" "Should we pull our ad from the NBC sitcom episode with the gay character because it might upset viewers?" "Will doing so encourage the producers to give us only characters conducive to our ads in the future?" "Should we produce our own media content to guarantee the best symbolic ambience?"

You also want control over the other ads that run near your ads. You might ask, "In our network TV ads, is there a Vidal Sassoon ad running in the same advertising 'pod' [the same block of consecutive ads] as our commercial for Stick 'EmUp?" You might be concerned that viewers will not pay as much attention to the Stick 'EmUp message because a competing ad is too close. You might even want to have a talk with the TV networks that carry your ads to ensure the best placement. If necessary, you can always threaten to pull your money from the networks and place your ads (and your dollars) elsewhere if the nets do not cooperate.

Advertisers want control over the viewing environment in which consumers are exposed to the ad. So if you decide to advertise on television, you might ask, "Will our potential customers worry about their hair more at night or in the morning?" "Should we advertise on Thursday night to reach people who are starting to think of weekend activities, including new hairstyles?"

But again, what advertisers want most is control over the buying habits of the audience. Perhaps because this final event, with which the institution is most concerned, is ultimately *out* of its control, the advertising industry seeks to gain the most control possible over the other elements of life.

In fact, when critics talk about advertising being "out of control," what they really mean is that advertising has too much control. Advertising is out of control when it has successfully wrested power away from other social institutions or individuals on the above mentioned issues (and even on other issues, as well). Such concern with the degree of control that advertising has is not new, of course. As Presbrey (1968) notes, one critic in 1867, practically at the infancy of the industrialized age, found advertising so pervasive and accepted that he called it "the monomania of our times" (p. 259). The issue of advertising control is one that has consumed critics of advertising almost since they began aiming their guns at the commercial target.

What I argue in this chapter is that changes in the environment of the advertising industry in the 1980s have opened new locations and techniques of control for today's advertising that later chapters will explore. Specifically, I argue that there have been changes in media, in viewing technology, in the amount of advertising and in regulation that have altered the conventional wisdom of advertising control techniques. In the 1990s, we are witnessing the results of these changes. Ultimately, advertisers' reactions to the 1980s have allowed them, even encouraged them, to consolidate their traditional forms of control in new and potentially powerful ways. This chapter will explore some important ways in which the 1980s changed advertising's approach to persuasive influence.

Advertising and Control: A Typology

First of all, what is *control?* It is a term that obviously has very strong connotations. The image we often have of someone who is in control, is that of a person with complete power. Certain advertisers would like to have this kind of control over buying behavior. By *advertising control,* however, I do not mean that advertising is all-powerful. Advertisers try to control perfectly the symbols in their ads, or the symbols around their ads, or our viewing of the ads or our spending triggered by ads, but they often fail in their control attempts. (They also often succeed, as we shall see.) If advertising did have absolute control, then advertising campaigns would always be successful and no advertised product would fail. We would never think a campaign was stupid, deceitful or offensive. Likewise, if advertising had complete control over media, then the media would never criticize advertisers or advertising, even superficially, and would do anything advertisers wanted.

Nevertheless advertisers *try* to exert as much control as they can. The definition of *control* used here is adapted from a definition given by Beniger (1986): "influence toward a predetermined goal" (p. 12). This discussion will not use exactly the same full definition as Beniger: He argues that intention is necessary for control, and that it is not control if the attempted controller is not purposefully and specifically trying to influence behavior in a particular way. This book will argue that unintentional control is also an important effect of advertising.

The control that advertising exerts, or at least attempts to exert, involves three dimensions: internal versus external control; operational versus allocative control; and intentional versus unintentional control. This typology of control is not necessarily mutually exclusive. In fact, the different types will often overlap in very real ways.

Internal control involves the skillful manipulation of symbols *within* an advertisement. Here control involves influencing how the viewer or listener perceives the ad, the images in the ad, and, of course, the product. Advertisers spend millions each year struggling to control the images in their advertisements. Complete control never occurs—but if it did, every potential consumer would immediately be drawn to the ad and then would accept the intended meanings of the ad, rushing out to buy the product. Chapter 2 will explain in more detail the processes and effects of advertising's attempts at internal, symbolic control.

External control focuses on advertising's attempts to shape the media environment in which the advertisement is embedded. Advertisers want their ads to be surrounded by media content that attracts desirable consumers and that complements the ads. Advertisers especially want be to be near media content that puts people in a mood receptive to seeing and liking their ads. But advertisers are not just concerned over the non-advertising media content; advertisers also want to control the other ads that are near their ads. Advertisers believe that the effectiveness of their messages decreases if their competitors' messages are too close or if too many other promotional messages swallow up their message. As we will see, advertisers often attempt to exert their economic clout over media to gain this form of control.

Another dimension of control involves *allocative* versus *operational*. These are two concepts that have been applied to the media in general by Murdock (1982) and to advertising specifically by Leiss, Kline and Jhally (1990). Allocative control is the control over the direction and philosophy of an organization. A person, organization or institution that has allocative control has the power to define what the goals of an organization are and what that organization is designed to achieve. Because allocative control defines "the big picture," it is the more powerful of the two. Operational control, on the other hand, is control over the day-to-day running of an organization: how the allocative direction is routinely implemented. It involves hands-on control of the operation of the organization, but within the limits of the resources and direction that have already been allocated. Obviously, someone who has both allocative and operational control is very powerful.

It is valuable at this point to compare the two dimensions of control already mentioned. Internal control involves, again, the placement of symbols in an ad. Here an advertiser may have both allocative and operational control, depending upon the situation. The advertiser definitely has allocative control: The creation of an advertisement, after all, is designed and structured to meet the needs of the advertiser (selling a product). And the advertiser may also have operational control if the advertiser does the ad in-house or is highly involved in the creation of the ads. Many advertisers, though, use an advertising agency, in which case the agency assumes responsibility for the day-to-day operations of creating the campaign and its symbols. Around 40% of advertising expenditures flow through ad agencies (Ducoffe & Smith, 1993).

Advertising might also have external allocative and operational control. Advertisers might have allocative control over the media if the media have been set up and designed for advertising's benefit. This book will later argue exactly that: Broadcasting, for example, has evolved in this society to be a carrier for commercials. The "ad carrier" purpose of broadcasting is embedded at the core of the system and affects, at some level, almost everything broadcasting does. The presence of advertising, and advertising's money, shaped broadcasting's development in such a way that it became the sole funding system, and whoever pays the piper also calls the tune.

Do advertisers have operational control over media? Sometimes they do, when advertisers produce programs themselves. In this case, advertisers have day-to-day operational control over media content. Later this book will explore the operational, external control that some advertisers may have (and an increasing number of advertisers do).

Finally, a last dimension of control centers on the issue of intentionality. *Intentional control* involves the controller purposefully attempting to influence something in a particular way, and successfully exerting this influence. *Unintentional control* occurs when something is altered in a way that the controller desires but did not specifically try to influence. In the internal, symbolic realm, intentional control reigns. Very rarely does an advertisement have a positive but unforeseen and unintended effect for the advertiser. In the external realm, advertisers may quite often try explicitly to influence media decision makers. Usually such crass attempts happen behind closed doors (Chapter 2 discusses such attempts). On the other hand, advertisers often will have unintentional control over the media content. Media creators will frequently shape content in such a way that they *believe* advertisers might want. As Baker (1994) argues, a new, specialized magazine created to appeal specifically to advertisers who desire to reach a particular consumer group is an unintentional exercise of control by advertisers. The advertisers did not initiate the magazine (the magazine's creators may never even have contacted advertisers during the planning stages), but advertisers nevertheless influenced the creation process. Obviously, if advertisers have allocative control over a media system, unintended control may happen frequently as media creators, working in a system thus defined, alter content for advertisers' needs.

These are a few of the types of control that advertisers might have, or at least might attempt, as part of their activities. Beginning in the 1980s, though, many "rules" for advertising control began to change. Many of the things that advertisers believed they were in control of began to decay during this decade. This panicked advertisers. Yet at the same time, many of the mechanisms that limited advertisers' control also began to deteriorate. This delighted advertisers. Whatever advertising's stance toward the changes, in combination the eighties' trends and occurrences set up advertising's new controlling strategies and directions in the 1990s. The next section discusses the decade of the 1980s as a necessary precursor—a transition decade—to the new forms of control that advertising is attempting in more recent times.

The Fluid Dynamics of Advertising Control During the 1980s

The 1980s and early 1990s had a split personality for the advertising industry, reflecting both the reduction of advertising's control in some sectors and the freedom from previous restrictions in others. Ultimately, though, both trends converged into a movement that encouraged advertising to explore new venues for promotion. This movement could make advertising, as an institution, potentially more powerful than ever (or, at least, give advertisers the ability to exercise new forms of power). Before advertising was motivated to explore these new directions of power, though, the stage had to be set.

FACTORS IN THE 1980s THAT DECREASED ADVERTISER CONTROL

Several factors during the 1980s seemed to upset advertising's institutional applecart. As a look through the advertising trade journals (e.g., *Advertising Age*) suggests, advertisers began to notice many of these problems in the late 1970s, but the problems became much more salient for advertising in the next decade. During this time, advertising as an institution felt an increasing lack of control over media viewing behavior, audience demographics and the mediated environment of ads.

The Loss of Control Over Media User Behavior

One thing that advertisers want to control is the attention the viewer or reader gives to the advertisement. Advertisers know that the first necessary (but not sufficient) condition for persuading a potential consumer to buy a product is to force the consumer to notice the message. If the consumer does not see the ad or ignores the ad, then the advertiser's message is wasted. So the advertiser wants to control the audience's viewing of media, especially to turn that head and focus those eyes on the ads. Traditionally, this is accomplished by the media guaranteeing a certain audience and then, once this audience is delivered, by manipulating the internal symbols of the ads so that the initial message of the ad says, "Look at me!"

But especially in the electronic media, advertisers have lost considerable control over the audience's media behavior. Before the 1980s, television advertisers had a captive audience. Most markets had only four or five channels to choose from. Changing the channel involved physically moving to the television set and using the mechanical channel switch. Removing commercials from one's favorite program was impossible (the best one could do would be physically to leave the room). The issue of audience control over television viewing has, however, become more critical to advertisers as most of the population has become "empowered" through new technology. It is a limited type of empowerment, of course, because viewers cannot totally substitute non commercial-influenced programming for the commercial-influenced programming. On most broadcasting and cable markets, it is practically impossible to escape to programming that advertising has not somehow touched.

Nevertheless, advertisers are increasingly nervous about this recent, if superficial, level of power audiences have over their electronic media viewing. New viewing technologies have been introduced into the marketplace and have become ubiquitous in most households. These technologies are, in some ways, anti-advertising devices. One source of viewer power has come from video cassette recorders (VCRs). The ownership of VCRs has offered flexibility to viewers in two ways, both of which undermine advertiser control over viewing behavior. First, *time shifting* (recording a program at one time and watching it at another time) can ruin the carefully developed time placement strategies of advertisers. Part of the reason many food advertisements are aired during afternoon soap operas is to influence the family dinner decision maker about what to prepare that night. Viewers negate this strategy when they time-shift the soap to evening, after dinner. The importance of commercial timing partially explains why an episode of *Seinfeld* was the most expensive program on which to place a 30-second spot advertisement during the 1994-1995 TV season. A minor rationale for the $390,000 cost was that the 9 p.m. Thursday time period is a prime way for advertisers to reach people who are about to make a decision about weekend moviegoing and automobile shopping (Mandese, 1994d). Time-shifting Jerry and company to Sunday afternoon damages the placement strategies' effectiveness, wasting much of its planned symbolic power.

Even more problematic for advertisers than time shifting is the emancipatory power offered by the fast-forward button, which allows viewers to record television programming and then fast-forward (or *zip*) through commercials. The fast-forward button has become an impromptu video editor, letting people essentially remove commercials from their favorite programs, or at least abbreviate them. VCRs, then, undermine the entire rationale of television advertising and, thus, the entire economic rationale of television itself.

Advertisers also mutter about remote controls. Indeed, the very name of the device (remote *control*) points to viewer empowerment. Remote controls instantaneously allow people to *graze* (or *channel surf*) from one program to another. Grazing is a problem of control for advertisers because it messes up the predictability of audience viewing. Much of television programming is based upon the idea of audience "flow." If viewers like one program and another follows that is similar to the one they like, then inertia will keep them glued to the channel (and, presumably, glued to the commercials). In pre-remote days, the physical effort of rising out of the chair and switching the channel—especially just to see what else was on—prevented many viewers from grazing. The leaves of grass, to extend the metaphor, were just too far apart to graze on back then. And if audience "flow" worked between programs, it also often worked within programs: It would take a determined and active viewer to rise up physically and rotate the dial at every commercial break before the 1980s. Things have changed. Today, with but the slightest push of the thumb, the remote deteriorates strategies for audience "flow" from one segment or program to another. Audiences are no longer assumed to stick around. The lubrication of the remote control encourages modern viewers to overcome the physical inertia experienced by their earlier counterparts.

But a specialized form of grazing, *zapping,* is an even bigger problem for television advertisers than zipping (which is limited to only those TV programs that an audience member had videotaped earlier) and grazing (where the audiences at least might watch the commercials). Zapping is the active and purposeful use of the remote control to avoid commercials. Seen as a problem for advertising even in the early 1980s when only 18% of the U.S. population had remote controls (Kostyra, 1984), the concern has reached almost panic stage as most TV sets currently sold in this country offer that technology. The real possibility that people are routinely zapping ads worries advertisers.

Cable television exacerbates the problem. Some cable channels have tried to attract the TV generation with "quick" forms of television like MTV and CNN Headline News, which break up their programming into short, isolated segments. Unfortunately for advertisers, such soundbite and quick-image TV breaks up programming into very small bits, offering more opportunities to zap. The increased amount of sports programming on cable also may be encouraging zapping. By offering more sports stations that air games at the same time, the insatiable sports fan can graze from one game to another and thereby avoid commercial breaks (Banks, 1987). One study done in the mid-1980s found that viewership declined by nearly 8% on network TV and more than 14% on cable stations when commercials came on, with remote controls being viewed as a prime factor (Savan, 1994). In the 1990s, it is logical to assume that these numbers have increased. During the break between network programs, audiences can drop by as much as 25% (Mandese, 1994c). Radio, too, has experienced a technologically driven, listener mini-revolt. The computerized "scan" and "seek" buttons on most car radios also allow increased ease of grazing and zapping, raising the issue of that medium's advertising effectiveness (Ward, 1991).

There is evidence that many of these problems (problems for advertising, anyway) will get worse, especially for television. In early 1991, Japan announced the development of a VCR that can automatically edit out commercials while recording (Kilburn, 1991). Although that particular system probably would not work for U.S. televisions, an early parallel system is the VCR Voice Programmer, in which a viewer, while watching a prerecorded program, can simply yell "Zap it!" to a voice-activated remote control and immediately fast-forward through the commercial (Colford, 1993b).

The Loss of Control Over Audience Demographics

It is commonplace to read about "the fragmented society" in media textbooks and trade publications. Society has become more specialized, such works say, and people are now placed in different specialized groups. Rather than conceiving of society as a "mass," society is instead viewed as a conglomerate of demographic and psychographic groupings. In order to talk to "society," then, one needs to address the different groupings rather than the mass. Taking as their starting point the *postindustrial thesis* of Daniel Bell (1973) and Richard Maisel (1973), discussions of the fragmented society often refer to three characteristics of postindustrial life. The first is the switch from manufacturing to service industries in Western societies, leading to more specialized job skills and expertise. Law, accounting, public relations and other white-collar professions have increased in importance in postindustrialization. A second factor is the increased prevalence of higher education that leads to diversified interests and an exposure to different viewpoints and lifestyles. An additional characteristic of the postindustrial society is the growth of the information industry, including the mass media and the development of information technology (for a discussion of the movement from an industrial society to a service/information society, see Beniger, 1986).

Both media and commercialism have contributed to the notion of a fragmented, specialized society. For example, network television is traditionally very efficient in reaching the masses. To use advertising parlance, network TV has a low CPM, or cost per thousand. Because network TV reaches so many people, the cost of reaching 1,000 people via television—the measure of efficiency for advertising reach—is very low. In response to the mass audience efficiency of national television, magazines and radio—in order to survive economically—had to niche themselves as more specialized media. These media, in a postindustrialized, specialized society, can help specialized advertisers reach specialized audiences. Magazines went from being characterized by mass-oriented publications like *Life* and *Look,* to the demographically targeted *LA Baby* and *Thrasher.* Radio went from being the 1940s' equivalent of network TV, to format-defined Adult Contemporary, Album Oriented Rock or Country. In the 1980s, newspapers began fragmenting into suburban editions, often defined by commercially advantageous groupings rather than metropolitan, community or electoral groupings (Bagdikian, 1992, pp. 220-222). On television, specialization and fragmentation first were issues when PBS and UHF became viable and more targeted options in the 1970s (Leiss et al., 1990, p. 113). The big push toward the fragmentation of television, though, was the interpenetration of cable television into the television public, especially when the technology advanced enough for cable to increase channel selection as well as fidelity. In 1980, a little more than 28% of the TV households had cable; by 1990, this figure was more than 60% ("Cable Penetration Reaches 65%," 1993).

Similarly, the driving nature of commercialism has contributed to the niched society construction as marketers began working toward promotional efficiency in the fragmented society. In the 1970s, advertisers and marketers greatly increased awareness and systematic research of different consumer "lifestyles" (combining demographic and psychographic categories) (Leiss et al., 1990). Certain types of people (young, urban, professionals, for example) become more desirable and better defined as consumers than did others. Specific groups might have more disposable income, or a greater inclination to spend this income on certain products or more opportunity to spend this income, than other groups. Obviously, then, once these groups became better defined, they also became more desirable, and advertising placement strategies were often designed to reach them.

The fragmentation of the media and consumer audience has caused two overall problems for advertisers. First, the ideal "media mix" is much more complicated and unstable than before the 1980s. It is very tough to find the ideal strategy for placing ads that maximize both reach (attracting as many potential consumers to your ad as possible) and frequency (forcing the desirable markets, through repetition, to remember your ad). The television networks, for example, do not deliver 93% of the TV viewing audience as they did in 1977, the peak of their reach: By the end of the 1980s their share had dropped to 66% ("Prime-Time Network Television Viewing," 1991). The network audience erosion is continuing in the 1990s, as illustrated by comparing the ratings for the top program in the 1987-1988 season (*The Cosby Show*, with a 28 rating and 44 share), with the top program in the 1992-1993 season (*60 Minutes*, with a 21.6 rating and 35 share) (Kauchak Smith, 1993). Thus, reaching the same number of television viewers now, compared to 1977, is a much more complex placement activity.

A bigger problem, though, may be the elusive nature of especially alluring markets for advertising. Unfortunately for advertisers, traditional media—even traditional specialized media—do not reach many of the most desirable groups. Many of these markets are people with an active lifestyle, which by definition takes them away from TV and other home-based media. The number of non-advertising entertainment choices open to markets with disposable incomes further exaggerates this trend. Such options include premium-pay cable (HBO, Showtime) and pay-per-view cable (Wrestlemania!), home videos, CDs, laser disks, computer networks, CD-ROMS and video games. Few of these options existed in 1980. In 1970, consumers spent 49% of their media expenses on non-advertising supported media, such as movies and records. By 1992, this percentage had increased to 57% as the number of non-advertising supported media options increased (Bogart, 1994). Consumers, then, have more places to escape advertising and are often willing to spend the money to do so. And it was usually the consumers most desirable to advertisers who escaped their messages.

A good illustration of this trend is the *tween* market, or those between 11 and 15, a very desirable market for advertisers. Tweens are desirable because of the high level of disposable income they have and their propensity to spend it. Tweens, though, are difficult to reach through television because they are often out with friends, at the movies or at video game parlors. Even while at home, they often forsake traditional television. Many tweens are disdainful of children's programming, bored with adult programming and enamored of non-ad supported uses of television like videotapes and video games. Likewise, other demographic clusters, like the highly spend-oriented DINKS (double-income, no kids) couples, are notoriously disdainful of traditional mediated content.

Like the loss of control over media viewing behavior, the loss of control over audience demographics will also probably be exacerbated in the near future. Much talk has been made of cable systems, utilizing digital compression and fiber optics, offering as many as 500 channels from which to choose. As one advertising executive concludes about such developments, "There will be an erosion of audiences, but there will be an erosion of cable audiences as well" (Kim, 1993b, p. S2). Media analysts also view the next big market "bubble," the post-boomer, 20-something "Generation X," as a difficult market to reach with traditional media. And even when this group does consume traditional media like television, they tend to be especially advertising resistant. Because they have grown up with emancipatory technology such as remote controls, Jeff Jarvis of *TV Guide* has described this market as "the remote control generation. They are no longer captive to the networks" (Donaton, 1993b, p. 17). Their freedom from old-fashioned ad media frustrates advertisers. "Gen X" consists of 46 million Americans with an estimated disposable income of $125 billion ("Twentysomethings," 1995).

The Loss of Control Over the Mediated Environment of Ads

Advertisers have a stake in attempting to influence the "environment" of traditional media, and this influence has been very successful. Mainstream media and their content are very receptive symbolic receptacles for advertising. TV, radio, magazines and newspapers work hard to please their main source of funding, advertisers. But the irony is that advertising has been *too* successful; mainstream media are *too* receptive. Mainstream media have become so receptive that they now carry such an abundance of ads that the effectiveness of individual ads is reduced. For advertisers, then, *clutter* is a big concern. Clutter is defined as the amount of time devoted to nonprogram content on television, including product commercials, program promotions and public service announcements (PSAs). Although the concern over clutter has been on advertisers' minds since the early 1970s when the standard unit of buying for network television became 30 seconds, the 1980s greatly increased the salience of the issue for that group as network TV offered cheaper 15-second units in the fall of 1986, increasing the number of ads on TV.[1]

Clutter, especially on television (which is where most concern lies), has increased in three ways. First, there are more television outlets that carry ads. The addition of cable television channels has meant that, overall, television airs more commercials than in the past, because most of the newly created cable channels carry advertising: By 1990, more than 60% of the nation's cable systems offered 30 or more channels

(Hallmark, Mangum, & Worthington, 1993). Similarly, in the 1980s, there was a growth in the number of independent broadcast television channels, increasing from 115 at the beginning of the decade to 339 at the end (Hallmark et al., 1993). More cable and independent stations have increased the number of "advertising carriers" in the 1980s.

Second, there is concern that the previously existing advertising carriers, like the TV networks, are carrying more ads, increasing the amount of nonprogram time. The broadcast and cable networks try to squeeze in more ads, especially in popular shows (Mandese, 1991b), to slow declining ad revenues due to home video and cable competition. Also to slow declining ratings, the networks have increased their efforts at self-promotion, like program plugs. Both of these strategies have caused clutter to increase. Also, though there has been an increase in the number of advertising supported media (like cable), there perhaps has been an even greater growth in non-advertising supported media (like videos), which might encourage advertisers to place more ads in the media that will accept them.

One study by General Motors, which the company planned to use in ad price negotiations, found that an average network prime-time hour had nearly 4 minutes more clutter in 1992 (totaling more than 14 minutes) than in 1983 (Brunelli & Kiley, 1992). In addition, something that has alienated advertisers from the networks on the issue of clutter is that both ABC and NBC admitted they sold more ad time in the 1980s but did not inform advertisers of the increase (Mandese, 1991b, p. 42). The fourth network, Fox, is also a clutter magnet. In May 1994, for example, Fox was the first network to go over 15 minutes of clutter per hour in prime time (Wallenstein, 1995). Yet those working in advertising are not just concerned with increased TV clutter on the networks. First-run syndicated TV shows—programs like *Wheel of Fortune* or *Star Trek: Deep Space Nine,* which are sold to local TV stations individually—also have increased the number of ads they carry. In 1992, the typical load for first-run syndicated shows was 12 minutes of spots per hour; in 1994 the industry standard had increased to 14 minutes per hour (Robins, 1994a). Syndication producers will often increase the number of ads to offset the rising costs of first-run production.

Clutter has affected other media besides TV. During the eighties, the number of magazine advertising pages increased by nearly 50% (Danna, 1992). There were more ad pages in consumer magazines in 1994 (more than 180,000) than in any other year in history ("Magazines Set

Ad Page Record," 1995). There is also a perceived problem with clutter in other advertising supported media, as illustrated by "more and more free-standing inserts falling out of newspapers, magazines stuffed with bound-in and blown-in response cards, mailboxes overflowing with unsolicited advertising, and so on" (Miller, 1989, p. 34).

A final standard for measuring clutter involves what is done with the total amount of time devoted to nonprogram content. From an advertiser's perspective, not all pods (or clusters of ads) are created equal. If there are numerous 15-second commercials placed in a commercial break instead of a few 30- or 60-second commercials, or if there are commercials for competing brands in the same break or if the break is extraordinarily long, then the clutter problem increases. So comparing daytime television with prime-time television, the clutter looks different. Daytime television on the networks averages 31 spots per hour compared to 20 for prime time, but prime time is more likely to group commercials for competitive products together (Mandese, 1992a). Given that cable outlets are often more demographically targeted than the networks and therefore often attract products for the same market, cable channels have an even more pronounced problem than the networks when it comes to "competitive clutter" (Mandese, 1993l).

The length of uninterrupted advertising pods is also a concern. One study by the ad agency BBDO found more than 6 straight minutes of clutter—including both product promotions and program promotions—between the popular ABC programs *Full House* and *Home Improvement* (Mandese, 1992b).

The rising costs of TV advertising time have increased the negative effects of clutter as well. For example, in the 1994-1995 season, the media time for a 30-second spot on *Seinfeld,* the most expensive TV show on which to advertise that season, cost $390,000—which was $65,000 more than *Home Improvement,* the most expensive show the previous year, and $80,000 more than the ad champion in 1992-1993, *Murphy Brown* (Mandese, 1992h, 1993h, 1994d). The recession of the early 1990s, which hit the advertising industry especially hard, has also increased the salience of the clutter issue. Because costs had risen for TV and other media, and because some advertisers had cut back on ad expenditures during this recession, advertisers looked for ways to stretch their ad bucks. One way is to decrease the length of each ad. Thus, many advertisers on television use 15-second spots instead of 30- or 60-second spots to maintain TV visibility while simultaneously cutting costs. This strategy also increases the overall number of commercials on television.

Clutter is a major concern for advertisers because of the possible effect it may have on viewers and their relationship to the ads. Increased clutter may cut down on consumers' attention to and retention of individual ads. People notice an ad when it stands alone; people may reach information overload when 15 ads are strung together. What makes the problem even worse for advertisers is that zapping and clutter are positively correlated: As clutter increases, so does the viewer's tendency to escape ads via the remote control ("Clutter Suffers Zap Attacks," 1992).

FACTORS THAT HAVE INCREASED ADVERTISER CONTROL

Although advertisers' new strategies for control in the 1990s partially reflect their perceived loss of traditional audience control, a further explanation for the institution's recent forays into new territories of control is their new-found freedom in other arenas. Two factors, especially, have increased advertising's effectiveness in wielding control. One involves the weakening of two of the most powerful advertising media, television and newspapers, thus allowing advertising to have more of a voice in media decisions. The other involves the stance toward advertising and media taken by the federal government.

Increased Media Desperation for Advertising Dollars

As discussed earlier, the overall share of the television audience by the Big Three networks has declined from 93% to around 60%. One consequence of this decline is that advertising placement is more complicated for advertisers trying to find that ideal mix. Another consequence is the potential decrease in clout by the TV networks and their subsequent willingness to be even more servile to advertising than in the past. The new television players that have contributed to the networks' decreased ratings (e.g., cable) likewise often show their willingness to bend for advertisers.

Network TV faces competition from other ad-supported television outlets, which is a relatively new situation for them. From 1955 (when Dumont, the early fourth network, folded) until the mid-1980s (with the rise of the Fox network and ubiquitous cable penetration), the networks went unchallenged as the main televisual advertising vehicles.

But then national cable networks became serious competition for both audiences and advertisers. Some cable networks—like USA and TNT—essentially try to be mini-networks, appealing to the same mass demographics and mass advertisers. Others attempt to draw away more specialized demographics (and the advertisers targeting these demographics), like children (Nickelodeon), tweens and teens (MTV), men (ESPN) and women (Lifetime).

The creation of the fourth, fifth and sixth broadcast networks (Fox, the United Paramount Network and the WB Television Network) has also taken away audiences and advertisers and will increasingly do so. What makes this situation especially distressing for the traditional networks is that the new networks, especially Fox, are targeting audiences who are desirable to advertisers. Programs like *Melrose Place* and *The Simpsons* skew toward young viewers and thus are especially advertising desirable. Similarly, the development of network-quality first-run syndicated programs, like *Babylon 5,* has often bled ratings from the networks as independent stations or Fox affiliates have snatched up these programs.

Why would increased competition lead to an increase in advertiser control? Normally, increased competition in media organizations might lead to increased content innovation. Those in the most competitive situation are often the most willing to experiment (Turow, 1982). Indeed, at one point the networks seemed to respond to the increased competition by introducing content innovations in their programs. In 1990, more auteur-driven programs like *Twin Peaks* and *American Chronicles* (from filmmaker David Lynch), *Cop Rock* (the mutant TV program from Steven Bochco), John Sayles's *Shannon's Deal,* and James Earl Jones's downbeat *Gabriel's Fire* generated industry excitement, at least at first. But these shows were expensive, did not draw large ratings and were a little too somber and offbeat for advertisers. By the next season, TV industry observers were noting the lack of innovation in programs. One ad executive noted, "The fact that there's no 'Cop Rock' or 'Twin Peaks' this year doesn't upset me" (Robins, 1991, p. 1). Television learned an unfortunate economic lesson from the 1990 season: Generally, innovative content in the new competitive environment does not work.

If innovation does not come in the form of content, where is innovation in the new television milieu found? It comes in the innovative ways that television can be subservient to advertisers. The flood of "advertising-friendly programs" on TV points to this increased servitude.

Advertisers generally love sitcoms, for example, with their half-hour format, humor and frequent family orientation. And the rule of thumb in modern television is, what advertisers want, advertisers get. In the 1993-1994 season, 21 of the 36 new prime-time network programs were half-hour sitcoms; in the 1994-1995 season, the proportion was 13 of 28. The sponsorship and cross-promotional deals that the networks are increasingly making with advertisers also show the "innovative pliancy" of the networks to advertising. Such deals will make up much of the discussion in later chapters.

If the powerful networks are more willing to bend for advertisers, then smaller cable networks are practically pretzels. In an attempt to cultivate relationships with advertisers, cable channels like Lifetime, Discovery and Comedy Central have struck deals with them, giving advertisers more of a promotional (even programming) voice in an effort to win advertising moneys (Bryant, 1993; Moshavi, 1993; Stern, 1993).

Television has not been the only medium hurt by the increased competition for advertising. Newspapers, the medium that still draws the largest share of advertising dollars because of its attractiveness to local advertisers, is finding itself in an advertising crunch. On the surface, though, this does not seem to be the case. In 1994, newspapers brought in more than $34 billion in ad revenue, or 22.9% of advertising dollars. Newspapers increased their advertising revenue by 7.3% from 1993 to 1994 (Coen, 1995).

What makes newspaper decision makers nervous, however, is that there is much faster growth in their direct competitors for local advertising money, like cable TV networks (up 17.8%), non-network cable stations (up 20%), local radio (up 11.2%) and direct mail (up 8.7%) (Coen, 1995). Newspapers are worried that their failure to keep pace with their competitors in 1994 could suggest a longer trend. From 1987 to 1992, inflation rose faster than newspapers' local advertising revenue (Coen, 1994). Reflecting the medium's diminished attractiveness to advertisers, newspapers' total share of advertising revenue has steadily declined, from 29.4% in 1970 and 27.6% in 1980 (Szathmary, 1992).

Part of the reason for this decline is that services that newspapers have traditionally had a lock on, like classified ads, can now be delivered by other means, such as telephone or local TV cable or computer networks (Fisher, 1993b). Next, powerful retailers, most notably Wal-Mart, have successfully publicized their wares without aid of the local newspaper. The Wal-Mart strategy involves bypassing local newspapers, instead using direct mail and even word-of-mouth to increase the store's visibility and community loyalty (Fisher, 1991). Wal-Mart's success often had a destructive trickle-down effect on newspapers. As Wal-Mart took business away from local businesses that did advertise in newspapers, these businesses were often forced to cut back on their newspaper advertising budget. A final reason for newspapers' ad decline is that newspaper readership has been on the decline for several decades as well, which decreases the medium's attractiveness to advertisers. In 1953, for example, the circulation of newspapers per 100 households was roughly 125—the average household, in other words, subscribed to 1.25 newspapers. By 1973 this number was 97, then 84 in 1977 and 68 per 100 households in 1990 (Baker, 1994). As one would guess from these figures, the number of Americans who read newspapers regularly has also declined, especially for those under 35 (again, the most desirable for advertisers). In 1970, the number of those under 35 who read a newspaper regularly was 76%; by 1990 that number was 29% (Mann, 1992).

Like television organizations, newspapers might try to compensate for these factors by becoming more advertising friendly. The "USA-Todayness" of newspapers, where newspapers try to copy the factoid, lifestyle, good-looking orientation of television, may be one variation of this temptation. Likewise, the creation of advertising liaisons—like the Newspaper National Network, a newspaper cooperative designed to recruit national advertisers for newspapers—may be another indicator of increased vulnerability to advertiser demands. As one newspaper executive noted about the creation of such efforts, "instead of simply selling space, we're listening carefully to advertisers and marketing those newspaper environments that best fit an advertiser's marketing goals" (Szathmary, 1992, p. 59). Such an attitude could grant advertisers even more influence over the content and readership of newspapers than before.

Deregulation

Besides the increased acceptance by traditional media of advertising influence, another factor in the 1980s that increased advertising's control was deregulation. With the dawn of the Reagan era in the early 1980s, the philosophy of "less government" and "more free marketplace" became official federal government policy. Advertising gained control in the 1980s as government relinquished control. Deregulation, in its most complete form, means taking two forks down the same road: For advertising, both forks have led to increased social influence. One obvious deregulatory path involves decreasing the regulation of commercial organizations and enterprises. For-profit, private institutions are allowed much more leeway in times of deregulatory zeitgeist than in times of more active governments. For advertising, the two most important manifestations of this deregulation involve the tolerance for corporate mergers and growth, and the decreased enforcement of rules against advertising.

In 1980s media and advertising, the big became bigger. Corporate mergers that might have been prevented by antitrust policy in earlier periods of active government were permitted in the Reagan eighties. For advertising agencies, this was the era of the "Big Bang" in mergers and acquisitions (Leiss et al., 1990, p. 163). One goal became "one-stop shopping," where one agency could supply all possible advertising, marketing and promotional services and even management consulting (as with the huge Saatchi and Saatchi) (Mattelart, 1991, p. 23). The two largest ad organizations in the world illustrate the growth in agencies. The WPP Group, the world's largest agency with 1994 worldwide gross income of more than $2.7 billion, is also the owner of the Ogilvy & Mather and the J. Walter Thompson agencies. Interpublic Group, number two, owns Lintas, Lowe Group and McCann-Erickson ("World's Top 50 Advertising Organizations," 1995). Almost three fourths of the top 20 ad agencies in the world were involved in at least one merger during the 1980s (Ducoffe & Smith, 1993).

Such mergers and growth have several potential effects. One obvious effect is that as an advertising agency grows, so does its potential influence over media—especially advertising-hungry media. Media may be more willing to heed the demands of large advertisers and large advertising agencies wielding multimillions than smaller ones. As Shoemaker and Reese (1991) note about the size of media funding sources, "the bigger the advertiser [and, presumably, the ad agency], the more muscle it has" (p. 164). A second effect of the growth of the mega-agency is that such growth allows easier handling of *integrated marketing,* in which the agencies can implement multimedia advertising and promotional strategies and accommodate worldwide global accounts, which in turn are encouraged by the increased growth and globalization of major advertising clients. Mega-agencies, then, can be equally comfortable with handling nontraditional promotional tactics such as direct mail and point-of-purchase (POP) as traditional media placements (Mattelart, 1991, p. 23). Because of this diversity in promotional expertise, the rise of the mega-agency has encouraged many of the trends discussed in later chapters. Mattelart argues, in fact, that the important and most valuable division in such agencies is not Creative, but Strategy, where all options for spreading the client's message to its market—through whatever vehicles possible—are explored and integrated (Mattelart, 1991, pp. 28-30). A final effect of agency growth involves the short-term financial consequences of mergers and acquisitions. The borrowing and decrease in cash flow that results from sudden corporate growth often leave the biggest agencies especially susceptible to recessionary pressures (Mattelart, 1991, p. 13), perhaps leading them to cut costs through cheaper media options. Such an incentive might lead to more clutter as advertisers buy smaller ad units. It might also encourage agencies to explore more alternative forms of advertising and promotion that have become characteristic of new advertising tactics.

The government tolerance for corporate growth in the 1980s has also greatly affected media organizations. The size of media industry leaders has increased tremendously since 1980. GE bought RCA and by extension NBC in 1986, for instance. ITT's attempt to acquire ABC in a similar manner in the mid-1960s was denied by the government because such corporate control "could compromise the independence of ABC's news coverage of political events in countries where ITT has interests" (Lee & Solomon, 1991, p. 77). Despite the fact that GE likewise had such global interests, its merger was allowed with a minimum of governmental and public discussion (Lee & Solomon, 1991, p. 77).

Similarly, in 1989 Time Warner Inc. was formed when Time bought Warner Communications Inc., bringing under one corporate umbrella magazines, motion picture and television production companies, cable TV networks, book publishers, record companies and a major comic book company, among other media holdings. Rupert Murdoch and his News Corp. have built a media empire of newspapers, magazines (including the country's largest in total revenues, *TV Guide*) and television (the Fox network, most notably). Ted Turner has built up his organization with the cable operations WTBS, CNN, TNT and The Cartoon Channel. Concerns about the concentration of ideas and communication, of course, followed such media activity,[2] but perhaps most important for this exploration is the diversity of the holdings of such media conglomerates. It is easier to move content *across* media when one organization owns several different media outlets. This element will especially impact upon the discussion of cross-promotional strategies.

A second way that media and advertising organizations benefit from deregulation, besides the encouragement of growth of such organizations, is the decreased attention by the state to commercial activities—especially in broadcasting, which is traditionally the most regulated of the mass media. As a point of contrast, during the Carter administration the chair of the Federal Trade Commission, Michael Pertschuk, was quite aggressive in attacking incomplete or inaccurate advertising. Such a stance changed with the new administration. President Reagan later named James Miller to head the agency; Miller toned down the agency's activism. The agency also had its staff cut in half during that decade (Jacobson & Mazur, 1995). Similarly, the Federal Communications Commission (FCC), the agency in charge of regulating broadcasting, also embraced a "free enterprise" philosophy with the leadership of chair Mark Fowler during the 1980s.

The lax attitude of the state toward broadcast commercial messages can be seen with changes in the amount of commercial time recommended by the FCC. The FCC relaxed restrictions on underwriter messages in public broadcasting in the 1980s (and again in the 1990s), making public television a more attractive promotional device. Similarly, restrictions on commercial television were diluted. In the 1970s, although no formal rules were put into effect, the FCC did highly recommend industry self-regulatory guidelines, especially for children's programming. The FCC implied that it would impose formal rules if broadcasters did not comply with these self-imposed restrictions. The self-regulatory organization for broadcasters, the National Association of Broadcasters, set up rules to pacify regulators, recommending that advertising total no more than 12 minutes per hour on weekday programming and just under 10 minutes per hour for weekend programming. Despite the rules, though, in the late 1970s the amount of commercial time on children's programming increased, and the FCC began formal procedures to evaluate the amount. The Reagan-appointed FCC Chair, Mark Fowler, abandoned this process in 1983-1984, however, thus sanctioning, through policy, such things as children's "program length commercials." The resulting programs, like *He-Man and the Masters of the Universe* and *GI Joe,* served as promotion for preexisting toy lines and were essentially 60 minutes of commercial time per hour (Engelhardt, 1986; Kunkel, 1988). Although Congress did resurrect restrictions about advertisements on children's TV programs in 1990, the FCC's lax implementation of these rules is at issue. For example, a 30-minute children's program is defined rather conservatively as a 30-minute commercial *only* if an ad for toys featured in the show is inserted in that show itself.

One factor that accentuated the deregulation of broadcasting during the 1980s was the role of cable. Technologically, the spread of cable had some interesting implications for deregulation. Because cable TV programming is not, strictly speaking, over the airwaves, such programming is often not subjected to the same rules as over-the-air broadcasting. Whether or not the public owns the airwaves is irrelevant to cable operators: The only owner of cable properties is the economic owner. Regulators permitted certain cable stations to bend or ignore certain rules about advertising and promotion because of the difference in their delivery system. Thus, for example, it was safer to show infomercials on cable stations in the mid 1980s than on broadcast stations, simply because any possible threat of regulatory danger against overcommercialization, however remote, was completely removed by the technological peculiarity of cable.

The beginning of this section stated that deregulation could involve two paths. One path, discussed above, involves the relaxing of regulations against industry. This path has led to increased growth and increased leverage in broadcast advertising. Another path impacts a second group: public, not-for-profit institutions. Cutting off public institutions from public funds was characteristic of government policy in the 1980s. The percentage of individual state and local budgets that came from federal aid, for example, dropped from 22% in 1979 to 16% in 1989 (Colastosti, 1993). Institutions normally dependent upon governmental funds—like education, museums and public broadcasting—found the well dry during the deregulatory decade. This, combined with the recession of the early 1990s, forced many public (and even private) institutions to turn to private sources of funding, leading to a "privatization" of public institutions (Mattelart, 1991; Schiller, 1989). In 1973, for example, corporate underwriting made up 3.3% of the Public Broadcasting Service's budget; by 1991 that figure was more than 16% (Aufderheide, 1991). Often, such privatization involved selling the public institution to advertisers as a promotional vehicle.

Although the Bush and the Clinton administrations slowed the pace of deregulation down a bit, most evidence points to continued movement in that direction. A report to the Clinton transition team about the Federal Trade Commission (FTC) recommended no serious overhaul of the agency, an agency described by *Advertising Age* as considered "fairly benign by the marketing community" (Colford, 1993a, p. 1). Similarly, on the issue of privatization, the 1994 budget proposed by the Clinton administration included a provision for selling frequencies of the radio spectrum, considered part of the public good for nearly 70 years, to private interests to raise as much as $7.2 billion. A plan to privatize Internet, the computer network, with equally promising (but often mutually exclusive) emancipatory and commercial possibilities, has been looked upon with favor by the Democratic president (Schiller, 1993).

The Republican control of both houses of Congress after the November 1994 elections seems to promise even more deregulatory movement. Even before the newly elected took office in 1995, some deregulatory measures were passed. In December 1994, for example, the FCC proposed looser restrictions on television station ownership, with at least one analyst suggesting that "the new Republican majority in Congress was responsible at least in part for the depth of the deregulatory proposals" (Stern, 1994, p. 6). Newt Gingrich, the conservative Speaker of the House, who began his tenure in 1995, has said publicly that he wishes to deregulate cable even further and to privatize public broadcasting. Gingrich has said that he wants to "zero-out CPB [The Corporation for Public Broadcasting], which has been eating taxpayers' money" (McAvoy, 1994, p. 48).

Conclusion: Advertising's Control in the 1990s

The issue of control was more prominently placed on advertisers' agendas beginning in the 1980s. With such issues as remote controls, clutter, advertising-free media and deregulation, advertising moved toward redefining—or at least rediscovering—its mechanisms of control. These new mechanisms of control often involve attempts at manipulating both internal and external factors and garnering allocative and operational control. Effects of such control are often unintentional but nevertheless significant. As will be seen, advertising has tried multidimensional techniques in an attempt to maximize its control in the new promotional and mediated environment.

But before these new forms can be explored, it is useful to review what advertising critics have said about advertising's more established forms of control and the effects upon democratic society and culture that such forms have had. The next chapter views the key criticisms social critics have aimed at advertising in modern society.

Notes

1. Before 1986, 15-second units had to be bought in "Split 30s," where a company bought a 30-second slot but then could split it into 15-second slots for two of its products (Banks, 1987, p. 51; Paskowski & Pfaff, 1986). Obviously, offering isolated 15-second units allowed smaller companies to advertise on network television.

2. In his 1992 edition of *The Media Monopoly*, Bagdikian notes about such media concentration that,

> Since 1983, the number of companies controlling most of the national daily circulation has shrunk from twenty to eleven. In magazine publishing, a majority of the total annual industry revenues, which had gone to twenty firms, now goes to two; in book publishing, what had gone to eleven firms now goes to five. (pp. ix, x)

2

ADVERTISING'S EXTERNAL AND INTERNAL CONTROL
Social Implications

ADVERTISING is firmly entrenched in our society. This is not anything new, and it does not take an exceptionally perceptive social critic to figure this out. A couple of obvious signs point to advertising's grip on our society.

One apparent indication of the entrenchment of advertising is the amount of money it contributes to the mass media. Advertisers in general are a main source of revenue for the media, and for some particular media they are *the only* source. Advertisers in 1994 contributed nearly $87 billion to newspapers, TV, magazines and radio combined (Coen, 1995). Although some of these media also receive money from other sources, like newsstand sales or subscriptions, the majority receive most of their revenue from advertising. Newspapers, for instance, garner about 75% of their total revenue from advertising (Baker, 1994). Other media, like commercial broadcast radio and television, receive virtually 100% of their income from advertising.

Another indication of the ubiquity of advertising is our daily exposure to an enormous amount of advertising messages. This is a big price that we pay for advertising's above contribution to media. We are overexposed to these promotional symbols: If we were to sum up the total number of product advertisements we are exposed to on TV, radio, newspapers and magazines, the number could be as high as 400 per day (Pratkanis & Aronson, 1991). If we were to add up *all* promotional messages—including logos on products, program promos and ads on billboards and in the Yellow Pages (two media that carry nothing but advertisements)—this number could reach 16,000 (Savan, 1994). Jacobson and Mazur (1995) argue that typical Americans will spend almost 3 whole years of their lives just watching commercials on television. The United States, in fact, is ad burdened. This country accounts for 57% of the world's advertising spending, yet the U.S. population makes up less than 10% of the world's population (Pratkanis & Aronson, 1991).

What effect does a discourse that is so economically and symbolically pervasive have upon us? What has been the impact of the advertising institution upon democracy? These questions are too complex to address comprehensively here, but some of the more salient points made by social critics about advertising can be summarized. Many of these points are even more applicable to advertising in the post-1980s world, and later chapters that discuss advertising's new forms will return to many of these arguments about advertising's social effects.

In media studies scholarship, there are many differing ways to study mediated phenomena. Political economists and symbolic critics represent two such ways. As Golding and Murdock (1991) note, critical political economists tend to be trained in economic or sociology departments, whereas symbolic critics—or, to use the term in its most general sense, cultural studies scholars—are more likely to come out of humanities programs. Although both traditions are interested in the relationship of the "cultural industries" to social power, their respective foci reflect the different training and perspectives of the two positions. Political economists emphasize studying the media as profit-driven economic entities, often showing how the forces of capitalism push media organizations—despite their self-trumpetings as purveyors of democracy—toward monopolistic control and economic safety in decision making. Symbolic critics focus on the manipulation of meaning and signs in media, sometimes highlighting the media's symbolic perpetuation of the status quo. At other times, these scholars stress the symbolic resistance allowed by the media's textual open meanings and the diversity of audience interpretations.

Advertising criticism as such can also be divided, although the two perspectives are more often blurred than in other realms of media studies because advertising texts are the most overtly economic of all media symbol systems. The explicit purpose of advertising is, after all, to sell products (see Kellner, 1990, and Jhally, 1987, for examples of advertising criticism that have as a stated purpose the combination of the two perspectives). Nevertheless, despite the blurring, two intellectual camps delineate critical advertising scholarship. Each camp has its own writers and ideas but both stress as an important theme advertising's imperatives of control and expansion.

The two critical camps hark back to the earlier discussion of external versus internal forms of advertising control. Political economists, including Herbert Schiller, Armand Mattelart, Ben Bagdikian and C. Edwin Baker, focus on the external control that advertising wields and the social and cultural effects of such control. This perspective asks, "How does advertising as a major funding system affect media content and the media's role in a democracy?" Symbolic critics, on the other hand, focus more on advertising's internal control. They look at how advertising attempts to manipulate symbols to influence a potential consumer's perception of a product. Such a perspective is not simply interested in an ad's effectiveness as a selling message, however. These critics often ask, "How do advertising's symbolic techniques affect our perceptions of not just the product, but also of social groups and social relations?" The remainder of this chapter will explore the most central arguments of each perspective.

Advertising, Economic Critics and the External Control of Media Content

One key assumption of the economic critics of advertisers is that the industrial structure of media affects its content. How a media industry makes its money will influence the types of messages that it produces. If the economic incentives encourage the production of one type of message over another, then it is a safe bet that the medium will generally produce the economically advantageous content.

Given this assumption, it is important when studying the economics of media to separate several different industrial elements. For instance, a good starting point is to divide a media industry into five different elements: the producer, the market, the product, the content and the audience. Such an analysis is crucial to figuring out what the different economic constraints and connections are. For most media, though, these categories overlap. If one were to look at a medium that is purely subscription or pay-per-item driven, like the magazine *Consumer Reports,* then the analysis would look like the following. The seller is the producer of CR. The buyers are the subscribers or (ultimately) those who purchase it at a newsstand.[1] The product is the magazine content itself: Buyers receive a copy of CR for their money. In this case, the intended audience is the market and the content (a CR news article) is the product. Because the economic structure of this system is such that the reader is the sole market, then it is logical to conclude that the incentives of the producer are to create a product (the magazine's content) that will appeal to the market (the reader).

As many economic critics of advertising such as Smythe (1977) argue, however, advertising-supported media are different. Ad-supported media include newspapers and magazines that receive most of their income from advertising, and media like broadcasting that receive all of their income from advertising. How are the five elements of producer, market, product, content and audience defined with advertising media? Some elements are the same in advertising-supported media and subscription-oriented media. The seller is the media producer in both; the audiences are the readers or viewers. But the market and the product are crucially different. In advertising-supported media, the advertiser is the market: The advertiser gives money to those who make decisions about media content. What does the market—the advertiser—receive in return? It is not content, as in subscription media. It is not even advertising slots, as one might believe on the surface. Advertising slots are just the means to the end product. The product in advertising-supported media is the audience. Advertisers want audiences. To illustrate briefly, the price of a 30-second slot on *Friends* is not determined by whether the advertisers like the program, or whether it is critically acclaimed or who produced the program. Ratings determine the price. Ratings measure the product being delivered: the audience.

Advertising-supported media, therefore, to please their revenue streams, try to deliver the best possible product. Because the audience is a nondurable good (Smythe, 1977), media must constantly work to produce an audience and to produce the audience that advertisers desire. It is in the media's best economic interest to do so. The media know that the hook for delivering this audience is their non-advertising content: the magazine article, the sitcom, the Top 40 rotation. They must work to grab this audience continually to deliver the goods to advertisers.

As with any sort of commodity transaction, not all product is equal. Buyers are looking for the biggest bang for their buck. Specifically, advertisers are looking for product that fulfills three criteria. The best deal for advertisers, then, are media that deliver audiences that score high on all three criteria: audience size ("product poundage"), audience type ("product purity") and audience susceptibility to the message ("product pliancy"). Media decision makers know that advertisers will pay prime dollar for this quality product. Economic critics of advertisers also know that the media often will shape their content to draw in the types of audiences advertisers want, based on these three criteria. Unfortunately, these criteria often lead to the creation of mediated content that may be desirable to advertisers but not desirable for an ideal democratic society.

PRODUCT POUNDAGE: DELIVERING THE MASS AUDIENCE

Obviously, advertisers want to reach as large an audience as possible when they place a commercial on television or a print ad in a newspaper. The farther the "reach" of the ad, the more promotional value they get for their money. All things being equal, TV advertisers want the highest ratings possible, and newspaper advertisers want the highest readership possible. The smallest drop in national television ratings can potentially cost the networks millions of dollars. Ad-supported media, then, try to shape their content to deliver mass-produced product. In what ways is the content shaped?

There is one overwhelmingly consistent message in advertising-supported media. Every program on television, every magazine article—no matter its genre or political persuasion—says the same thing. This message is "WATCH ME, WATCH ME, WATCH ME!" Advertising media are designed to glue that eyeball to the screen or the page or that ear to the speaker. Media decision makers know that in order to reach desired levels of revenue, they must deliver audience numbers. Their economic existence depends upon it. On the other hand, their economic existence does *not* depend upon educating us or informing us or challenging us. The bottom line is, they must get us to attend to media above all. Television ratings make this clear. Ratings overwhelmingly determine advertising costs. TV ratings measure the degree to which audiences are watching. Because television economics are based on ratings, it makes perfect sense that getting people to watch is the defining goal.

This leads media to be extremely entertainment oriented. The media must get us to watch, and if this means seducing us with entertainment, then so it goes. Media content is primarily designed to appeal to our desire for pleasure. In this sense, the media are demagogic. They are so desperate for our attention that they will give us what we want, repeatedly, even if what we want is not always what we need. Television producers know that if programs—or segments in programs—are too long, or too difficult to comprehend or too boring, people might switch channels. Newspaper publishers know that if they continually publish stories that are too dry, circulation may drop. Topics that are entertaining or intriguing (O. J. Simpson-esque) dominate the media; topics that are complex or difficult to grasp or involve historical discussion, must run a more difficult road for media exposure. It is easier to find out what happened last night in Madison Square Garden than in Bosnia. Situation comedies are the most prevalent genre of programming found on prime-time television.

This situation is exacerbated because the audience-product is non-durable; it must be constantly replenished. The media must predictably deliver the big audience every time, which means always drawing us back. But just maintaining the same level of entertainment might not be enough to guarantee audience size. Media do not want us to get bored with the same old thing. Keeping us entertained, day in and day out, may mean that the entertainment quota has to be higher today than it was yesterday. So they work to refine the entertainment value; content needs to be funnier, faster, sexier, more visceral. When this happens, non-entertaining messages often suffer. To adopt a phrase from Postman (1985), media's entertainment imperative might be "amusing us to death." [2]

If topics are not inherently entertaining (i.e, topics without elements of sex, humor or violence), then ad-media's need to be entertaining frequently transforms the topics. Newspapers, faced with declining readership, often turn to the more entertainment-oriented media as a role model in demagoguery. *USA Today,* the "McPaper," has led the way in entertainment-modeling behavior. News stories are shortened when in *USA Today* mode, with some newspapers even enforcing a strict word-length on stories and cutting down on "jumps," where a story is so long it cannot fit on one page. Factoid journalism, using colorful pie charts, summarizes interesting tidbits in short segments. Color graphics (and information that can fit into color graphics) and other "eye candy" take center stage. The sections of the newspaper that are the most entertainment centered, like (literally) Entertainment news, "Lifestyle news" (the catch-all category), Sports or Fashion, may increase in size. Conversely, the traditionally more hard news sections like Metro or International may take up a smaller proportion of the paper (Hammer, 1991; Kurtz, 1993).

Television, a purely advertising-funded medium, leads the way in the "Entertainment-ization" of information. News and other programming on television are presented in short, easily digestible chunks to keep viewers' attention. Postman pointed out that the average length of a camera shot on television is 3.5 seconds. Or at least it *was* 3.5 seconds in 1985 when Postman published this observation; there is every reason to believe segments on TV are even shorter a decade later, with the entrench-ment of MTV and CNN Headline News presentational styles. A study by Hallin (1992) researched *sound bites,* or uninterrupted video segments that show a news source talking about an issue. In 1968, the average sound-bite length on network TV reports of the presidential election was more than 43 seconds; in 1988 the average length was less than 9 seconds (Hallin, 1992). Such fast-paced news is fun to watch, but is it what news should be? Postman (1985) does not think so. He points to the contradiction that, "Americans are the best entertained and quite likely the least well-in-formed people in the Western world" (p. 106).

Besides the entertainment imperative of ad-supported media, the product poundage criterion also stresses a middle-of-the-road orienta-tion to media content. Anything that would exclude potential audi-ences—including extreme political partisanship to the left or right—is discouraged in much advertising-funded media.[3] Media want to em-brace possible consumers, not alienate them, so any real extremism in media content tends to be avoided and a centrist perspective cultivated.

Baker (1994) argues that newspapers' dependence upon advertising—and the middle-of-the-road pressure that accompanies such dependence—

is one reason for the development of objectivity as a defining news writing norm. Any basic journalistic writing course emphasizes an objective writing style: an emphasis on facts, on direct quotes, on the summary lead and inverted pyramid structure, and most of all on removing the reporters' political biases from the story. Taking a longitudinal perspective, Baker maintains that as newspapers increased their reliance on advertising revenue, they also increased the percentage of objectively written news stories. Although reading an explicitly partisan newspaper might help readers interpret news events and place them in a critical framework, it also excludes readers who do not agree with the specific political perspective of the paper. Thus, Baker speculates that to avoid offending readers and (worse) encouraging them to look elsewhere for news, the advertising-enhanced need for big audience numbers encouraged the newspaper industry to develop a more objective orientation.

Is this desirable? Certainly, democracy needs objective information (McQuail, 1991). But Baker argues that too much objective information encourages passivity among the citizenry. Too much decontextualized and factual information may smother the passion evoked by partisan communicators. Although the evidence is correlational, Baker points to the higher political participation in countries that have a higher percentage of explicitly partisan news outlets compared to our own more objective and more advertising dependent news outlets. Has American interest in voting declined as we are overwhelmed with isolated bits of information but not given the interpretative schema to prod us into action?

Television adopts an especially dominant middle-of-the-road alignment (Postman & Powers, 1992). If print readers come across an article that does not appeal to them, they simply scan the paper for another article. The nature of print encourages readers to stick with the original paper until they notice something more appealing. Adding the occasional specialized item might even attract readers. Television, though, is a time-based medium. If a TV program or news story comes on that the viewer does not like, the viewer has to wait until the program is over to see what is on next on that particular channel. Of course, such devoted viewer loyalty rarely happens. More likely, the viewer will leave that channel and go to another one. There goes the viewer and (more importantly) the viewer's contribution to the ratings. The nature of broadcasting, then, makes it economically intolerant of diversity: Specialized items might repel viewers. In television and radio, *every* news story, sitcom, drama program, music video or song must have some appeal for every member of the audience, or they might lose that audience.

Such a middle-of-the-road incentive could explain why heavy viewers of television tend to be "mainstreamed" compared with light viewers, as argued by an oft-cited cultivation analysis research project (see, e.g., Gerbner, Gross, Morgan, & Signorielli, 1986). According to this perspective, as television habitually exposes people to its overwhelmingly centrist perspective, people themselves begin to adopt a non-extremist perspective on the world. Television cultivates a mainstream perspective in its heaviest viewers, decreasing the diversity of political opinions.

PRODUCT PURITY:
DELIVERING DESIRABLE DEMOGRAPHICS

Although advertisers want the largest numbers possible when placing ads in media, they also want the audience to be "pure." As discussed in Chapter 1, some people are more attractive to advertisers than others. Even mass-oriented advertisers like McDonald's want to reach certain consumers more than others. More specialized advertisers like Infiniti are even more in tune with the demographics of audiences. Advertisers especially want audiences with three characteristics: disposable income, the willingness to spend it and the opportunity to spend it. Advertisers, then, encourage the media to deliver demographic groups (combinations of gender, race, class and socioeconomic indicators) that have these three characteristics. When the media deliver this audience, they are rewarded; if they do not deliver, advertisers ignore the media. In fact, the particular demographics of a media audience may be more significant than the raw numbers. As one advertising executive bluntly stated, "the most important thing for our clients is the demographics" (Sharkey, 1994, p. B29). The emphasis on demographics explains why, at the beginning of the 1994-1995 TV season, a program like *Melrose Place*—when compared to a higher-rated show like *Murder, She Wrote*—can garner more advertising dollars. *Melrose* appeals to more younger viewers than does *Murder*.

The emphasis on advertising-desirable demographics skews media content. Specifically, audiences who possess these characteristics have a louder or more refined voice in the media than those that do not have these characteristics. Media create content to echo the voices or interests of desirable audiences. Audiences who are not "demogenic" are ignored or seriously underrepresented by advertising-supported media. Those who are poor, elderly or live in rural areas have less media options designed to appeal to them than those who are rich, young and urban. This is especially true for the issue of class. Those among the lower or working classes face a double hardship when it comes to mediated information (Baker, 1994). First, because they do not have a high level of disposable income, paying for subscription-oriented media, such as magazines, newspapers, books, cable TV, movies and videos, is problematic if not impossible. Advertising, however, makes the mediated division between rich and poor worse. Advertising is much more likely to subsidize, with advertising revenue, media aimed at the upper class than media aimed at the poor. Both subscription and advertising revenue are increased for the well-to-do. As Baker (1994) concludes about this dynamic in newspapers, "The result is that advertising subsidizes newspapers designed for the people most able to pay without a subsidy" (p. 69). The availability and the quality of media designed for the poor will suffer as a result. Obviously, such a discrepancy has implications for the equality of political knowledge—and potentially for political participation—of the rich compared to the poor (Baker, 1994).

An infamous example of how demographics dictated the availability of media content for certain audiences is the purging of "rural-oriented" television programs on CBS in the late 1960s. At the end of the 1970-1971 season, CBS had 9 of the top 20 highest-rated television programs, including number 15, *Mayberry R.F.D.*, and number 16, *Hee Haw*. Besides these top 20 programs, there were also such solid audience drawers as *Green Acres* and *The Beverly Hillbillies*. By the next season, all 4 programs were gone from the network's schedule, even the 2 in the top 20. The reason for the programming massacre was the demographic battle that CBS was losing at the time. The shows appealed to an audience too old and too rural for advertisers. NBC and ABC were both cultivating programming that skewed younger and more urban with programs like *Rowan and Martin's Laugh-In* (NBC) and *Mod Squad* (ABC). Thus, despite the popularity of the rural programs with millions of viewers, the tyranny of advertising dictated that the programs had to go. The viewers were not the right ones.

The moral of all this is, when the media claim that they simply "give the audience what they want," they lie. At best what they do is "give only certain audiences what they want." Even more precisely, the self-serving media motto should really be amended to, "We give advertisers *who* they want."

PRODUCT PLIANCY:
DELIVERING SUSCEPTIBLE AUDIENCES

So far, the discussion has focused on two important product characteristics, audience size and demographics, emphasizing how advertising's desire for these characteristics may affect non-advertising content. A third characteristic has to do with the audience's susceptibility to the advertising message. Advertisers want audiences who are pliant: audiences who have a mental and emotional disposition to accept the sales pitch of the commercial message. How can such a product be delivered? There is no guarantee, but advertisers desire media content that puts viewers in a mood that is receptive to advertising. They do not want the environment surrounding their ads (the media's non-advertising content) to interfere with their carefully constructed sales pitch. Advertisers believe that their persuasive messages work best when the media content that comes before and after the advertisement puts potential consumers in a certain mood and avoids discussing certain negative ideas. Because advertisers are so concerned about the mediated symbols that surround their advertising messages, they often serve as agenda setters: They encourage media to cover some things and ignore others. Sometimes this agenda-setting role is explicit. Intentional control is manifested when advertisers withdraw their support for a particular TV show or magazine because of its content. Media creators might later think twice about a similar program or article. Sometimes, though, the control is unintentional, such as when media creators self-censor based on the kinds of messages they believe advertisers will like or not like. Regardless of whether it is intentional or unintentional, media practitioners often add or delete specific ideas at the request, or the believed request, of advertisers. Such content alterations serve to induce the most desirable state of mind in audiences so they will be receptive to sales pitches. To restate this idea, advertising has an ideological effect upon media content. Advertising's economic presence significantly influences the view of the world that media present, a view embedded in and influenced by social power and social relations.

What is this ideology? What messages or tones are inserted in advertising-driven media because of the revenue source? Critics have argued that media content often includes specific ideas conducive to consumerism. Ben Bagdikian (1992), in his classic *The Media Monopoly,* lists ideas that have been successfully inserted in content on the behalf of advertisers—messages like "All businessmen are good or, if not, are always condemned by other businessmen" (p. 154). Similarly, certain TV genres that promote commercialism, such as game shows ("Shoppers, Come On Down!") and talk shows ("Of course I'm excited about my latest movie, Jay! Want me to set up this next clip?") blend in quite well with the commercials. In newspapers and magazines, sections like Entertainment, Lifestyle and Fashion are often commodity driven. News stories about commodities—like the latest movies, toys, clothes or cars—complement the advertising for these very same products. Sometimes advertisers make explicit demands for such product-oriented content. The Chair of the Tandy Corporation (parent company of Radio Shack) implied exactly that in a 1994 public speech to the Newspaper Association of America. In this speech, he hinted that little of Tandy's $500 million advertising budget would go to newspapers unless that medium "gave significant coverage to new store openings and important press releases" (Stein, 1994, p. 13). Presumably, however, coverage of such events from a consumer advocacy point of view would not count.

Besides the pro-advertising ideas in the media, the tone and style of much of the mass media, especially television, are receptive to advertising. Barnouw (1970) argues that critically acclaimed "anthology" television series like *Kraft Television Theater* in the 1950s ultimately did not survive because the tone was too consistently disturbing, downbeat, controversial and unpredictable for television advertising. A drama like the anticorporate teleplay "Patterns" was not very advertising friendly. Situation comedies, on the other hand, increasingly the most prevalent genre on television, mesh perfectly with the needs of advertising. Unlike the 1950s anthology series, every week one finds in the sitcom the same likeable characters, the same premise, and, presumably, the same audience (give or take a few million). The situation comedy is designed to be broken into thirds, with commercials easily slotted between trivial cliffhangers. In addition, everyone feels good while watching a sitcom: It is designed to make people laugh. So when you see the commercial for Camay Soap in between bits of *Full House,* you are in a receptive mood to be hit up for money. Of course, the more "sitcommy" (read, the more warm and fuzzy) the program, the more desirable for advertisers.

Illustrating this is the 1993-1994 television season, when it was more expensive to advertise on the ABC program *Home Improvement* than on *Roseanne* ($25,000 per 30 seconds more expensive), despite the fact that the *Roseanne* vehicle had had higher ratings the previous year. Although certainly one reason for this discrepancy is the slightly more desirable demographics of *Home Improvement,* another reason could be the darker tone of *Roseanne,* which undermines the buying mood of the public. As one advertising executive speculated about the differences in the two shows vis-à-vis advertisers, *"Roseanne* [like *Home Improvement*] also has a family setting, but it's a much more dysfunctional family" (Mandese, 1993h, p. 26).

Thus, advertising encourages ideas favorable to selling to be included in media, and it influences the tone and style of media. Advertising also has the effect of discouraging the inclusion of certain ideas in media content. As one advertising critic argues, "Despite the potential danger and occasional occurrence of government censorship, private entities in general and advertisers in particular constitute the most consistent and the most pernicious 'censors' of media content" (Baker, 1994, p. 3). Topics that are explicitly anti-advertising, or even anticorporate, must often meet a higher threshold of journalistic certainty, artistic achievement and viewer interest than more innocuous topics. Advertisers hope that media creators will heavily screen such topics. If, however, critical ideas occasionally make it through the media industry filter, advertisers will often not hesitate to yank advertising dollars from the offending media organization. For instance, NBC criticized Coca-Cola in a documentary on farm workers in 1970. Although the documentary was accurate, the beverage company pulled many of its commercials from the network. It was years before NBC aired another documentary criticizing a major advertiser (Baker, 1994). Cigarette manufacturers have also displayed a quick trigger finger when criticized by the media (Bagdikian, 1992; Baker, 1994).

Many advertisers do not want *any* sort of explicitly political or disturbing idea at all near their advertisements, even if it is not specifically anti-ad. Advertisers essentially want viewers who are politically and emotionally "sleepy," not mad as hell and really quite willing to take it some more (Selnow & Gilbert, 1993, p. 140). Viewers who are too charged up might question specific advertising claims or even the role of advertising in society. In addition, protests and boycotts targeted at advertisers but designed to influence the ideological content of media content, make advertisers very nervous. Advertisers do not want any group to threaten a boycott because an advertiser places spots on particular programs. Thus, political ideas—especially ones that lean too heavily to the left—may be advertising poison. Rush Limbaugh, certainly, can find advertisers for his radio show, but leftist or liberal counterparts have a more difficult time (Wilke, 1995a). Even Limbaugh faced some advertising backlash, apparently because of his extremely political persona, however. Although the Florida Department of Citrus denied that politics entered into the decision, in July 1994 the organization pulled its advertising buys on Limbaugh's radio program amid protests over the program's sponsors (DeNitto, 1994a).

Likewise, advertisers might avoid media content that they consider potentially too unpleasant or disturbing for consumers. Major advertisers like Procter & Gamble and Kodak have official guidelines about what media content is acceptable—and more importantly, unacceptable—as carriers of their ads (Baker, 1994; Selnow & Gilbert, 1993). Kodak's "Guidelines for Television Program Acceptance" include avoidance of programs in which "members of the clergy (ministers, priests, rabbis, nuns, etc.) are portrayed in a manner that clearly denigrates or satirizes their position" (quoted in Selnow & Gilbert, 1993, p. 156). Kodak also prohibits gratuitous sex, violence and profanity—and a laundry list of other taboos.

Television advertisers invest in certain techniques to ensure their desired level of control over content. Although advertisers cannot make explicit demands for script changes in the shows on which they advertise, they often do read scripts or preview already taped but not yet aired programs. Once a buy has been made, large advertisers will frequently hire firms, like The Advertising Information Services, to screen programs to check for ad placement, juxtaposition of commercial ideas with program ideas, and the technical quality of the broadcast (Robins, 1992).

It is useful at this point to update an argument made earlier about the television networks and their willingness to accept advertising influence. Observers have noted about the 1993-1994 television season that, as advertising revenues tightened for the networks, the networks aired more "safe" programming in an attempt to placate advertisers. When Johnson & Johnson threatened to pull its ads from the 1992-1993 CBS program *Hearts Afire* because of the implication of premarital sex, the program returned the next year with the main characters married. In a sitcom originally planned for NBC, *Monty,* the main character's daughter was a lesbian. Fox picked up the show mid-season with the character transformed as straight. As one Disney executive concluded, "[The schedules were] so safe because there's a fear of losing advertising. You mix that with a society that is much more [economically] conservative and a recession and you get a recipe for safe programming" (Brodie & Robins, 1993, p. 65).

Network programmers may have learned the same lesson from *NYPD Blue*, one of the few truly innovative shows that season, as they did from 1990's *Twin Peaks* and *Cop Rock*. *NYPD Blue* was highly controversial, pushing the network envelope for nudity and harsh language. The controversy heated up when Donald Wildmon and the American Family Association targeted the show as immoral. Although *NYPD Blue* was a ratings and critical success, it was slow to attract advertisers because of the controversy, and this tardiness cost its network, ABC, significant revenue. As one network executive noted about the gritty program, "Terrific show. Terrific ratings, and ABC lost money on it last year because too many advertisers were scared away by the Rev. Wildmon and the rest of the lunatic fringe." The same executive observed about the next season's programming that, "this year there's nothing that comes close to [*NYPD Blue*]" (Robins, 1994b, p. 42).

TWO FINAL POINTS ABOUT EXTERNAL CONTROL

Two more arguments about the external influence that advertisers have over media content are especially critical. An important theme for many economic critics of advertising is the increased growth of individual advertising organizations. A company that puts in one ad for one product may not have much influence, but a company that places a hundred ads for a hundred products could (Leiss et al., 1990). Thus, researchers have noted that even though tobacco ads have been banned from broadcasting, the electronic media may be hesitant to criticize tobacco products because the large diversified cigarette companies spend so much money in the media to advertise their other products (Shoemaker & Reese, 1991). Philip Morris, for example—the second largest U.S. broadcast ad-space buyer in 1993 behind Procter & Gamble—spent more than $700 million that year to reach broadcasting audiences ("100 Leading National Advertisers," 1995). Similarly, to stress a point from Chapter 1, individual advertising agencies can possess clout through the sheer number of dollars they represent. Leo Burnett, the top agency in placing ads in U.S. media, had more than $2.1 billion in billings in 1993 ("U.S. Agency Brands," 1995). Such economic weight could allow particular advertisers and agencies a powerful voice in media operations.

A second point involves the influence of advertising upon non-advertising media content, like CDs, motion pictures and videos. Advertising is a powerful social institution, and it affects other media, even those it does not traditionally finance. For example, many advertising-free media, to compete successfully, may have to copy the entertainment style of advertising media. Even if motion pictures never accept advertising revenue, they will be affected by advertising in that advertising media influence the definition of expected entertainment. But advertisers will often try to get their economic claws in these media, too. Later chapters, in fact, will highlight advertising's economic intrusiveness into these normally advertising-free media. Motion picture producers, for example, now routinely assume revenue will flow from advertisers interested in placing their products on the motion picture screen. Advertising, then, is not just interested in a depth of control (nearly complete allocative control over media systems, for example), but also in a breadth of control (turning new media technologies or even social institutions into promotional vehicles). Schiller (1989) notes how museums and public celebrations are often turned into sponsored corporate events. Mattelart (1991) highlights how international media systems previously run and funded by the state are now privately sponsored through advertising.

These, then, are a few of the most central arguments of the economic critics of advertising. We will see these arguments recur throughout the different chapters. But another strong critical strain focused on advertising is the work of critics who concentrate on the semiotic manipulation that occurs in advertising. Like the economic camp, symbolic critics of advertising emphasize the imperative of control, but rather than concentrate on the control that occurs outside of advertising texts themselves (such as the influence of advertising upon media content), these critics concentrate on the symbolic expansion and control *in* the advertisements.

Advertising, Symbolic Critics and the Internal Control of Commercial Content

Advertisers of most mass-produced products face a serious dilemma selling these products. One product (like Pepsi) is not materially different from the competing product (like Coke). So how does one differentiate, promotionally, one product from another? One way to differentiate the product is to lower the price permanently but, frankly, manufacturers do not normally like to go for this strategy. The lack of real differences between the ingredients of competing products creates a problem for advertisers, who usually turn to the world of the symbolic to solve this problem.

Several critics have written about the symbolic solution advertisers have devised for their problem. Davidson (1992), using industry terminology, calls it the "branding" of a product (p. 23). Hayakawa (1972) termed it the "poeticizing of consumer goods" (p. 225). Leiss et al. (1990) describe it as the application of the "Product-Image Format" (p. 244). R. Goldman (1992) explores the "commodity-signs" of ads (pp. 37-60). In probably the most extensive discussion, however, Williamson (1978) writes about the process as the linkage of products with desirable "referent systems," a term this discussion will adopt.

ADVERTISING AND REFERENT SYSTEMS

Manufacturers' solutions to the differentiation dilemma have created a contradiction in product advertising. To differentiate one product from another, the advertisement must avoid talking too much about the product. The product itself, after all, has few differences from competing products, so talking just about the product would reveal this lack of distinction. What do ads for the product talk about, then? In order to strengthen the "uniqueness" of the product, advertising must go *beyond* the product and focus instead on the needs and wants of the consumer. Ads are not as much about the products as about the consumers—their likes, dislikes, aspirations and social anxieties. Advertisers ask, "What are the most desired values and goals of our customers, and what symbols can we use in our ads to represent these values and goals?" Advertising seeks symbolic control over the perceived differentiation of a product by linking the product in the ad with something "outside" the product: a socially desirable object or value for the audience. By symbolically placing the product with the object or some other icon representing the object or value (like Cindy Crawford for "hip"), advertisers hope that, through association, the audience will link the qualities of the object/value with the product. Cindy, representing hip, is the referent system for Pepsi in Pepsi's ad. Cindy is the symbol, hip is the referent, and Pepsi wants to get in the middle of this symbol-referent connection. Thus, although the product is not materially different from other products, if successful the positive social image of the product (Hip Pepsi) is different from the negative social image of the competitor (Square Coke). Advertising attempts to construct the image of the product through referent systems in this way.

Often, the ad just tries to associate the product with the referent system. Cindy Crawford is drinking Pepsi in this ad; consumers like to be hip; consumers believe Cindy Crawford is hip; consumers like Cindy Crawford; the hipness and likability of the symbol Cindy Crawford will (hopefully) be transferred to Pepsi in consumers' minds. The ad works as an *enthymeme*—an implied connection between symbols—that the advertiser hopes the audience will make. Nowhere in the ad are these symbolic linkages made explicit: A narrator does not say, "Here's Cindy Crawford. We all know she is hip. And because she is drinking Pepsi in this ad, you should think Pepsi is hip, too." Such an obvious narration would sound absurd. So rather than tell us these connections, the advertiser hopes we, the audience, will make these connections in our heads. Through the juxtaposition of elements in the ad (Cindy, in a hip outfit, drinking Pepsi and having a refreshed expression), an implied linkage is made. Advertisers are banking on our previous knowledge of icons of hipness. They are hoping that we already know that Cindy = hip. The advertiser hopes that the audience will merge the product symbol (a Pepsi can) with Cindy as symbol and finally with the meaning of "hip."

Sometimes, though, the ad tries to do more with the connection between the product and the referent system. Sometimes the ad implies that the product "generates" the value. The consumer can become part of the symbolic linkage when the product generates the referent system. All the consumer has to do is buy the product. Joining the Army allows you to "Be All You Can Be." To achieve self-actualization (the desired referent), the ad implies, you need to join the Army (i.e., buy the product). You own the referent system when you own the product. In other cases, the product is the necessary "currency" to achieve the desired value. The product gives you something to trade to achieve the referent. Gleem leads to white teeth, which make you romantically desirable. White teeth alone are not the desired referent, but you need white teeth to achieve the referent (romantic success). In these ways the link between the product and the referent system is strengthened:

The product is necessary to gain access to the referent system, either directly (product as referent system generator) or indirectly (product as referent system currency) (Williamson, 1978, pp. 36-38).

THE IDEOLOGICAL EFFECTS OF REFERENT SYSTEMS

The referent system strategy is interesting in and of itself as a persuasive tactic. But symbolic critics of advertising focus on a more significant issue: the potential ideological effects of referent systems in advertising. Such critics often argue that advertising as a symbol system affects not only our view of the product, but also our view of society, of social power and of social relations. This section will discuss four ideological effects of advertising: (a) the pure referent system, (b) the devalued referent system, (c) the infected referent system and (d) the hegemonic referent system.

The Pure Referent System

Williamson (1978) and others note that it is not enough for advertisers simply to link their product with an external referent system, because a referent system will often contain elements that are *NOT* desirable to the advertiser. Thus, advertising offers a "purified" or ideal view not only of the product, but of the referent system itself. By decontextualizing the referent system, the advertisement removes any possible detrimental element of the referent system for the product.

This purification process can be so complete that advertisements can even use referent systems that are often critical of advertising—for example, feminism ("You've Come a Long Way, Baby"). R. Goldman (1992) describes the purification of feminist symbols in advertising:

> When advertisers appropriate feminism, they cook it to distill out a residue—an object: a look, a style. Women's discourses are thus relocated and respoken by named objects like *Hanes* hose, *Nike* shoes, *Esprit* jeans. Sign-objects are thus made to stand for, and made equivalent to, feminist goals of independence and professional status. (p. 131)

At its most extreme, then, advertising can gain symbolic control over a referent system by "recuperating" its values (Williamson, 1978, p. 167). The positive elements of the referent system are highlighted in the ad; the potential antiselling drawbacks are symbolically removed. Thus, as Ewen (1988, p. 98) explains, this recuperative and decontextualizing technique is what allowed IBM to use the Little Tramp character from Chaplin's *Modern Times* to sell computers, despite the fact that the original movie was about the horrors of technology and industrialization. A similar point can be made about the use of rap music in advertising. When an ad uses rap (when the Campbell Soup kids sing their jingle to a rap beat), it is not really using rap—it is using advertising's version of rap. The beat is there, as is the "look" of rap and hip-hop, but the advertisement has removed the political meat of the genre. Rap becomes a sound in advertising but is no longer a political battery.

Another issue related to the purification of referent systems is the expansive tendencies of ads. I discussed briefly in the previous section that advertising is externally expansive. In this economic perspective, the expansion is physical: Ads are placed in movies or on the outside of a bus or in a museum. In the symbolic perspective, however, a referent system can be expansive. *Any* referent system is open to advertising co-optation. Traditionally, peer acceptance, individual self-actualization, sexual appeal, religion, history and art are possible referent systems that have been co-opted by advertisers. Advertising even has an incentive to expand symbolically. Because advertising wants to plug into the popular value systems of its audience (at least, a purified version of the value systems) and because advertising wants to grab a viewer's attention (and often uses its version of "the new" to do this), advertising seeks to expand its control over new social symbols. Dinosaurs become the rage in ads after *Jurassic Park's* theatrical run; the grunge look is found in ads at the height of the Seattle scene; the Persian Gulf War is exploited in ads when it looks like the result will be U.S.A. All The Way (McAllister, 1993). Of course, the purification and recuperative processes mentioned above partially explain the vast range of referent systems available to advertising. Ads, through symbolic manipulation, are easily able to decontextualize and remove any non advertising-friendly elements from new referent systems.

The Devalued Referent System

Wernick argues that there is another consequence of the linking of the product to social referent systems in advertising. The obvious purpose of an advertisement is to sell a product. This is its very reason for existence. *Everything* that is in an advertisement, then, is subordinated to that purpose. By definition, to put a referent system in an ad is to devalue it. When used in an ad, according to the ad's inherent symbolic hierarchy, the referent system is subordinate to the purpose of selling the product (Wernick, 1991, p. 189).

Benetton, the clothing manufacturer, caused quite a stir in the 1990s with its controversial "United Colors of Benetton" social issue ads. In these ads, only a small logo for Benetton in a lower corner signals what the ad is selling. The rest of the ad presents a man dying of AIDS, or a blood-stained Bosnian uniform, or a nun and priest kissing or an interracial kiss. The concept of the devalued referent system highlights the social dangers of Benetton's campaign. No matter how noble the intentions of Benetton's advertising creators, showing images of race relations in the ads symbolically positions racial issues as lower than, and existing for, commercialism. The man with AIDS becomes a Benetton referent system used to sell a product. In fact, when explaining the justification for the ads in the midst of heavy criticism in Europe, a Benetton spokesperson revealed the ease with which the commercial imperative can devalue the social topics. According to Benetton, a rationale for the ads is not their effectiveness as a consciousness raiser, but rather their effectiveness as a selling tool: "Benetton products are doing better than others thanks to its advertising" (Mussey, 1995). Good sales end the argument.

The example of celebrity endorsers—and the contamination effect of such endorsements—also illustrates the "devaluation" process of advertising. Advertisers love to use motion picture celebrities as referent systems. Movie stars know, however, that appearing in commercials dilutes their star quality. When you see a movie star shilling for a product, the glamour and allure of the star decreases. Because such commercially active stars are tainted, they often find they have fewer offers for future projects or perhaps command less of a salary. For instance, media industry analysts have argued that Cher's appearances in both short-form 30-second commercials and long-form infomercials somewhat derailed her Oscar-winning career as a movie actress (Murphy, 1993). Other big-time movie stars who want the dollars that product endorsements offer but do not want to dilute their celebrity mystique will appear in television advertisements abroad, as in the examples of Eddie Murphy, Arnold Schwarzenegger, Kim Basinger and Woody Allen. They believe that such international endorsements minimize the danger of devaluing their Hollywood image by marginalizing their commercial appearances.

The Infected Referent System

Other critics have pointed to the "infectious" nature of advertising, or the ability of a successful ad to turn the referent system itself into an ad (R. Goldman, 1992, p. 19). When advertisers successfully link their product with a socially desirable image/value/object, at the very least what they want is the "goodness" of the value to rub off on the product. When we see Michael Jordan in a Nike commercial, because we like Michael Jordan we will like Nike, too. But advertisers, ideally, want more than this: They want "Nike-ness" to infect Michael Jordan. Advertisers want the link in our heads to be so strong between Nike and Michael Jordan that not only do we like Nike better because it is associated with MJ, but when we see MJ we automatically think, "Air Jordan/Air Nike." Michael Jordan becomes a walking advertisement—on and off the court (or the baseball diamond), in and out of commercials—for Nike.

The infectious nature of advertising symbols is one reason using "oldie" songs for commercials is such a good idea, promotionally. It is not just that such songs (like the Beatles' *Revolution*—for Nike, again) have nostalgic value for such lucrative markets as baby boomers. The song might also become popular again because of its exposure in the commercial (Cook, 1992, p. 126), and every time it airs on the radio as radio content, it is a free plug for the product. For this reason the Woody Allen movie *Manhattan* is forever tainted for me. I think of United Airlines whenever I see the movie: Both United and Woody used George Gershwin music, but United used it more explicitly and more ubiquitously, and the connection is permanently linked in my mind.

The Hegemonic Referent System

A key concept for critics who focus on the ideological import of media systems is hegemony. *Hegemony,* though, is a pretty slippery term. It can have varied shades of meaning depending upon the goals and assumptions of the critic. In this context, hegemony refers to a circumstance where the power differential of a social system is made to appear natural and inevitable. For those with power and those without power, the system is hegemonic when the power difference appears to be the natural order of things: the way things have always been done, always are done and always will be done. The referent system strategy used by advertising encourages advertising to have a hegemonic function. This section will focus specifically on how advertising legitimatizes capitalism. Advertising, as a totality, often creates an image of capitalism that naturalizes it. Capitalism is a given in advertising and is often explicitly celebrated. Though this section will not focus on the these issues, other critics have focused on the hegemonic function of advertising regarding gender (Bretl & Cantor, 1988; Lovdal, 1989) and race (Kern-Foxworth, 1994). One point to stress here is that advertisers are not conspirators trying to oppress the powerless in society. Any hegemonic effect of advertising messages is not purposeful. Advertisers really just care about selling their products. Often, though, the techniques they use to sell their products have social effects that go beyond selling.

Advertising as a whole celebrates capitalism. This celebration takes a couple of different but related forms. First, many advertisements explicitly trumpet capitalist institutions. Commercials for banks obviously celebrate banking; commercials for credit cards celebrate that industry. Because financial advertising links the product with things that audiences find positive (as any advertisement does), the capitalistic products are placed in an unwaveringly positive light. To illustrate briefly: A 1994 TV commercial for Visa Gold presents the ubiquity of automatic teller machines (ATMs) abroad and how useful Visa Gold is with such machines. In the commercial, two Americans are faced with a broken-down car in a Middle East desert. A local boy comes to their rescue, however, and points them to a money machine. The ad ends with a crowd of natives from the country watching in admiration as the two Americans successfully withdraw money. The indigenous people literally applaud the Americans for their financial resources. The magic of "ATM" (pronounced *Ettiene* by the small boy) and a Visa Gold card rescue the Americans. In this commercial, Visa specifically and money lending generally is associated with security in a foreign country, security during mechanical breakdown, international reverence for the United States and social approval. Other commercials celebrate capitalist institutions because the ads are targeted at those in business. Television commercials aired in 1995 for Microsoft self-servingly attempted to appeal to financial and corporate leaders by declaring (twice) that, "Business is the engine of society."

Besides such pro-capitalist commercials, a much more significant legitimation of capitalist ideology occurs in the way advertising discusses consumption. Consumption and commodities are presented so uniformly in advertising that the discourse perpetuates a capitalistic worldview. Advertisements link the product with a socially desirable referent system. Often, the symbolic strategy of the ad implies that the product will *generate* that referent system—that is, if one acquires the product, then one acquires the valued meanings or goals. If the referent system in a commercial is social acceptance, then the ad implies that the product will generate social acceptance. Advertising constantly implies that values like love, security, peace of mind, fun, peer acceptance and hipness can be acquired with the product. In other words, consumers can *buy* love, security and the other values. All they need to do is spend money . . . on the advertised product, that is. Cumulatively, advertising overwhelmingly endorses the consumption ethic. In the world of advertising, self-actualization is achieved not through political participation or intellect or world awareness, but through consumption. It is a one-solution discourse, with that one solution—spending—being presented in the mass media over and over. Advertising encourages active buying, and, by extension, discourages participation in other interventionist arenas like politics.

Another way to describe the emphasis that advertising places on consumption is to apply the concept of the *fetishism of commodities* to advertising. This term, adapted to advertising by Jhally (1987) and others, has several implications, but the most relevant issue for this discussion involves the specific images of consumers and consumption that advertising presents. Because advertising is most interested in getting people to buy products, it makes perfect sense that the messages in advertising emphasize and celebrate the consumption of these products over their production. Advertising, using socially desirable values, makes consuming its products appear as desirable as possible. What many symbolic critics argue, then, is that advertising—as a main source of product information for most Americans—skews our view of product commodities. We fetishize the product. We can see the products only in terms of consumption.

Advertising lacks any sort of discussion of what Schudson (1986, p. 6) calls "externalities," or the social costs of mass producing a commodity. It is very logical for advertising, given its purpose, to exclude such discussions. Why would an ad include information about the amount of pollution caused by the production of its product? Or the investment policies of the company that produced the product? Or the ownership patterns of the company? Or the labor policies? Or the amount of raw materials (including animal lives) that went into the product? If they aren't forced to include the information, they won't. Instead they talk about how great it would be to consume the product. They talk about how consuming the product will get us a date, financial security or a cool image.

Because advertisers do not include this information and because advertisers so heavily stress consumption views of commodities over production views, we as users of the advertisements may perceive commodities and products overwhelmingly in terms of consumption. When we see a diamond ring, we usually do not automatically think, "I wonder if the diamond was mined under exploitative working conditions?" Instead we often think, "I wonder how that would look on my finger?" or "I wonder if I could afford to purchase that ring?"

The fetishism-of-commodity perspective is an argument for the hegemonic effects of advertising. Consumption-oriented thinking protects the producers of the products. If advertising trains us to think of products in terms of consumption rather than production, then the production process may often go unexamined and, therefore, unquestioned.

These, then, are the main arguments of the economic and symbolic critics of advertising, arguments that I will return to in later chapters. But despite the traditional separation between the political economic and the symbolic traditions, recent trends in advertising lend themselves to a combination of the two schools. In the 1990s, mechanisms for external and internal control are merging, a merging that is being manifested in the new and renewed advertising techniques. Panicked over the loss of influence by such factors as clutter and audience activity, but delighted by deregulation and media subservience, advertising is exploring new techniques of control that involve both economic and symbolic elements. Chapter 3 discusses one such tactic of control: place-based advertising.

Notes

1. The economics of magazine publishing is a little more complicated that this, of course. Technically, magazine distributors are the producer's immediate customer for newsstand sales, because these distributors give the producers of magazines money. For the purposes of this specific argument, though, such distinctions are not critical.

2. Postman's explanation for why television is so entertainment oriented is different from the emphasis here, however. Postman is a neo-McLuhanist, which means he stresses the technology of television as its central characteristic. Television as a channel for communication, according to Postman, shapes information in a way that makes it more image oriented and entertainment driven. Postman views the commercial imperative of media as secondary to the monolithic effects of the pervasiveness of television technology.

3. Rush Limbaugh's popularity is an obvious exception to the middle-of-the-road orientation of ad-supported media. In this case, one could argue that the entertainment imperative of media supplanted the middle-of-the-road imperative. Limbaugh's personal charisma is appealing to many people and so overcomes the potential offensiveness of right-wing ideologue discourse.

3

PLACE-BASED ADVERTISING
Control Through Location

As you climb aboard an exercise bicycle at your local health club, you get mentally ready for a hard workout. Around you are other like-minded health enthusiasts, those on the go, those who do not stay home very much, but also those investing the time and money for a physically active lifestyle. Gearing up for the first electronically simulated hill, you notice the television monitors in front of you for HCTV, or Health Club Television, a satellite-delivered medium. On the screen you see not only programming about health-related issues, but also commercials for health-related products and other merchandise for active yuppies with plenty of disposable income. The people in the programming and commercials, you notice, are often idealized versions of the people around you: All just doing it, all believing sweat is sexy, all wanting to taste it all. If you want to zap to another program, too bad.

You do not have a remote control, and there is nothing else on. Literally.

HCTV is an example of place-based advertising, a recent advertising trend expected to become a significant media placement strategy for advertisers in the 1990s and beyond. This chapter will analyze this "new medium," as it is called in the advertising trade journals, arguing that the best way to understand the dynamics of "place-based"—its origins as well as its possible effects—is through a combination of both political economic criticism of advertising and symbolic criticism of advertising. This combination is especially useful for the new trend because place-based combines the economic and symbolic influences of advertising in a more aggressive way than in the past. The possibilities for new levels of internal and external control by advertising through place-based strategies and technologies will also be discussed.

The Rise, Fall and Rise of Place-Based Advertising

Traditionally, most advertising-supported media are "home based." The consumer is exposed to the advertised message while at home watching television, listening to the radio and reading newspapers and magazines. Advertising, then, was often physically tied to the home. Yet there are more and more "place-based" media options available for advertisers. One ad industry executive defines a place-based medium as "one where the demographics of the reader, viewer or listener are controlled by the location in which the message is delivered" (Cortez, 1992e, p. 25). Place-based media can take many forms, including televisual (such as in the notorious school-based project, Channel One); magazines (including McDonald's *McMagazine*); radio (like Kmart's in-store KMRT); posters (such as the display boards placed in senior citizen centers by The Senior Network); bags and sacks (like In-Flight Humor!, which places ads on airsickness bags); interactive kiosks (like The iStation found in music stores); and even floor tiles (brought to you by two companies, Floor Focus Media and Indoor Media). The creators of the media will often provide free media technology and programming, and will in turn rake in money from advertisers wishing to reach those potential consumers who visit the place. Sometimes the controlling organizations of the place (the school, the music store) are monetarily compensated for allowing the media to be there. Sometimes those organizations are given free media time to plug themselves on the media in their own place. Sometimes those organizations create the place-based media themselves.

Out-of-home advertising has probably existed as long as there has been advertising. A London clothing merchant in 1740 placed his shop bill alongside the town crier during announcements, for example (Presbrey, 1968, p. 490). Place-based techniques increase during times of promotional frustration for advertisers. In England during the mid-1800s, for instance, many manufacturers found that applying assembly-line industrial processes created a glut of goods that outpaced consumption. This glut of manufactured product was coupled with a London press that still placed many restrictions upon advertising. As a result, advertisers looked elsewhere for new advertising vehicles—and outdoor advertising prospered. Dyer (1982) notes about this period that, "At one time in London billposting was so popular that it seemed you might never get to see a building at all" (p. 32). Later that century, British advertising could be found in some places normally not thought of as advertising carriers, such as theater safety curtains (Dyer, 1982).

In the United States, the height of the industrial revolution saw its share of out-of-home promotion and place-based strategies. Manufacturers during this time sought different ways to promote their product before the rise of broadcasting solved many of their advertising problems. In the 1860s, "sandwich men," who literally wore advertisements, strolled visibly down big city streets and passed out handbills (Presbrey, 1968, p. 258). At the retail level from the 1860s onward, manufacturers attempted to socialize people to the idea of buying mass-manufactured, branded goods. One technique was to flood retailers with point-of-purchase (POP) displays for such products as Uneeda Biscuits or Ivory Soap (Strasser, 1989). Such strategies continued to be used, of course, and are still used today. Similarly, advertising printed on paper bags utilized in retail outlets became prevalent in the 1880s to promote these new industrialized products. Billboards, too, became more of an institutionalized form of advertising during this time, as billboard companies systematized payment plans and location strategies. Besides buildings, manufacturers placed their messages on such transportation devices as horse-drawn cars and trolleys to reach commuters (Strasser, 1989).

Other strategies were even more creative. In U.S. theaters in the 1880s, manufacturers might not advertise on fire curtains but did "produce" plays with free and open admission, in which a product, like a Willcox & Gibbs sewing machine, would be featured heavily in the plot (Presbrey, 1968, p. 303). Even in routinely produced plays, in what may be the closest 19th-century precedent to the "place-based" strategy (i.e., designed to reach well-to-do theatergoers through ad placement in media), the printed theater program often included advertising by at least the 1850s (Presbrey, 1968, p. 518).

In this century, besides the continued use of out-of-home advertising such as the Goodyear blimp,[1] billboards and POP displays, ads might precede motion pictures in theaters in the 1920s. One such example is the film short *Brushing the Clouds Away,* plugging Fuller Brushes (Ewen, 1976, p. 73). These early precedents, though, were limited. They tended to be scattered and "gimmicky," not really an indication of an established advertising trend. When broadcasting became a viable national advertising medium in the mid-1920s, the incentives for aggressively exploring place-based strategies declined as radio and television sucked up advertising dollars. Because of broadcasting's effectiveness as an advertising medium, most major promoters saw little use in the mainstream application of advertising on fire curtains and play programs. Such place-based strategies became the domain of the small business looking for the cheap gimmick or were limited in scope to billboards and POP techniques.

No longer. Place-based, just a few years ago labeled "new media," "alternative media," and even (ironically) "environmental media," is becoming a more established option for advertisers. The 1990s have seen an incredible proliferation of such media for several reasons. The increased economic and technological sophistication, including im-proved satellite technology that allows programming and ads to be easily beamed to places with electronic place-based media, has encour-aged the strategy's growth. Similarly, the decreased effectiveness of broadcasting as an advertising medium—caused by such factors as clutter, remote controls and VCRs—has also been a factor in the tactic's renewal.

Place-based advertising is a hot tactic for the 1990s. Advertisers spent between $350 and $500 million on place-based media in 1991 (Cortez, 1992e, p. 25) and by 1994 were spending $700 million annually, with a projected annual growth of 50% (Kelly, 1994). As one advertising executive noted about the trend, "Place-based media is like the Wild West of the American frontier. It's an exciting freewheeling brawl, and there's a new idea coming to town every week" (Kelly, 1994, p. 12).

Actually, advertising in different social locations is becoming less of a frontier and more of a civilized promotional option. The increased institutionalization of place-based media points to its continued acceptability. For example, advertising industry trade journals, such as *Advertising Age,* have included a section on place-based media in their annual "round-up" reviews of media (Cortez, 1992f). Many organizations, such as Actmedia and Catalina Marketing, focus on creating place-based options for their clients. Advertisers have hired advertising agencies specifically to coordinate place-based strategies, such as Frito-Lay's hiring of BBDO for such duties (Syedain, 1992). Perhaps the strongest indicator of acceptance is the fact that powerful establishment media organizations, including Turner Broadcasting, NBC, CBS, ABC, Time Warner and Gannett, are investing in or setting up place-based organizations. Turner Broadcasting System is investing so heavily in the place-based phenomenon that it has created a subsidiary, Turner Private Networks, to coordinate its efforts in that realm. Established media organizations have found that they can exploit their copyrighted hardware and, especially, software (stock programming) to gain market advantage in the place-based wonderland.

There is an ever-growing list of sites where place-based media can be found and, increasingly, several choices of media in any given place. Thus, for example, place-based media exist in the social places listed below.

ENTERTAINMENT PLACES

Advertisers like to place their ads in entertainment media. Such media provide a nonthreatening symbolic environment for the advertising. They make audiences pliant for advertisers. Because of this, it follows that one of the most common venues for place-based advertising is in out-of-home entertainment places. When people are ready to be entertained they are often in a good mood, relaxed, and perhaps receptive to persuasive messages.

In movie theaters, several options for place-based strategies exist and at least two of these strategies are antagonistic toward each other. One logical option is the showing of ads on the screen *before* a movie, because people are often in their seats staring at the screen minutes before the movie starts. In addition, moviegoers are accustomed to movie trailers that advertise upcoming features. Accordingly, National Cinema Network's On-Screen Entertainment is an organization that derives revenue from the coordination of slide ads before movies (Magiera, 1990a). Another pre-movie option is Screenvision Cinema Network, which can boast the placement of filmed commercials in more than 6,600 theaters for companies such as Coca-Cola, AT&T and Reebok (Magiera, 1993b).

Many movie studios and distributors, especially Disney and Warner, frown upon pre-movie ad activity. These studios have banned on-screen ads before their movies since 1990 (Magiera, 1993b), for a reason to be discussed below. Despite such mandates, theaters have actually increased the number of pre-movie commercials since the bans (Magiera, 1993b). The increase illustrates the financial benefits of the strategy for theaters and perhaps the irresistible movement of place-based strategies generally. But some theaters that have complied with the studios' wishes—and seek to replace lost ad revenue because of that ban—have looked to other place-based strategies. *Movies USA* is an ad-supported magazine distributed in theaters (Magiera, 1990a), and Cinemedia Corporation has experimented with placing ads on popcorn bags in movie theaters (Magiera, 1992b). UA has created the Lobby Monitor Network, which places ads on TV monitors in movie theater lobbies (Mandese, 1992d).

Another way advertisers can reach viewers in movie theaters is through product placement, in which the advertisers pay a fee to have their product featured in the movies themselves. Product placement, although found in movies since at least the 1930s, took off after 1982, when E.T.'s cinematic love of Reese's Pieces increased sales by 70% (Schudson, 1986, p. 102). The attractiveness of product placement explains the economic logic behind Disney's and Warner's ban of pre-movie theater ads. In pre-movie ads, the theaters benefit economically. In product placement, the studios benefit. So studios have tried to flex their theatrical muscles to make product placement advertisements stand out in an ad-free environment. Ads before movies would dilute the attractiveness to promoters of ads in movies. Disney aggressively markets product placement *in* its movies: For $40,000, for example, marketers could have had a character use their product in the Disney movie *Mr. Destiny* (Magiera, 1990b, p. 8). High-profile movies like *Total Recall, Back to the Future: Part II,* and *Wayne's World* feature prominent product placements. Sometimes a product placer will not specifically pay for the ads, but will trade for them: *Fortune* magazine gave the movie *Wall Street* free advertising space in exchange for favorable placement in the movie (one character calls *Fortune* "the bible") (Miller, 1990). Chapter 5 will argue that product placements often become important parts of cross-promotional deals. In fact, product placement has become institutionalized to such a degree that there are several dozen companies that *coordinate* product placement for advertisers (Slate, 1993, p. 77).[2]

Ad-supported media are also found in entertainment places besides movie theaters. Channel M (for Minotaur Promotions) is a very successful televisual ad medium placed in video arcades, positioning music videos and video game tips around the ads. When the service began, an advertiser would pay $650 per location to have a TV spot played more than 300 times a month (Kelly, 1991; Goldman, 1994a). In ski resorts, Resort Network Sport has established Ski TV nationwide, featuring ads from such marketers as Chrysler and Anheuser-Busch (Kelly, 1991). Advertisers such as Lubriderm Lotion can also buy outdoor billboard ads along the chair lifts at these resorts ("Just Don't Try to Lubricate Your Skis With the Stuff," 1992). Six Flags Entertainment, owned by Time Warner, has 150 TV monitors placed along waiting lines for rides in each of its amusement parks, plugging Time Warner merchandise (Donaton, 1993a). A company in California, Ocean Advertising, sells ad space on banners and the sails of sailboats after the owner of the company "began to wonder what good the small beach signs were doing when everyone on the sands was facing the water" (Cray, 1990, p. 4).

TRAVEL PLACES

If an advertiser wants to reach travelers either in the air or on the ground, there are several choices. Because air travelers are on average affluent (they can afford an airline ticket, after all) and/or business representatives, they are a very desirable market. One of the most successful of place-based media for this market is Turner Broadcasting's airport-based medium, originally called The Airport Channel but later renamed CNN Airport Network to reflect its non-advertising content. CNN Airport Network consists of television monitors placed at the gates and luggage claims of 17 domestic airports (as of mid-1994) and features material from Turner-owned CNN shown around the ads (Goldman, 1994a; Grimm, 1992d; Mandese, 1993l). An advertiser with a particular aversion to Ted Turner, however, can go with the Flight Channel instead—originally found in the Syracuse/Hancock International Airport but later with monitors in other New York airports (Cortez, 1992e, p. 25; Kelly, 1994). And once the consumer is in the air, besides the on-flight magazines that carry ads, there is the

Sky Radio option, run by Gannett, which carries news, sports, weather and ads. Sky Radio will play eight commercials per hour, with a ninth reserved for the host airline (Fisher, 1992). On longer flights, passengers may see commercials or other promotional videos on the movie screen in the cabin.

Advertisers also want to reach desirable earthbound travelers. For urbanites who have to travel by train to work every day, there is the Commuter Channel. Like the Flight Channel, it features news and commuter information wrapped around commercials for products like TheraFlu. This company is attracted to the Commuter Channel because it is "able to reach people who are suffering from cold symptoms just when they realize they might need a cold remedy—on their way to work" (Cortez, 1992e, p. 25). Eastern Lobby Shops investigated the implementation in 1993 of a place-based television system in its 150 magazine newsstands located in areas where commuters travel (Donaton, 1993d). Also, the New York subway system has developed plans with Gannett to make transits more "advertiser friendly" to reach those commuters (Martin, 1991, p. E6).

Finally, for those advertisers who want to reach people who are *about* to travel, there are place-based options at travel agencies. One particularly innovative system, provided by Travelview International, is the Travel Preview System, in which customers of travel agencies can pick up free videos, carrying ads, about a particular location. An advertiser can become part of the Travel Preview System for a little over $150,000, excluding the cost of the production (Lawrence, 1993).

RETAIL PLACES

Promotion at retail is not new. Shoppers have spent many a Saturday in grocery stores going from one promotional food display to another, picking up a free piece of pizza here or a free sample of instant orange juice there. POP displays like promotional signage and *endcaps*—stand-alone displays placed at the ends of aisles—are likewise a long-time retail staple. Because there is a long tradition of on-site promotion at retail outlets and other consumer purchasing places, it is not surprising that this social place should generate perhaps the largest amount of place-based activity. Several different categories of retail places have been active in this realm.

Advertising media are latching onto many department store outlets. The Kmart point-of-purchase radio signal KMRT mentioned earlier, labeled as "extremely successful" by one Kmart executive, includes 12 minutes of ads per hour and reaches 4 million people daily (Fitzgerald, 1993, p. 8). In addition to the radio network, Kmart also tested a television version in its stores, and its competitor, Venture, has a TV monitor system in its stores that plugs its products in all 93 of its outlets (Fitzgerald, 1993). Besides these two retailers, J. C. Penney, Sears, Foot Locker and R. H. Macy have tested or implemented televisual place-based systems in their stores, many of them open to external advertisers (Donaton & Fitzgerald, 1990; Lipman, 1992b; "Penney Prepares Video Network," 1992). AdVenture Media, a place-based advertising firm, provides programming and advertising to television sets already existing in retail: those electronic or department stores that sell TVs, such as Sears' Brand Central and Montgomery Ward's Electric Avenue ("What's Hot," 1992).

Supermarkets are also a hot space for place-based technology. The increased technological sophistication of place-based media has raised the stakes for this promotional location. NBC has funded a checkout-placed television system (McCarroll, 1992). The project, NBC On-Site, features silent television monitors placed strategically in retail outlets and has been tested in 69 retail sites in eight states (Mandese, 1993j). Other grocery store ad placement systems include ActMedia's instant coupon dispenser and cardboard grocery cart ads; In-Store Advertising's electronic signage system; and the Audio Coupon Dispenser, which kicks out an on-site coupon while playing a short jingle for the product (Fahey, 1990; "What's Hot," 1992). Advertisers like Nabisco have explored ads on floor tiles, mentioned earlier, in 10 eastern U.S. supermarkets (Davis, 1993a). One company even places ads on grocery check-out conveyor belts (Lawrence, 1994).

Although Turner Private Networks is in its infancy, it has been aggressive in testing place-based media in fast-food chains. The organization flirted both with Burger King to test an on-site advertising system (Fahey & Hume, 1991b) and with McDonald's to test a system they called McDTV. A prototype system for the mediated McDonaldland was tested in mid-1992 in 14 sites and offered different types of programming for monitors placed in different sections of the restaurant (including a children's option—featuring segments with Ronald McDonald and Turner-owned Hanna-Barbera and MGM cartoons). Advertisers participating in the test included Mattel and Hasbro; if fully implemented the system could be placed in all 9,000 McDonald's across the nation (Grimm, 1992d). The fate of McDTV is still uncertain, however, because McDonald's put the project on hold (Donaton, 1993c). More promising for muncher-oriented advertisers is Food Court Entertainment, a coordinator of commercials on TV monitors in food courts in shopping malls (Kelly, 1994).

Finally, there are several miscellaneous place-based retail locations, including Blockbuster Entertainment (formerly Blockbuster Video, with the name change signaling the company's diversification), which has promoted MTV on its in-store monitors (Hume, 1992b); and Admax Network, a closed-circuit video system placed in various warehouse outlets (Fahey, 1990). In 1992, MTV exploited monitors in record stores by creating the New Music Report, an ad-supported program of short music videos (Miller, 1992). First Interstate Bank of California has toyed with the idea of selling ad time on TV monitors above bank teller lines (Johnson, 1992a). Tyme Corporation, an automated teller machine network, will sell ads on ATM screens to banks, savings and loans and credit unions; they may later sell ads on the ATM receipts ("Coming to Your ATM Screen: Ads," 1993).

HEALTH PLACES

Because people are ego-involved in their own health and are willing to spend money to improve and maintain their health, advertisers have encroached on places that center on medical issues or healthy lifestyle promotion. This chapter began with a description of Health Club Television, a TV system placed in front of stationary exercise machines in health clubs such as Bally's and featuring 12 minutes of ads per hour for Coca-Cola, Mazda and NBC, among others (Schlossberg, 1991c). The owner of HCTV, Health Club Media Network, has had previous success with the place-based radio system it pipes into more than 70 health clubs in the United States ("Merger Plans for HCTV," 1992).

But if, despite health club membership, consumers need to see a physician, then they might be exposed to other health-place media. One highly publicized attempt at such strategy was Special Reports media, founded by media entrepreneur Christopher Whittle. *Special Reports Magazines* were placed in doctors' waiting rooms beginning in 1988; later the service evolved to multimedia, including the placement of content and ads on television monitors and in magazines, posters and pamphlets. At its height in 1992, 32,000 doctors' offices carried at least one of the Special Reports media. Advertisers included Quaker Oats and Nutri/System (Donaton, 1992c). The system might have been too ambitious, however: In February 1994 it was completely shut down except for the poster medium (Kelly, 1994). Other options filled the gap. The Good Health Channel is targeted at pediatric offices, with additional plans for a similar system for veterinarians' waiting rooms (Kelly, 1994). A more specialized version of place-based in the health realm is the Newborn Channel, aimed at new mothers and placed in hospital maternity wards (Kunkler, 1992).

EDUCATIONAL PLACES

No doubt the best known, and the most controversial, of all place-based examples is Channel One, another place-based option founded by Whittle and then later sold off to K-III Communications Corporation. Channel One has been extensively discussed and critiqued elsewhere (Barry, 1989; Rudinow, 1989a, 1989b). Although it involves a public institution (education) and has been the most publicized of the place-based systems, its basic logic is similar to all such strategies. Participation in Channel One offers a high school around $50,000 worth of electronic media equipment and a daily 12-minute news show. In exchange, the school submits to a mandatory showing to the class of the televised advertisements that are aired with the news program. Despite the boycotts and controversy over the project, Whittle had little trouble attracting interested schools and advertisers, and Channel One was his company's most profitable venture. By mid-1992, Channel One was in approximately 12,000 schools, reaching 8 million students, with plans to add to this number. It had brought in about $100 million in ad revenues during the 1991-1992 school year (Donaton, 1992c). Advertisers on Channel One included Burger King, Gatorade, M&M/Mars, Pepsi, and several movie studios ("On the Air at Channel One," 1992). Whittle sold Channel One to K-III in 1994 for $260 million ("Whittle Communications Empire Now Gone," 1994).

Despite its notoriety, Channel One is not the only place-based ad strategy positioned in schools. Scholastic Teen Network magazines claim to reach 8 million students. The *Wall Street Journal* offers a "classroom" edition in which advertisers can purchase space (Donaton, 1991). The organization Modern Talking Picture Service can place sponsored media in elementary and high schools and in colleges. With the college system, Modern College Television, a college will receive a television monitor and kiosk, along with a small fee, in exchange for agreeing to show a certain number of sponsored videotapes per week. The televisions are usually placed in college bookstores but can also pop up in university recreational facilities (usually in a strategic location, like in front of exercise bikes). In elementary schools, Whittle has nailed up The Big Picture, a sponsored wall display that features such products as M&Ms (Kleinfield, 1991). In Atlanta, a test was conducted in which ad-supported video screens were placed near public phones at local high schools, with Coca-Cola, Pizza Hut and Reebok signing on (Bayor, 1990). Finally, the College Television Network, available in 1994 at 200 campus cafeterias, is an interactive kiosk featuring music videos and commercials (Goldman, 1994a).

PLACE-BASED FAILURES

The above sections illustrate the scope of place-based advertising but do not include minor miscellaneous examples such as place-based advertising found in coin laundries—like Whittle's advertising-supported posters (Kleinfield, 1989), and gas stations—where pumps have been equipped with miniature color screens to show commercials while consumers fill their tanks (Rickard, 1994a). But the strategy has not been without its setbacks. Christopher Whittle did not succeed with Special Reports in doctors' offices. One outrageous—and short-lived—example of place-based strategies was Privy Promotions, a firm that proposed setting up ad posters on bathroom walls in sports arenas and stadiums, especially above sinks and urinals (Cortez, 1992d). Perhaps because of the lack of an attractive ad "environment," Privy could not pull in the needed sales volume and had folded by late 1992 ("What's Not," 1992).

More surprising is the failure of Ted Turner's Checkout Channel. By September 1992, The Checkout Channel, featuring video screens placed above checkout lines in grocery and drug stores, had been installed in 150 stores, with advertisers including *People* magazine and Life Savers candy (Grimm, 1992d; Wussler, 1992). At the beginning of 1993, however, the project was scrapped, with losses estimated between $20 and $40 million. Reasons given included poor planning and the obtrusiveness of the sound of television, problems that NBC's in-store video systems may correct (Donaton, 1993c).

The Trucker's Network was another misfire. This strategy, a system of monitors fed content via satellites, featured weather and travel information as well as commercials for Slim Whitman records and *Sports Illustrated* at initially 43 truck stops around the country (K. Goldman, 1992). In April 1993, the system was shut down, perhaps due to management problems but with the possibility of being reinstated at some later date (Farhi, 1993).

One problem with place-based advertising that many advertisers raise is the lack of reliable research on its effectiveness. Christopher Whittle, attempting to counteract this hesitation, had begun brandtracking and results-measurement techniques for his health-oriented Special Reports. Similar measurement plans were also in the works for Channel One (Spethmann, 1992). The Advertising Research Foundation, too, formed a subcommittee in late 1992 to study place-based media and establish measurement guidelines (Banks, 1992). And in what may be yet another indicator of the mainstream acceptance of place-based measurement, Nielsen completed tests in November 1993 of a standardized measurement procedure for place-based effectiveness, using the CNN Airport Network as its testing grounds (Mandese, 1993l).

Despite these missteps and problems, place-based advertising has grown into a pervasive and established advertising strategy. In explaining Whittle's failures, industry analysts pointed to his idiosyncratic long-term planning rather than the flaws of place-based strategies. One marketing consultant argued that, "Whittle had some good ideas. It's just that he was too grandiose and couldn't wait until tomorrow. He tried to run before he was able to crawl" (Kelly, 1994). As an editorial in *Advertising Age* concluded about the demise of The Checkout Channel, "Skeptics quickly began casting aspersions on the viability of all place-based media projects. They're wrong" ("Turner Checks Out," 1993, p. 16). Place-based advertising will continue. Based upon the work of economic and symbolic critics of advertising, how might one understand the social and cultural dynamics of the place-based phenomenon?

The Imperative of Control
in Place-Based Advertising

One theme of this book is that advertising is driven by an imperative of control. Externally, advertising economically influences the content of traditional media to encourage the most receptive environment for commercialism. Internally, advertising tries to control the symbolic construction of products so that audience members associate the product with desirable values and objects. The advantages of place-based media for advertisers can be best understood by this imperative of control, although—as will be argued—what is in the best interests of advertiser control is not always in the best interests of a democratic society. Advocates of place-based advertising hope that the strategy allows those in the commercial sector to gain control over four different areas. Certainly, control is not always achieved, but even the unfulfilled assumptions of the would-be controllers present a frightening image of advertising goals.

CONTROL OVER DEMOGRAPHICS

Reaching desirable groups—especially those groups with disposable income and the willingness to dispose of it—is problematic for advertising in the 1990s. Tweens and businesspeople, for example, are difficult to reach with common advertising choices. There are simply too many places for them to escape the advertising in traditional media. Place-based helps solve this problem.

For the tween market, place-based media can be found in amusement parks, video game parlors and schools. If advertisers can reach the market in these places, there is no escape. Illustrating this tactic, a trade ad for Scholastic Teen Network magazines, appearing in a July 1992 issue of *Advertising Age,* features the headline, "Mousse Season Opens Today," with the text,

> So does makeup season. And lip gloss season. And almost every beauty category you can name. In fact, when school opens kids go to town, on everything from mousse to makeup and more. And you can be there, too. Right where they live. Inside the classroom. In the pages of the Scholastic Teen Network magazines.

This ad is aimed at potential advertisers for Scholastic Teen Network magazines, distributed in schools. The language of the trade ad reveals modern advertising's assumptions about buyers, sellers and advertising in social places. The dominant metaphor of the ad implies that selling is really hunting, especially in the age of place-based tactics. Marketers are the hunters, tweens and teens are the hunted and school the traditionally inaccessible hiding place for the hunted. It is not really "mousse season" that opens, it is student-consumer season. With The

Scholastic Teen Network, the marketer-hunter now has access to the consumer-prey's formerly impervious lair. The place where the prey gather is school. They cannot be reached at home, the ad implies, because they do not really "live" there, but they do "live" in school and thus can be reached/hunted/sold to. In addition, the place is valuable because it encourages consumerism. In the world of place-based advertising, the school does not function as an educational place, it functions as a place for consumption. Before students can successfully "live" in school, they have to "go to town" to acquire their commodities for living. They have to acquire the goods to help them look the part. The place in this instance serves a dual function: School is where this market can be reached, and it is a center where the market displays its consumption skills. To extend the hunting metaphor—school is the home of the prey, and it also the place where the prey go to gorge themselves. They gorge themselves on spending. Marketers can thus sneak right "inside the classroom," and fire at will.

In fact, two trade ads for Modern, a company that places sponsored media in schools, imply that reaching this demographic group, in this place, is especially important to advertisers. It is important because of the market's vulnerability to long-term persuasion: a vulnerability of age accentuated by place. Place-based advertising in schools, because of the demographics it reaches, is like an investment, according to these ads. One ad (reflecting subtle stereotypes) shows a small 5-year-oldish Asian boy in a business suit and carrying a briefcase. The copy reads, "Reach him at the office. His first day job is kindergarten. Modern can put your sponsored educational materials in his lesson plan." The assumption here, obviously, is that commercial messages ingrained in the child's "work" setting now will stay with that child forever. The child has already been corporate groomed: The job of the Modern marketer is to groom him for its specific corporation. Another ad sells this point even more. Featuring an older schoolgirl, the headline of the ad reads, "Reach her before she gets credit," with the copy elaborating, "Modern product sampling can help you develop brand loyalty even before she becomes a serious shopper." Place-based, then, allows advertisers to socialize this group, difficult to grab otherwise with traditional media, for future profitability. Brand loyalty is the end; education is the means.

Place-based media can reach other desirable demographics. HCTV can help advertisers reach the 11 million health club members who have a median household income greater than $47,000 and who are "harder to reach because of their lifestyle" (Schlossberg, 1991c, p. 1). Likewise, a trade ad for Turner Private Networks, appearing in a September 1992 issue of *Advertising Age,* trumpets the demographic advantages of its media choice: "In major airports across the country, *The Airport Channel* features customized programming for the frequent traveler and affluent business audience. Here, you'll reach the heaviest purchasers of up-market goods and services." If someone is on the road too often to watch TV, then go on the road with that person. The indications are that demographics and narrowly targeted strategies will continue to grow more salient for advertisers: One survey of auto makers found that 90% believed "niche" media, including place-based, will become more important in the future as advertising tools (Cortez, 1992c).

CONTROL OVER MEDIA VIEWING BEHAVIOR

Place-based media also help disempower the viewer (and, by extension, re-empower the advertiser) by taking away the viewer's time-shifting, grazing, zapping and zipping technological choices. Because place-based advertising offers only *one* channel, with no fast-forwarding allowed, it recaptures the glories of advertising past when broadcasting offered limited choices and channel changers were an entire coffee table away.

Sales pitches for place-based media often stress the behavioral control within the advertisers' grasp. Much of the discourse surrounding this media reveals a "master/slave" rhetoric describing producers and consumers. Place-based advertising works because the medium is able to put physical shackles on consumers' viewing behavior. As place-based advocates almost gleefully point out, viewers cannot escape place-based ads. For example, an executive for the airplane-based Sky Radio argues that, "There's lots of talk by other media about [having] a captive audience, but we are going to have people literally strapped to their seats at 30,000 feet above the ground" (Fisher, 1992, p. 26). An executive of Six Flags boasts about the company's TV monitors over park attraction lines: "This is the ultimate zap-proof TV. No one can change the volume, no one can change the channel and they can't go to the bathroom because they'd lose their place in line" (Donaton, 1993a, p. 13). A 1994 trade ad for Delta Air Line's *SKY Magazine* points out that, "At 33,000 feet, there's simply no getting away from

SKY Magazine . . . " Any emancipatory power offered by the remote control is taken away. It is a return to the Good Ole Days of the Ante-Zapping Era.

But place-based does not just allow advertisers to recapture the eye-locking control they had in the past; this strategy also offers new forms of control over media behavior. Specifically, advertisers may feel that they can control consumer postviewing behavior much more effectively with place-based than with other media. The point of advertising, after all, is to get people to buy things. With place-based media, the mental disposition of consumers—their "pliancy"—may be increased for advertisers because the place may encourage a certain type of thinking. In the home, viewers might ignore commercial messages if inertia prevents the "Buy This" message from being immediately relevant. In a place where "Buy This" can be acted upon instantly, however, and people are in a buying state of mind, the consumer might be more susceptible to advertising messages. If advertisers can influence people closer to the buying decision than before, then they will feel they have that much more control.

Accordingly, elements of place-based rhetoric have stressed the new control that advertisers might have over a consumer's buying routines. It was described earlier how the makers of TheraFlu liked the Commuter Channel because it reached people who realize on the way to work that they might have a cold. Likewise, a trade ad for Healthlink Television, an early doctor's office medium, told the advertiser that, "research shows that for half of the consumers, a visit to the physician is 'the stop before they shop.' " Thus, this message implies, place-based reaches people who are thinking about shopping and about to enter an environment of shopping.

Of course, with this logic, the media that can claim the most timely control over consumers are the retail-based systems, where advertisements can reach the consumer immediately before the purchase. An early electronic place-based option for retail was VideOcart. VideOcart would install small electronic screens in shopping carts. A VideOcart trade advertisement to potential advertisers featured the headline, "A 15-Second Spot at the Moment of Decision—A Million Times a Week." A competitor, In-Store Advertising Network, also claimed in its ads that their messages would "catch the consumer's eyes where two out of three purchasing decisions are made—right at the point of sale." Another trade ad for Actmedia's Instant Coupon Machine brags that, because of its location, it "creates impulse purchases as well as trial and brand switching like no other consumer promotion." Although puffery characterizes advertising, even trade advertising, the language of this quotation is revealing. The Instant Coupon Machine does not merely encourage impulse purchases: The backer of the machine wants us to believe that its placement *creates* impulse purchases. These ads assume, and hope, that the consumer is so malleable in these consumption places that the messages placed there will have direct effects. Such strategies are meant to undermine our ability to make reasoned consumer decisions.

Based on the way place-based executives talk about their medium, it seems as if the messages are so powerful they come not from a mediated source, but from a charismatic super-seller standing next to the would-be buyer. The descriptions of place-based impact tend to be very physical, as if a real person were literally pushing the consumer to buy. An executive for Food Court Entertainment, the mall-based TV system, argues that this system maximizes consumer vulnerability in this way: "We're hitting people when they are relaxed, sitting down to eat with $100 in their pocket" (Kelly, 1994, p. 12). Given the emphasis on reaching the vulnerable consumer by place-based advocates, *hitting* may not be the appropriate term: *blindsiding* is a better description of their goals. Similarly, placing ads on floor tile in retail outlets will give "the consumer the extra nudge" toward the sale (Rickard, 1994b, p. 53). Actmedia's POP display, according to a 1994 *Advertising Age* ad, "can close the sale" for the product. The place-based advertisement is more than an ad: It becomes a virtual salesperson.

ECONOMIC AND EXTERNAL CONTROL OF PLACE

One thing that advertising strives to control is the external environment of the ads. With traditional media, this means influence over the media stories and portrayals that accompany the paid selling messages. Place-based advertising, however, has allowed advertisers to gain economic control over *two* external realms: the media content that surrounds the advertising on place-based media and even the place itself.

Advertisers influence, either obtrusively or unobtrusively, the symbols of the media content that encompass the ad, simply because of their financial role in the media system. Advertisers want the surrounding media environment to be a properly commercialistic cocoon, keeping consumers in the proper frame of mind to receive the ads. Because the place-based medium's sole purpose for existence is to be a carrier for advertising, the non-advertising content of place-based is often very advertising friendly. The importance of place-based media's advertising friendliness is especially salient in a place that has anti-advertising elements. One such potential place, for example, is school. Advertising encourages impulse behavior; school encourages reasoned behavior. Non-advertising content on Channel One, therefore, serves as a womb for advertising in this potentially hostile environment. Its pace and style serve the dual function of grabbing students' eyes and of making advertising in an educational place more palatable.

One study of Channel One's news content found that only 1 or 2 minutes a day of the newscast tended to be "hard," issue-oriented news. The rest was made up of soft news, often pushing the latest innovations in commodity technologies, such as the making of Nike shoes (Murray, 1991). The pace of the newscasts, in addition, matched commercials: short and fast paced (Murray, 1991). In fact, one critic argued in 1991 that Channel One privileged the commercials over the news in that the average commercial on the place-based channel was 30 seconds long but the average news story was only 18 seconds long (Murray, 1991). Despite the early quick pace of Channel One, Whittle retooled its news content in 1992 to give it an even more "MTV-ish" tone ("Channel One's Education Plan," 1992). Thus, the "Watch Me! Watch Me!" entertainment imperative of advertising-supported media applies to place-based content perhaps even more than to home-based media. Channel One illustrates this. In a social place where an informational and educational imperative is meant to dominate, the mandate of eye-candy imagery takes over.

If the external control of media content is so easily accomplished in an educational place, such control is even more assured in commercial spaces. One of the strengths of the proposed *McMagazine,* produced by McDonald's and distributed at their stores, was that it would allow the corporation to "control the editorial environment in which their ads appear" (Donaton, 1992b, p. 45).

A similar concern about product placement in films, a form of place-based advertising, is that the marketers seeking product place-ment might further water down artistic control, supposedly central in film (Miller, 1990). Does product placement encourage movies to be more welcoming to advertising? Promoters, obviously, want to place their products only in advertisement-receptive movies: Movies that have bad endings or movies that are too grim or movies that critique consumerism or capitalism they generally want no part of.[3] For example, as one product placer notes about TV product placement (to be discussed further in Chapter 5), "We work for McDonald's. We wouldn't want a situation where McDonald's would be used to show that a character is a jerk and a job at a McDonald's restaurant is the only work he could get" (Slate, 1993, p. 77). Such selective buying could put additional pressure on moviemakers to make movies that have happy endings or scenes receptive to product placement. Product placement as a form of place-based advertising thus limits the diversity of motion picture content. It creates incentives for certain types of movies, but not others.

Some advertisers even grouse about the lack of control they experience in product placement. Black & Decker sued the producers of *Die Hard 2: Die Harder* when the scene featuring their product was cut from the final version, alleging that the cut scene cost them more than $150,000 in promotional costs for tie-ins planned around the product placement (Colford, 1990). Orkin pest control sued the makers of *Pacific Heights* when a fictional Orkin employee in the movie said the word *shit*. The suit was settled out of court, and the word was removed from the video release (Busch, 1994). In order to maintain product placers as a funding source, moviemakers might have to shape their content for this new market.

There are even occasions where a marketer is heavily involved in the production of the movie, although this is still rare. The most notorious example of this is the aptly titled *Mac and Me,* made with investment money from McDonald's and loaded with references to the restaurant and its cross-promotional partners, Sears and Coca-Cola. The title of the movie is a subliminal McDonald's slogan. A young, very attractive romantic interest for a main character is a McDonald's employee in the movie. Ronald McDonald appears in the movie. A central scene, where everybody (except the villains) is having a great time, takes place in a McDonald's. "Mac," an alien child, is last seen wearing the now-defunct clothes line, McKids. Coca-Cola is used to revive the ill but sympathetic aliens in the movie's climactic scene (The Berkeley Pop Culture Project, 1991, p. 18).

In addition to the economic influence advertisers may have over place-based content, there is a danger that advertisers could begin to affect the place itself. Chapter 1 described the role that deregulation has played in the expansion of advertising in society. In the 1980s, marketers were simultaneously given more leeway to "push the envelope" of their economic behavior while the funding for many public institutions was cut, leaving those institutions searching for new sources of revenue. Many private organizations have also come under financial strain during the recession of the early 1990s, forcing them to generate alternative sources of revenue. One conclusion about these trends is that creators of place-based media, and those who advertise on them, have sparked this trend simply because they are no longer denied access.

The need for commercialistic private interests to save the day for public institutions has been advanced by both the private interests and the public institutions in their justifications for place-based intrusion. Christopher Whittle himself pointed to the lack of public funding for education in his pedagogical rationalization of Channel One, citing the statistic that the United States allows 10 times more funds for the military than for education (cited in Barry, 1989, p. 41). Without his commercial involvement, Whittle argued, many schools that now have video equipment would have no equipment. In justifying the placement of ads at public beaches (Horovitz, 1990), subways (Martin, 1991) and state office building elevators ("Buckeye Ad Bucks?" 1991), public officials discuss, first and foremost, the lack of public funds that makes such selling necessary.

Different places, then, will allow place-based media in their domain. This could have at least two effects on the place, one unintentional and one intentional. First, when a place opens itself up to place-based media, the place, in essence, must "compete" with the mediated discourse. It is not just the Channel One content that is affected by the advertising; the nontelevised educational content of the school is also affected. Suddenly, with Channel One, the discourse in schools—teachers' lectures, textbooks, other videos—must compete with flashy newscasts. Because they are funded by advertising, these newscasts are designed, above all, to get students to watch. That is their first and foremost economic goal. Postman (1985) argues that the entertainment stakes of education have already been raised by the prevalence of home-based television. How high do the stakes rise when televisual amusement is literally brought into the classroom?

At the intentional level, there is evidence that advertisers and the representatives of advertisers (the owners of the place-based system) will exert as much economic control over the place as possible. When the sound level of video games was drowning out the commercials of the arcade-based Channel M, the video game volume was turned down (Goldman, 1994a). Channel One is perhaps a more insidious example. Although the organization makes much of the free equipment that the schools use, Whittle Communication retains ownership of that equipment and will revoke the majority of it if the contract is canceled (Rudinow, 1989b). This contractual form of control can supersede pedagogical interests: In Detroit, four science teachers were reprimanded by their school for allowing students to work on science projects rather than watch Channel One (Jacobson & Mazur, 1995). For complete economic control, of course, the place-based media organization or the advertisers themselves would actually own the "place": This would give them both allocative (long-term) and operational (day-to-day) control. This control would not just be over the ads or the media content around the ads, but also over the place. This makes Whittle's Edison Project, the proposed for-profit private school system that he wants to establish, very interesting. Although the Edison Project has been seriously scaled back from its original conception, Whittle has said that his Channel One would likely be shown in his Edison Project schools (Donaton, 1992c). Would Edison schools be a more "advertising- and corporate-friendly environment" than public schools, given the nature of the ownership that has been proposed? Some critics believe so. As Jonathan Kozol concludes about Whittle, Channel One and Edison:

> Whittle is dangerous—very dangerous—for American education. He's dangerous because he is selling the idea that the public schools can be used as a marketing place for commercial products. He's opening the doors for a massive new industry—the Educational Industrial Complex. (cited in Brodinsky, 1993, p. 546)

And even if Whittle himself might not walk through the doors, there are plenty of marketers who will take those steps.

SYMBOLIC CONTROL OF PLACE

A final form of control that place-based media offer advertisers is over the symbolic realm. The symbols in the place-based ads become more effective because of the advertising-free nature of many of the places. Also, the new media offer very strategic and effective forms of internal control over the symbols that appear in the ads themselves.

Addressing the clutter problem, for example, many place-based organizations point to the benefits of advertising in symbolically virgin territories, away from the clutter. One executive for the ad agency Saatchi and Saatchi points out about the Airport Channel that, "There's not a lot of other advertising when you're sitting at a gate, so it's relatively uncluttered" (Fahey, 1991b, p. 44). Trade ads for Cinespot, a theater ad placement company, and Healthlink also bragged about their clutter-free places. Advertising is in this sense geographically imperialistic, looking for new territories it has not yet conquered. When it finds such a territory, it fills it with ads—at least until this new place, like traditional media, has so many ads that it becomes cluttered and is no longer effective as an ad medium.

Another symbolic issue is the matching of symbols in the ad to the tone and expectations of the place. It was noted earlier, for example, that some advertising analysts believed The Checkout Channel failed because its ads did not blend well enough into the supermarket environment: The audio elements combined with the visual elements were too obtrusive for the place. Refining the technique, then, NBC On-Site will provide silent video monitors to merge better with the place. Likewise, product placement companies warn advertisers to make their commercials for movie theaters longer than usual and "cinematic," so that the look of the commercial matches the look of that place's media content (Lev, 1990).

The most interesting symbolic control that place-based offers, however, is hinted at in the work of such symbolic critics of advertising as Judith Williamson (1978). To reiterate, advertising links its products with what is socially desirable in society. In an individual ad, marketers hope that the product will be symbolically associated with this desirable object or value in the consumer's mind. Place-based strategies offer a depth to this internal linkage that is frightening.

In traditional media, manipulation of symbols can occur at two levels. The first is in the commercial itself, where the creators of the ads manipulate the symbols of the product directly. This is the internal control for which advertisers strive. Advertisers also try to manipulate at a second level: They match up the symbols of the ads with the media content that surrounds the advertising. This involves external control.

Besides these two levels of control, place-based offers a third level: the use and manipulation of the symbols of the *place*. The physical and social place becomes a symbol system—a text—that advertisers can purify, recuperate and link in a self-serving way to their product. The place becomes an even larger symbolic cocoon than the media content. This symbolic linkage and co-optation of place have at least three implications.

First, often the place—whether it is a health club, a doctor's office or even McDonald's—is a positive and/or credible one for the audience. Advertisers, looking to associate with the positive and the credible, take advantage of this. Desirable social places become referent systems for place-based ads, whether the ad specifically mentions the place or not. Place-based media bank on this positive textual association. The owners of on-site media try to convince potential advertisers that their ads are more credible simply because they are shown in a particular social place. About the would-be McDTV, Turner Private Networks claimed that by placing ads in McDonald's, "you'll reach folks in one of the friendliest family environments ever cooked up." At least one advertising executive, for AT&T, concurred when he said, "The environment of McDonald's is very compatible with our audience. It's a brand that kind of communicates and conveys warmth and family and togetherness, and that's just the profile of what we're after" (Grimm, 1992d, p. 13). Ads in doctors' offices also hope to plug into the symbolic goodwill of the physical context. The Healthlink company argued in a trade ad that advertising for health products would especially benefit from a health-driven environment, because, "The physician's office is trusted, credible and authoritative, so your message will be heeded."

Is this claim valid, though? Does the credibility of a social place "rub off" onto the ad? At least some research points to this effect. One study has found that students exposed to Channel One believed that the products advertised on the medium were "good for them because they were shown in the classroom" ("Students Give Passing Grade," 1991, p. 34). A separate study by Greenberg and Brand (1993) found that students exposed to Channel One valued products that were advertised on the medium more than students not exposed to Channel One. Channel One students were also more likely to express an intention to buy the products. Perhaps most disturbing, though, is the evidence that exposure to advertising in schools may legitimize consumerism in general. The study found that students subjected to Channel One were more likely to express materialistic attitudes than those students in Channel One-less schools. And why should students not accept these values? They were, after all, learned in school. With Channel One, commodity fetishism becomes a part of the curriculum.

Another implication of using the place as a symbolic system goes back to a point made earlier. Some advertisements do not just link their products with desirable values, they also sometimes imply that their products generate, or are currency for, these values. In these ads, the consumer *must* have the product to have the value. Ads using this strategy may find a unique opportunity with the environment of the new place-oriented media.

The consumption of home-based ads is often very private and individualized: The consumer may be reading the newspaper by him- or herself or watching television alone in an environment of the consumer's own shaping. Consumption of place-based media, on the other hand, is not usually done alone; it is often a very public and open exposure, unlike home-based media. The environment is not individualized: In fact, the environment is often constructed based upon the social needs or image of a group. Advertisers on place-based media use the environmental predictability of the technique to their advantage. If advertisers want to imply that their products offer particular skills useful in the place, or a particular type of social acceptance by people in the place, then they can incorporate the symbols of (a) the ad, (b) the media content and (c) the place itself in a kind of synergistic textual dance.

If a person is relaxing at home and sees an ad for the hippest exercise outfit, the effect may not be that great. To someone lying on the couch, eating ice cream, an ad for ThighMaster may seem intrusive, even silly, in that setting. The ad is out of context. But in the health club, when the person is doing a ThighMaster-like exercise, and sees people in the *commercial* "thighmastering," and then sees people in the *media content* thighmastering and then sees people in the *place,* the health club, thighmastering (or the equivalent), the effect could be quite different. In the health club, quite literally everywhere a person looks reinforces a message of adopting a fit lifestyle, including consuming fitness commodities. Thus, the social anxieties, the need to "fit in," that advertising attempts to create in consumers can be heightened even more if the place is strategically used. If advertising is indeed more about consumers than products, ads in a place-based context drive this point home. Like-minded consumers fill the ads, the content and the place.

This has implications for critical thought and reflection. With retail-based ads, our critical thinking ability might be dulled by the fact that we receive persuasive messages so close to a place where we can act on the persuasion. Ads on a mall television set may encourage us to plunk down money right then and there. With other types of place-based systems, our critical abilities may be dulled by the intensified commodity norms that fill the place. We become surrounded by displays of consumption in the media content, the ads and the place. And because we match the demographics of those portrayed in all three display modes (we would not be in the place if we did not match), commodity pressure further increases. Place-based advertising may exploit this anxiety by saying, "You *must* have this product to fit in *here, now!*"

Advertising thus views the social place not just as a place for selling, but as a tool for selling as well. Another trade ad for the placement service Modern invites this utilitarian viewpoint when its copy, placed under the picture of a stylish high school girl, declares, "Her social life revolves around high school. Modern can make sure your sponsored video plays there." With this strategy, school as a referent system is purified: Its purpose is to increase the effectiveness of the placed ad. High school becomes a symbol system for advertisers, nothing more. Advertisers in high schools have an incentive to co-opt the look of the "typical" high school student, commodify that look, and, ultimately, transform that look to match the advertisers' products.

There is one final implication of the use of place as symbolic referent system. Wernick (1991) claims that advertising devalues referent systems, because the ad implies that the referent system, no matter what it is, is *always* subordinate to the purpose of the ad (i.e., selling the product). Place-based advertising uses the place itself as a referent system, sometimes explicitly, always implicitly. And place-based media's pervasiveness and conspicuousness make an even louder statement than traditional mediated advertising about commercialism's symbolic superiority over its environment. It may not be very important that place-based advertising devalues Kmart, but what is the long-range cost of a symbolic as well as economic subordination of education and medicine, or even a public beach, to commercial messages? How is the student-teacher relationship affected when the teacher turns on a TV commercial in the classroom and portrayals of teachers appear in the commercials?

Conclusion: A Commercial Sense of Place

One last issue that it is important to deal with here and that ties into issues previously discussed, is the relationship of place-based advertising to divisions in society. There are two schools of thought about the relationship between media and social division. On the one hand, media are said to create or widen already existing social divisions. Those who highlight the role of media in a postindustrial society, discussed in Chapter 1, are an example of this camp.

Then there are the theories that say that the media dissolve social distinctions. George Gerbner's cultivation analysis perspective, for example, argues that heavy television viewing uniformly distorts beliefs about the world in the same way for everyone (Gerbner et al., 1986).

Similarly, the work of Joshua Meyrowitz (1985) points to the extremely open access to information that television offers compared to other media. TV offers increased physical access to information: Once a TV is in the home, we have access to an unlimited amount of programming. Television also offers increased symbolic access: It combines the visual, aural and verbal in a way that is very easy to comprehend. Both of these modes of access have tended to blur social distinctions. Television encourages sameness in society by demystifying the Other; we see groups not like ourselves on TV all the time. Before television, Meyrowitz notes, our social "place" (how we identified ourselves as a socially constructed man or woman, for example) was tied to our access to different physical places. Men would talk to men in "men places," like the poker table or the locker room, and reinforce what it meant to be a man in these "backstage," exclusive talks. Women were physically barred from these places and had little access to the information and perspectives presented there.

Not everyone had equal access to all physical places and the information shared about groups in these places, so social divisions therefore tended to be very distinct. But as television entered society, this technology allowed access to different physical places. In televisual plays, in documentaries, in sitcoms, women *could be* in the locker room. Likewise, men saw women's frontstage *and* backstage behavior (at least as portrayed on TV). Men became less strange to women and vice versa. And, eventually, things like androgynous behavior, the "sensitive" male and even populist women's liberation activism were encouraged as gender exclusivity eroded. Similarly, the distinctions between childhood and adulthood began blurring, and the distinctions between those with social authority (e.g., politicians) and those without began blurring. According to Meyrowitz (1985), as television ruptured the connection between physical place, information access and social division, it changed "the 'situational geography' of social life" (p. 6).

How does place-based advertising fit in with all this? Place-based is an explicitly commercial use of television, a use that Meyrowitz perhaps underestimates in his discussions (Kubey, 1992). Place-based, because of the control needs it satisfies for commercialism in general and for specific advertisers in particular, is a completely different use of television technology than Meyrowitz assumes. Place-based repairs the separation of physical barriers and social definition. Rather than opening information access, as broadcast television does, place-based limits access: Only health club members see HCTV; only school kids see Channel One; only skiers see the Resort Channel. Although magazines and cable also aim at specialized, marketable groups, they are *not* able to deliver a captive audience like place-based media do. Place-based marketers boast that they can glue eyeballs to information and advertising more than any other delivery system. They can also deliver pure demographics because of their physical location.

The messages in place-based media—both the advertising and non-advertising content—are often filled with stereotypes of the people who hang out in the place. Health Club Television features demographic stereotypes (young/urban) and psychographic stereotypes (perky, health conscious consumers) throughout the content. And such stereotypes are the only thing on TV. Meyrowitz (1985) says of broadcast TV viewing that, "people are much more likely to stray outside their traditional fields of interest when attending to television and radio than when reading books or magazines" (p. 12). With place-based it is just the opposite.

If people happen to bring a book or magazine to read, they can escape their social group information. But if they are bound by media in the place, they have no choice. Place-based television is closed-circuit, closed access and closed topic. Thus, people who have access to these physical settings, and the desire to go there, are being force-fed information and social role models about their predefined demographic/psychographic groups. Conversely, other groups not tied to that social place do not have access to the information or the portrayals. In fact, their exclusion is what makes place-based so attractive. If physical location were not controlling demographics, then place-based marketing claims would not be as attractive.

One critical thing to remember is who is defining these groupings. The imperative of consumption defines and drives these divisions. Divisions might be becoming more distinct, but the demarcations are along *marketable* lines. These socially defining lines are defined not so much out of the experience of the people, but out of advertisers' need to sell products. Place-based ties into the concepts of lifestyle, demographics and psychographics. Instead of putting a health club in a commercial, to tie into the product's link to yuppie lifestyle, why not put the commercial in a health club and make this link that much more explicit? In addition, if you put the health club in a commercial that is in a health club, you have a double whammy tie-in. If you show a commercial dealing with a kid's peers while he or she is surrounded by his or her peers, you similarly have a double-dipped symbolism. Place-based, then, strengthens the link between demographics and psychographics. It reinforces the stereotypes of a potential consumer type *while* a person is physically surrounded by the stereotypical demographics, in a stereotypical place of that type. Place-based media create new places and social groups. But these places and social groups are defined commercially. The point of their existence is not to encourage democratic empowerment through group organization. The point of their existence is to sell. They exist only when they are commercially viable.

Other, less marketable social groups, without the cohesion—even if artificially contrived—of place-based media, may be less well defined. If marketers divide the world according to their economically advantageous criteria, what happens to the groups that fall into the gaps? Will the less affluent, or those in rural settings or those less willing to part with their money, find that they have "no sense of place" while other groups have their senses overwhelmed with place?

Certainly place-based media would have to become much more prevalent than they are currently for such an effect to be widespread. But with the ability of the strategy to meet the problems of 1990s advertising, one wonders if it is moving in that direction.

Notes

1. The Goodyear blimp is an interesting example of both sponsorship and place-based strategies in one. It is sponsorship when the blimp itself, floating over some sporting event, gleams the Goodyear logo. It can also be a place-based (in this case sky-based) strategy, however, if Goodyear or other blimp companies sell the lighted signs attached to the blimp. Illustrating the changing dynamics of the time, it is interesting to note that in the 1990s other companies have copied Goodyear's decades-old strategy. Watching a sporting event, we are just as likely to see the SeaWorld, Fuji, Blockbuster or Metropolitan Life Insurance blimp as the Goodyear blimp. Some of the advanced blimps, in fact, are solely sponsored vehicles because they are internally lit, making the sponsored company's logo glow like a promotional moon in the sky (Spain, 1994).

2. Product placement is also evident in other countries' media. Inserted ads abound in Brazil's *telenovelas,* that country's equivalent of soap operas. The Brazilian television network Globo employs more than 30 people whose job is to survey up-coming programs for product placement opportunities (Mattelart, 1991, p. 132).

3. There are rare exceptions to this, depending upon the image of the product. For example, the original *Batman,* released in 1990, would not on the surface seem very concordant with product placement, given its dark, threatening urban setting. The subplot

of the villainous Joker poisoning consumables would not seem to help matters, either. But American Express, which positions itself as the shield against dark, threatening urban settings, found the movie perfect. In one of the first scenes a family is mugged, and the mugger, going through the stolen goods, holds up an American Express card and sneers to his criminal companion, "Don't Leave Home Without It." The company's fear appeal is thus given cinematic legitimacy.

4

CONTROLLING VIEWER BEHAVIOR
Creating the Zapless Ad

MUCH of this book might give the reader the impression that television as an advertising medium—especially broadcast television—is dead. Far from it. Although certainly the issues of clutter and audience emancipatory technologies have forced advertisers to explore other advertising options (such as place-based and sponsorship avenues), these issues have not mandated that advertisers give up on television. Instead, advertisers are searching for new ways to recapture the promotional value of the medium. Some of these ways seem contradictory. Some strategies ask, "How can we hide the fact that this is an ad?" With this strategy, the advertiser strives to make people forget or not realize they are seeing an ad. Other strategies do the opposite. These strategies ask, "How can we revel in and celebrate our advertisingNESS?" Advertisers here want a televised environment that is nothing *but* ads. As we will see throughout this chapter, television advertising has cultivated both strategies. Such techniques have implications for our sources of information in a democratic society.

Techniques of Clutter Crunching and Remote Restraining

Television and the other traditional mass media saw their stock drop in the advertising community during the 1980s, a decline that greatly concerned the advertising industry. For example, when the status of television's uncontested effectiveness as an advertising vehicle became, in fact, contested, writers for the trade journals began suggesting (and are still suggesting) ways around the clutter and zapping/zipping trends. Some of these suggestions have been implemented or still may be implemented.

A few of these suggestions involve rethinking the placement of television commercials. One proponent of new ad placement strategies argued that television advertisers need to avoid the beginnings and ends of programs, when it was felt that most zapping took place ("How to Avoid Being Zapped," 1984). Another strategy is the *roadblock,* developed to nab viewers who use their remotes to cruise television channels during commercial breaks. A roadblock is the placement of several spot ads for the same product on different television stations at the same time. Roadblocks force even the most ardent zapper to see some part of the ad. Some advertising futurists have argued that TV networks must change their ad placement strategies to adjust to the new environment. Kostyra proposed that all the television broadcast outlets standardize the times that commercials are shown, making it impossible for remote controllers to escape ads because every station would air ad pods simultaneously. This would apply to all programming with a few exceptions such as sports telecasts, which are less controllable than news and fictional broadcasts (Kostyra, 1984).

Other advertising critics have maintained that television ads simply need to get better. These critics say that the lack of creativity in commercials—the use of tired clichés and advertising conventions—encouraged people to avoid or ignore ads (Upshaw, 1990). One proposal argued in favor of economic incentives for advertisers who upgrade their creative efforts. The premise of the proposal was that if an ad causes a person to zap to another channel, the program and the other ads around it would also suffer. If advertisers create a spot "that is entertaining or interesting or compelling" and thus prevents zapping, then the advertisers would be awarded an "Audience Retention Bonus" for their efforts. Ideally, this proposal went, the more gripping the ad, the bigger the bonus (McNeely & Marshall, 1992).

Despite such suggestions, generally no large structural changes were made in television to increase its advertising effectiveness. Rather, advertisers gave more attention to manipulating the symbolic nature of ads to try to glue eyeballs back to the screen or page. Sometimes, as we will see, these symbolic manipulations involved an increase in operational control of television by advertisers.

Four Anti-Zapping Strategies

Four anti-clutter, anti-zapping strategies seem to stand above the rest, either because of their success or their ubiquity. Most of the examples of these four strategies come from television, the medium hardest hit by the 1980s' changes. These strategies involve (a) the co-optation of the written word by television commercials, (b) the use of audience anticipation, (c) the creation of camouflaged ads and (d) the creation of all-advertising television channels.

THE "LET'S SPELL IT OUT" STRATEGY

Several media observers have run with the Marshall McLuhan-esque idea that television is antithetical to the written word. One advocate of such a notion, Neil Postman (1985), believes that the television medium aggressively "attacks" writing as a mode of communication (p. 84). Writing and television are such different communicative channels that they encourage different orientations to information processing and to the world. With writing, we are forced to follow a sequence of information arranged logically. Sequential linearity is built into the very structure of written communication. The first word leads to the second, the first sentence to the second, the first paragraph to the second and so on from the first word to the last. We have to process this information one bit at a time (one word at a time). If other bits of information intrude upon the linear sequence, we become distracted. Many people cannot read in a noisy room.

According to Postman, television, with its ubiquitous image orientation, undermines the characteristics of print, including exposition and logical analysis. Television bombards us with disconnected images and sounds and music. Some television genres are decidedly nonlinear. Music videos are 3-minute chunks of often unrelated music and images. *Sesame Street* presents the alphabet in sound-bite form. And even hour-long, plot-oriented dramas on television—one of the most linear forms of network TV—have strong nonlinear elements. Commercials, completely unrelated to *anything* within the program, constantly interrupt the narrative flow. In addition, TV has naturalized its own nonprint style of communication in this society. Television is everywhere. It is ubiquitous in our lives.

Postman and others argue that television's mode of information has affected our abilities to process print. We become bored or confused by written communication. The emphasis on a nonlinear, holistic form of communication like television perhaps erodes our ability to follow linear argument easily or to think logically (as the written text requires). The written word and the televisual image are different paradigms, so the argument goes, and they encourage people to think in mutually exclusive ways.

Similar arguments have been made specifically about advertising on television. Cook (1992) believes that advertising by its very nature is more speech oriented than print oriented. Since the development of the electronic media, ads have privileged oral communication over written text and often use music and visual images as their sole form of communication, with no words at all. Cook offers as further evidence for the antiprint bias of advertising the disdain that television advertising seems to have for print when print *is* used in television advertising. Traditionally, print is used in advertising only when it has to be, such as in warning labels ("Drink Responsibly") or government-mandated qualifications ("Some Assembly Required"), and usually placed in a very small, inconspicuous corner of the commercial screen. Other commercials may use print in limited ways, such as for the price, slogan or name of the product.

But since the late 1980s advertising has rediscovered the written word as an important resource, even for television commercials. Many recent commercials on television use large and very obtrusive words—either on blank backgrounds or foregrounded over images. Sometimes whole sentences appear in the commercial; sometimes gigantic words cover the entire television screen in the ads. And the words do not come only at the end of the commercial. Indeed, as we will see, the whole point is to spread the words throughout the commercial. Print, seemingly, has become a new language for television advertising.

For example, a 1993 McDonald's commercial for "The New Deluxe Breakfast" constructed an imaginary dialog with the viewer. The narrator of the commercial asks orally, "Hey, what's for breakfast?" and the viewer "answers" via huge letters on the screen, "I'm not much of a morning person." The conversation continues like this, with the narrator talking to the viewer and the viewer responding with print. Similarly, the Army, in an amazingly hip MTV-style ad, tells the viewer-reader about the advantages of Army life in big letters across the screen (like "Earn Money for College,"). The ad ends with the Army's trademarked slogan, set to music, one *word* per screen, one screen per musical beat: "Be" "All" "You" "Can" "Be." Beer manufacturers have also noted the advantages of text, with Budweiser asking the viewer to hoist up a Bud for the toast, "To" "Teamwork," and letting us know that they are "Proud to be your" Budweiser bottle (which is how they end the sentence, in a mix of print and visual imagery). These are just three examples of scores of commercials in the 1990s that have used the written word prominently in their television commercials.

Why are television advertisers increasingly using print in their TV ads? Two reasons, both related to the problems of modern advertising context, have encouraged commercials to flirt with verbal literacy.

First, advertisers are aware of the remote-controlling and fast-forwarding TV audiences. Television commercials are worthless if people use their remote controls to avoid the commercials (or dilute them: My mother always turns the sound off on commercials, a behavior that I've noticed only since the remote has entered her house). The zipping of commercials that audience members recorded serendipitously with their tape-recorded programs also frustrates advertisers.

Textual ads undermine these strategies. Print-oriented commercials communicate even with the sound off or the fast-forward button pushed. They are designed to attract the eye in these situations. With print reinforcing the oral and musical message, the commercial is perfectly understandable with the mute button engaged. Print commercials also fit into a fast-forwarded environment. Often the words are huge on the screen, and linger there, seemingly to dare the viewer to fast-forward through them and just try not to be aware of the message. With one word per screen, fast-forwarding moves the commercial along at a comfortable reading pace so it is perfectly understandable as a selling pitch.

A second promotional benefit has to do with the Postmanian analysis of television imagery. One could argue that in the 1980s the McLuhan legacy of television had been reached: TV had become nearly entirely image oriented. Certainly specific forms of television, like Music Television or *Sesame Street* or CNN, have increased the visual-image nature of television to the point where critics hail television as the ultimate in postmodernity. TV is nothing but a series of barely related, quick-cutting images from this perspective. The commercial has contributed to this tele-bricolage: Often nonverbal, often copying the most visually flashy elements of television, often lasting only 10 or 15 seconds, TV commercials become a series of images that try to link sexy referent systems to a product in ways meant to dull critical thinking.

But it is precisely this image orientation of television that has encouraged ads (literally) to spell out their message. Media, especially television, have become *too* image oriented for advertising. What has happened to televised images is similar to the issue of advertising clutter. With the issue of clutter, television and other media are so receptive to advertising that these media were overwhelmed by ads to the detriment of the selling message of individual ads. With images, television has so shaped itself to an image orientation that the images are collapsing into each other. It becomes impossible to differentiate one image from another. For a form of communication that has as its first goal to attract attention, this sea of images is an oppressively swallowing sea. Thus, in part to escape a trap that they themselves have created, advertisers must turn to the written word (or at least their co-opted version of the written word) to stand out. We are so unfamiliar with seeing print on the TV screen that (advertisers hope) it stands out like a reference to Goethe in the middle of a *Baywatch* episode.[1]

Does this mean, then, that advertising will be in the vanguard in the verbalization of television? Will commercials counter the image-oriented monolith and turn around critics of televisual communication? At the very least, will such commercials help us become more intelligent buyers? Will the increased emphasis on print provide us with additional product information? Perhaps this new trend in advertising will increase the democratic purpose of media by providing more specifics about products and helping us make more informed consumer decisions. If images seduce, maybe the written word creates more separation between the consumer and the message. Maybe the increased use of print will encourage consumers to take more critical distance from the selling message. Will such commercials make a small contribution to literacy and to a more knowledgeable citizenship?

Of course not. The purpose and role of the verbiage in these commercials guarantee that the above questions will be answered in the negative. The words used in these new commercials are, essentially, images themselves. Television advertisers use words so fragmentedly, so decontextually, that they have the same effect as a series of images. Rather than encouraging linear thought and critical analysis, they discourage them. Rather than giving us more product information to make informed choices and give us a critical distance, such ads try to seduce us into viewing things from the advertiser's point of view.

The letters that appear on the TV screen during these commercials do not give the viewer product information, but instead are used to grab attention, reinforce the visual image of the product, appeal to the emotions or draw the viewer into the advertisement (more on this below). They function, therefore, in the same way as visual images. Instead of the verbal component making the image component more literate, it is the other way around. The words become more image-like.

A 1993 television commercial for "Planet Reebok" illustrates how this works. This commercial attempts to promote Reebok's version of women's empowerment, and by doing so it of course also promotes Reebok shoes. A series of images of athletic women (boxers, cross-country runners) is featured on the screen. The framing image of the commercial, though, is the first image, a slogan written in white letters backgrounded on a spinning Earth: "What is Life Like on Planet Reebok?" A series of visual cuts then serves to answer this question. In this 30-second commercial, there are 33 different camera shots (more than 1 a second), with dizzying camera movement and changing graphics in many of the shots. Twelve of the shots are different word-screens interspersed with the visual images. In each of these word-screens, a short phrase fills the screen—starting with black letters on white background, but then flashing from this to a white on black background and back again. The word-screens include such patronizing phrases as "No Biological Clocks," and "No Old Boy Networks." A frenetic rock score fills the speakers during the commercial.

In this context, the words *are* images. There is no time for reflection. The words are typographically flashy, constantly changing colors. They are only peripherally connected to each other and the visual images and even less connected to the product, at least from a product information point of view. In fact, the verbal component of the commercial encourages irrational reflection, if any. The words are used to reinforce the connection of the product to the referent system, women's empowerment. The words and images together tell us that "Reebok shoes" equal "Gender Equality." A word-screen tells us "No Boundaries"; cut to a close-up of Reebok walking shoes.

The final irony is that words are then used to deny the symbolic manipulation the advertisement engages in. The commercial is an exercise in product-claim hypocrisy. Despite the "What is Life Like on Planet Reebok?" opening slogan, which "lingers" on the screen for 4 seconds, longer than any of the other pseudo-feminist sound bites, the commercial attempts to use words to disavow its commercial-ness. The final slogan shown in this commercial is "No Slogans." The final slogan contradicts the entire selling technique of the ad. Words thus allow the commercial to have it all: the authority of words, the style of TV, the co-optation of a valued referent system and the ability to separate itself from commercial technique.

Advertisers have not increasingly used the written word solely for the remote control and VCR tyrant. Advertisers also use words to appeal to the faithful commercial viewer. Often the words and the visual/aural elements of the commercial combine in a way to "reward" the television loyalist. For example, in a Budweiser commercial, the words, "Proud" "to" "be" "your" "Bud," although appearing one after another on different screens, pop up on their screens to the beat of the Budweiser jingle. It becomes a music video in which the viewer can enjoy the image/aural synergy, but with words being substituted for, or added to, more traditional televisual images. The selling message (e.g., "Proud to be your Bud"), instead of being laid out for critical analysis, merges with the visual and aural elements to accentuate the acceptance of the message.

Other ads use words to draw the viewer into the commercial. Because the written words often encourage us, as viewers, to take the conversational place of the manufacturer or encourage us to feel we are engaged in conversation with the manufacturer, such commercials try to suck us into the image-text persuasion rather than giving us written modes of critical distance.

One clever example of this "verbal product identification" might illustrate this point more clearly. A TV ad for Oldsmobile begins with a blank screen and a narrator asking orally, "Can you find the Oldsmobile in this picture?" After an artsy image of the car appears on the screen, a word appears on a blank background: "Hmm . . . " This word-screen is our contribution to the "dialogue" the manufacturer is having with us in the commercial. The narrator asks again, "We'll give you another try." More sporty car images, then another word-screen, "Err . . . " The commercial encourages viewers to convey astonishment over the new hip Oldsmobile. But the end of the commercial really puts us in our commercial place. The narrator tells us, "It's the Achieva Sports Coupe. Surprised?" And we verbally respond, "Stunned is more like it." The narrator reminds us, "It's your money," and in a shift in perspective, the next word-screen presents the slogan of the manufacturer, "Demand Better." Perspective is thus seamlessly shifted from a contrived viewer-to-manufacturer dialogue, to a manufacturer-to-*manufacturer* dialogue. The final word-screen, meant to represent our voice, is the slogan of Oldsmobile. "Our" words became even more solidly the words of "Oldsmobile."

Such are the ways that advertisers use words themselves in 1990s ads. They want to have a word with us, and it is a discouraging word.

THE "ADVERTISING BY ANTICIPATION" STRATEGY

One of the first advertising campaigns to really show the selling potential of outdoor ads was the famous Burma Shave series of billboards of the 1920s through the 1960s. The billboards were red and white signs placed along the road at spaced intervals (at first 20 yards apart, but later increased to 50 yards as road speeds increased). Each sign contained one part of a complete sales sentence, encouraging viewers and passengers to anticipate the next sign in the series: "Every Day" (would say one billboard), "We Do Our Part" (would say the following one), "To Make Your Face," "A Work of Art," "Burma Shave" (The Berkeley Pop Culture Project, p. 15).

Although this anticipatory element has never completely gone away, the current context of television advertising has revitalized it. By manipulating *when* the ad is placed, with a clever "wink" to the audience about this manipulation, or by creating a feeling that a certain ad could pop up at any time, advertisers hope to stick out in the clutter. They hope that advertising by anticipation will hold thumbs off of remote control buttons by piquing the viewers' interest, just a little.

Some ads, for example, use a "bookend" ad placement strategy. Crispix cereal is a product that has as its unique selling proposition

(USP) that of a crunchy cereal even after several minutes of soaking in milk.[2] The cereal's television ad campaign tried to accentuate this point by using a two-part commercial, with the first part separated from the second by a commercial for an unrelated product. In the first commercial, the spokesperson pours milk on the cereal to see if it keeps its crunchiness and then hints to the viewer that the result of the experiment will take longer than the length of the commercial. Fade to black, and another TV commercial comes on. After this promotional intermezzo is over, the same Crispix spokesperson appears again, having waited patiently, and then smugly and loudly crunches a spoonful of Crispix in his mouth. Similarly, another set of commercials for Bud Light, airing in the fall of 1993, used this strategy. In the first commercial installment of the two-parter, a man on a beach with a cooler full of Bud Light encounters one of the stereotypical mainstays of advertising, The Deceptive Female. Using her sexuality, T.D.F. buries the man up to his head in sand and walks away with the cooler of Bud Light. The commercial ends with him helpless. After a commercial for an unrelated product airs, the head is shown again, still buried, pleading with people to give him a hand with a can of Bud Light, which is placed tantalizingly close to him but still out of tongue's reach.

The master of the television Ad-of-Anticipation strategy, though, is the Energizer Battery Bunny. This campaign, using the famous battery operated, drum beating, tireless Pink Bunny, has used the strategy in two ways. One is similar to the Crispix and Bud Light bookending tactic, where one or several nonrelated commercials are sandwiched in a two-part commercial for a product. In this case, the Energizer Bunny disappears in the Bermuda Triangle in the first part of the commercial and then pops out again in the second part, after we have seen commercials for other products in between.

The second, more successful strategy uses the intertextual knowledge of the viewer as a form of anticipation. Intertextuality in media content is the use of unexplained popular culture references to draw upon the audience's previously held knowledge. Such a strategy often sucks a viewer deeper into a program. When characters on *Seinfeld* joke about the plots of *Melrose Place,* the joke is that not everyone gets the joke. It draws in the "with-it" audiences and allows them to participate more deeply in the meaning of the show. The program "winks" at the viewers and essentially asks them, "Are you hip enough to understand this reference?" If the answer is yes, then presumably the jokes are funnier, the dialogue more involving and viewers feel good about the clever nature of the program and how smart they, the viewers, are.

The Energizer Bunny ads of the late 1980s and early 1990s worked in the same way. The purpose of many of the Energizer ads is to copy the formula of commonly known advertising genres (like pain reliever ads or beer ads). Such a strategy grabs the attention of the viewer by asking the viewer, "Do you get the parody?" Thus, a brilliantly derivative commercial for the faux pain reliever "Darnitol"—with authentic aspirin commercial clichés down pat—suddenly is interrupted by the sentient battery-operated toy. There were several ads in this series, including parodies of ads for diarrhea remedies, musical compilations and insurance companies.

Both anticipatory strategies—the bookend commercial and the intertextual commercial—are designed to piggyback on other ads, essentially increasing the reach of the ads. At least, they might increase the reach of the ad in the viewers' heads. Both strategies work by anticipation. They turn ads for other products into ads for the anticipated product. For a particular advertiser, clutter and unwanted technological manipulation become less of a problem when not only the advertiser's commercials, but also *other* commercials create the desired image in the viewer's mind. In the bookend strategy, even on the first viewing of the first part of the sequence, the viewer strongly suspects that a follow-up commercial will soon appear. The viewer, then, is thinking of Crispix or Energizer batteries even when the nonrelated middle commercial is on. It is the commercial equivalent of a soap opera cliffhanger, but with the resolution to the cliffhanger coming in 15, 30 or 60 seconds instead of the next day. Whatever the case, the commercials encourage the piqued viewer to stay tuned to, and be mentally primed for, the follow-up commercial. And after these two-part commercials have been aired often enough, the second part is really no longer needed. Viewers anticipate the second part, which is all that is necessary. All the commercials sandwiched within the two-parters—or believed to be sandwiched within—become part of the campaign. Whether the sandwiched elements are other commercials or public service announcements or even more television content, they become integrated into the campaign. The two-part commercial contaminates the content around it by planting the idea in viewers' heads that the punch line will soon follow once the filler is removed.

The Energizer intratextual parody ads are likewise designed to use other ads as promotional devices. When the campaign first aired, the main strategy was surprise: One would see a commercial for a nonexistent product that looked just like every other commercial, but then would be amazed when the commercial was interrupted by the Bunny. At this early stage, the hook of the commercial was its role as an eye-opener (or, again, eye-grabber). But part of the longevity of the campaign was due to the change in its strategic effectiveness. After the campaign had become successful and well known, the ads were not so much centered on surprise as on anticipation. People had seen the Energizer commercials enough to begin to recognize the clues about the real identity of the commercials. These clues might include the use of a fake product name or a series of images that seem just a little too hokey. Once these clues were disseminated, viewers tried to guess which new commercials were Energizers. This, then, affected how people viewed other, more conventional commercials. When successful, such ads created a feeling of anticipation and encouraged guessing in the viewer when a *real* (i.e., authentic) bad ad comes on. One viewer quoted in *Advertising Age* said that she hoped "that the bunny will come along whenever she's watching a particularly bad commercial" (Vadahra, 1993, p. 16). Both types of advertising-by-anticipation ads, then, contaminate other elements of television. Usually, the intertextual strategies simply affect our perceptions of other ads. The bookending strategy, though, may have the effect of turning anything around the ads into a part of the ads. It infects other parts of television. The strategy could influence our perceptions of non-advertising content as well as the ads themselves.

THE CAMOUFLAGE STRATEGY

Miller Lite, once its retired-athletes, "Tastes Great!" "Less Filling!" campaign finally itself retired, looked for other campaigns to rejuvenate the product. One that has been more successful than most has been the "Can Your Beer Do This?" campaign. A typical scenario involves two people or groups arguing over two programs on television that they want to watch ("High Diving Competition" vs. "Sumo Wrestling," for example). Finally someone says, "Let's watch both," bops the television with a bottle of Miller Lite, and the two TV shows are then magically combined ("Sumo High Diving") so that everyone is happy.

The commercial tries to make the point that Miller Lite combines two elements (Tastes Great, Less Filling) that are difficult to combine in one beer. Yet what the commercial also points to, inadvertently, is the recombinant nature of television. Television more than any other medium likes to combine disparate elements. To use Gitlin's (1985) recombinant metaphor, television tends to come up with show ideas by splicing the genes of shows together. Programs like *Dr. Quinn, Medicine Woman* combine one genre with others to come up with new ideas. *Dr. Quinn,* for example, was originally conceived as a combination of the Western show with the medicine show with the strong single woman show. Such a strategy has several advantages for television. It allows program producers to pitch their show to program buyers as something brand new, yet also just like past successes (*Dr. Quinn* is a *new* combination of *Gunsmoke, Marcus Welby, MD,* and *One Day at a Time*). Such a construction also allows the new show to be described quickly to program decision makers: "*Dr. Quinn* is *Gunsmoke* meets *Marcus Welby, MD* meets *One Day at a Time*." Finally, it also gives them two or more cultural formulae to pull from when generating individual episode story ideas each week—"Let's stress the Western part this week, and the doctor part next week, and the liberated woman against sexist ideas the week after!" (McAllister, 1992).

Commercials contribute to the recombinant nature of television (and, to a lesser extent, to all popular media that carry ads). Frequently, ads combine the ad form with the media forms that surround the ads; like the anticipatory advertisement, they are becoming intertextual, depending upon the audience's knowledge of popular culture. Ads are always looking for the socially familiar and desirable to link with their product: Advertising's use of symbolic referent systems is its central map in its search for symbolic, internal control. One possible referent system that advertisers may use is media content. Television ads will try to look like television shows; newspaper ads will try to look like newspaper articles. In fact, advertising has special incentives for co-opting the symbols of media—especially media that surround the ads—as the referents in ads themselves. First, our society has become very "media literate," but in a superficial sense of that term. As Andrew Hart (1991) notes, *media literacy* in this sense of the term means that we can "recognize television or radio genres, [or] know which pages of particular newspapers or magazines carry the material we want" (p. 2). Thus, we pride ourselves on knowing the names and birth order of all of *The Partridge Family,* but perhaps know less about the logic of TV economics. It is the first-level knowledge that advertisers are interested in exploiting. As our literacy increases, advertising has an incentive to use television and other media icons in their commercials because such icons and themes are so well known. Featuring Homer Simpson in an ad is a good strategy because people know, and enjoy, Homer. He's a widely familiar referent system.

A second, and more powerful, incentive for commercials to take other media forms is advertising's goal of making people *forget* that they are watching an ad. Advertisers believe that a sales message's credibility is immediately suspect when viewers realize they are watching an ad. In the era of audience viewing technology, such suspicion may well lead to the commercial being zapped away. Thus, especially in recent times, advertisers have an incentive to combine media genres with their advertising purpose to camouflage, at least at first, the fact that the viewer is watching an ad. More and more ads are recombining with media forms, using these forms as referent systems to try to blur the distinction between what is a program and what is an ad. Ads, then, have combined with the image of programs to create the recombinant "Ads as Programs." Even the names of these ads suggest their recombined origin: "magalogues"—which Mark Crispin Miller (1986) describes as "a direct-mail catalog as slick and startling in its graphics as any fashion magazine" (p. 189), "advertorials," "infomercials" and "documercials," for example. Television seems to be doing this the most, so the following examples will focus mostly on television, but there are increasing incidents of camouflaged ads in print forms as well.

Historical Precedents for the Camouflaged Ad

Ads that pretend to be non-ads are not new. Like many trends discussed in this book, the prevalence of camouflaged ads increases during times of "advertiser frustration" or, conversely, during times of "advertiser permissiveness." Usually, waves of camouflaged ads involve some of both characteristics. Print ads during the late 19th and early 20th centuries are examples. As advertisers felt that the traditional promotional techniques available to them were deficient, and as print media turned to advertising as the major source of revenue, advertisers turned to such techniques as camouflaged ads. Thus, during the height of the industrial revolution when assembly-line production techniques became more efficient but before such promotional carriers as broadcasting were implemented to promote the mass-produced products satisfactorily, camouflaged ads were not uncommon.

From the very beginnings of mass advertising, the middle of the 19th century, advertisers would hire journalists to write ad copy in a news-paper-story style to hide an ad's self-serving motives (Presbrey, 1968, p. 256). Some ads in these early days were not simply written like news stories; they often had the *form* of news stories as well. An ad for a patent medicine was headlined "HOW A LIFE WAS SAVED," followed by the sub-head, "THE LIFE OF CHAS. S. PRENTICE SAVED BY THE USE OF WARNER'S SAFE KIDNEY AND LIVER CURE," and included a byline and a dateline (Presbrey, 1968, p. 295). More systematized were the "reading notices" that appeared in newspapers at the turn of the century. Reading notices were announcements paid for by advertisers that were identical in appearance, and even published as, newspaper articles. Sometimes, in fact, reading notices would include more "newsy" information unrelated to the product to seduce people into reading the copy. Large corporate advertisers, who threw their economic weight around, could be especially effective in their demands for a high degree of similarity between the reading notice and the news article. When postal laws were changed to require a clearer designation of advertising material, reading notices tended to die out (Baker, 1994; Lawson, 1988).

Other forms of camouflaged ads appeared later in the 20th century. In the 1920s, during the peak of prosperity of that decade, advertising was such a common tool for captains of industry that clutter actually became an issue. More commonly labeled "saturation" at the time, advertisers were concerned then, as they are now, that individual ads would become lost in a crowded selling landscape. In this period, the industry stressed what the ad trade called "editorial copy." Ads in this mode included Palmolive ads that looked like newspaper advice columns, and Pond's Cold Cream ads that camouflaged themselves as editorial copy in *American Weekly* magazine (Marchand, 1985, pp. 94-103). Marchand noted about a Fleischmann's Yeast ad campaign that, "Sometimes the ads recapitulated the layout of the magazine or newspaper so perfectly that the reader might become thoroughly immersed in the ad before discovering that it was not an editorial issue" (p. 17).

One might also explain the existence of camouflaged ads by highlighting "advertiser permissiveness." Examples of advertising using camouflaged ads because certain social forces permitted the practice can be found in broadcasting from the development of radio until the early 1960s. In the early days of broadcasting, the distinction between programs and ads was often not distinct. The dominant funding system of early broadcasting was sponsorship, in which one advertiser funded one program. Sometimes the advertiser or advertising agency even produced the program. Thus, the financial tie between the advertiser and the content was very direct. In those days, advertisers had both operational and allocative control over much broadcasting content. Advertisers defined both the incentives and the logic of the system, and they often controlled the day-to-day operations. Chapter 6 will discuss in more detail the incentives of early sponsored broadcasts.

Sponsorship encouraged camouflaged commercials in broadcasting. Advertisers would often take full advantage of their operational control. In radio, "dramatized" commercials became popular in the 1930s as sponsors encouraged ads to sound like programs (Barnouw, 1966, p. 276), and the mood and pace of commercials often matched programs (Marchand, 1985). Stars would pitch their sponsor's product on radio ads and often would integrate the sales message into the program itself.

As television developed, the actors of sponsored shows, in character, would hawk their sponsors' products in commercials aired during the program. Andy Taylor and Barney Fife, on duty in the Mayberry sheriff's office, in uniform and accompanied by a laugh track, would pitch Grape-Nuts in television commercials aired during their show. Lucy and Ricky would explain why Philip Morris was *their* cigarette. Lucy, though, came across as slightly more domesticated—and presumably less troublesome (for advertisers)—than in her sitcom. "You see how easy it is to keep a man happy? Why not give your husband a carton of Philip Morris cigarettes?" she cooed. Rob and Laura practiced innocent domestic sparring while smoking Kents. In the most notorious example, Fred Flintstone and Barney Rubble, looking, sounding and acting as they always had, flacked the advantages to audience members (including children?) of Winston cigarettes during the cartoon's original prime-time run.[3]

One difference between these old camouflaged TV commercials resulting from sponsorship and those currently on the air is the subtlety of the pitch. In the old commercials there were strong hints that the viewer was, in fact, watching a commercial. Often the characters would directly address the audience, as in the *I Love Lucy* commercial; both Ricky and Lucy make eye contact with the camera. Other commercials would signal their true nature by having endorsers go on and on about the product. In the *Flintstones* commercial mentioned above, Fred at one point notes, "Winston is the one filter cigarette that delivers flavor twenty times a pack. Winston's got that filter blend." Replies Barney, "Yeah, Fred. Filter Blend makes the big taste difference, and only Winston has it. Up front where it counts. Here. Ahead of the pure white filter. Winston packs rich tobaccos specially selected and specially processed, for good flavor in filter smoking." Also, of course, there was a more direct economic incentive for such blurring in the early days of television sponsorship, as the sponsoring company would have strong say about using the talent and their characters in ads. Because single sponsorship rather than spot advertising was a major funding system in early broadcasting, blurred ads were commonplace.

From the mid 1960s through the early 1980s, such blurring of ads into programs declined, however. Part of the reason was the elimination of sponsorship as a funding mechanism; another part of the reason for the decline was the more activist stance the FCC took during the 1970s, which strongly discouraged such deceptive commercialistic tendencies. But beginning in the late 1980s, television and other media have experienced a renaissance of blurred ads, with such ads using a variety of media forms as referent systems. As Miller (1986) concludes about today's blurred ads, unlike the historical examples listed above, now "such practices have come to represent the ideal type of TV advertising" (p. 190).

Before these ads can be specifically discussed, it should be noted that a main reason for the effectiveness of camouflaged ads is the nature of media content in the 1990s. Ads that appear to be programs work so well in today's television environment because so many programs function as advertising. It is a mutually occurring recombination. In modern media, the non-advertising content often has strong commercial overtones that allow blurred ads to slip perfectly into media's ambiance.

The Flip Side: Programs as Ads

One incentive of advertising-driven media is to deliver "pliant" audiences to advertisers. Advertisers want potential consumers to be receptive to selling messages, and media content that encourages such receptiveness is especially attractive to promoters. The current competitive environment for advertising dollars in television may increase the incentives for advertising-friendly content.

Contemporary writers of media have noted the increase in the blurring between ads and programs since the mid- to late 1980s (Alter,

1989; Miller, 1986). Here the focus is on ads that try to appear as programs, but the complementary phenomenon likewise happens. Programs or other forms of media content frequently serve as promotion for advertised products. Programs that have the characteristics of ads make ads that have characteristics of programs less jarring. As one side blurs into the other, the invasiveness of the advertising imperative becomes complete. Television and most other advertising-supported media forms have always been very advertising friendly, but now viewers are often likely to see explicit plugs in the programs themselves.

For example, Chapter 3 (on place-based advertising) discussed advertising in movie theaters. One specific version of this advertising strategy was product placement in movies to reach the motion-picture-going public. Product placement, though, appears in television shows as well. In a way, the prevalence of product placement in television is surprising. The FCC has regulations against producers receiving payments for product plugs on their shows, and the networks could alienate an advertiser by placing a competitor's product in the network's programs, seemingly giving the competitor's product preferred treatment (Slate, 1993). Yet the prevalence of recognized products on television programs is significant, showing the desperation of TV organizations to please advertisers. Trainer and entertainer Jake Steinfeld actively promised product placement for cooperative advertisers on his cable show *Big Brother Jake*. In this case, such blatant product-placed concessions were simplified by the fact that the program was a cable, not broadcast, program and therefore not subject to FCC regulations (Magiera, 1992a). Broadcasters have participated in the activity, though; sometimes with enthusiasm. Wayfarer sunglasses appear on *Seinfeld*, and Giorgio Armani glasses surface on *Murphy Brown* ("Product Placement Brings Movies, TV Shows to Life," 1992; Slate, 1993, p. 77). The computer that Doogie Howser used was an IBM. Characters on *Law & Order* and *Murder, She Wrote* use Pelican pens (Slate, 1993, p. 77). Perhaps one of the most blatant examples of product placement was found in NBC's 1993-1994 mid-season replacement show *Viper*, which featured a mutated version of the Dodge sports car of the same name (Elliott, 1993).

Product placement on TV has increased in recent years, despite incentives against the activity. One study of television product placements in 1993 found more than 900 product plugs in the Big Three network television shows during a 24-hour period, with nearly 75% of the placements being "very clear." This was up from around 820 plugs in 1990 (Fawcett, 1993, p. 21). The advertisers may not be able to pay for the product placement, though, so compensation is generally made by providing the products for free, both to be used on the show and for talent use in general—Jerry Seinfeld, for example, gets a free supply of Nike shoes for wearing them on his show ("Ad Time Giveaways," 1993).

Other examples of ad-like programs besides those with product placements can be found in media content. Both television and print news often serve as promotional vehicles in their acceptance and discussion of public relations material that promotes particular products. This furthers the total blur of programs and advertising. Video news releases (VNRs), by providing news with attractive but slanted news visuals of cool new products, often are too good for news producers to turn down. One study revealed that 80% of TV news directors use VNRs several times a month; overall, promoters made available around four thousand such releases to television stations in 1991 (Lieberman, 1992). Similarly, with the increase in "soft news" and specialty news programs on cable television, such activity is increasing. *Entertainment Tonight*-like shows that center on fashion or leisure issues are increasingly attractive to television outlets.

Furthermore, again reminiscent of the 1950s and 1960s, more talk shows are using talent to plug products during the shows. This trend heated up with the rise of the "talk show wars" of 1992 and 1993, when Jay, Dave and others were positioning for ratings. Cable talk shows on The Family Channel and The Nashville Network have made such plugs since the 1980s, but more widely watched outlets, like *The Tonight Show with Jay Leno,* have rediscovered the technique. The NBC late-night staple, for example, features the announcer of the show, Edd Hall, plugging advertisers like Certs (Mandese, 1993a). The increase in radio talk shows has also encouraged product plugs by talent. The teen drink Snapple has been promoted with live, unscripted plugs by radio talk show hosts Rush Limbaugh and Howard Stern during their shows (Winters, 1993).

As media become enmeshed in diversified and wide-ranging ownership webs, the temptation to plug other holdings of the parent company may become too great to resist. Thus, ABC's *Monday Night Football* has been explicitly plugged on ESPN's *NFL Prime Monday,* to the point where the announcers of the ABC game, Frank Gifford, Al Michaels and Dan Dierdorf, have visited ESPN electronically to preview the upcoming matchup. Both ESPN and ABC are tied into the same parent company, Capital Cities. Likewise, NBC was able to sneak in references to its experimental Interactive Network on *Fresh Prince of Bel-Air* (a program that is coproduced by NBC) and even during the network's broadcast of *Super Bowl XXVII*. Two programs that NBC has produced or coproduced are *Saved by the Bell* and *Fresh Prince of Bel-Air*. It is not surprising, then, that NBC used one show to plug the other. A character on a 1993 episode of *Fresh Prince* invasively mentioned the inane *SBTB* by name.

Ads as Media Content

With commercialistic elements embedded in programming and media content, it is no surprise that programming elements have been pervading commercials with increased frequency since the mid-1980s. These "Ads as Content" copy a variety of program genres—often with a remarkable degree of sophistication. Ads as media content are appearing more frequently in both print media and television.

In magazines, for example, the most common form of camouflaged ad is the *advertorial*. An advertorial, sometimes called in the trades a Special Advertising Section, is defined by the American Society of Magazine Editors as "text/advertising packages focusing on a particular topic but *not* created by a magazine's editorial department" (Bailey, 1992, p. 18). In other words, the advertisers themselves often may have a strong say, if not total operational control, as to the complementary nature of the advertorial section, a nature that is designed to blur editorial with ads. Advertorials are preplanned symbiotic tools created to make the editorial seem like advertising and the ads seem like editorial. Some magazines, such as *Sports Illustrated*, plan several such sections every year, and in 1991 these sections accounted for about $230 million in ad revenues (Bailey, 1992, p. 20). Sparked by times of increased competition for advertising dollars, advertisers will sometimes demand the placement of advertorials as part of their negotiations with the magazines (Donaton, 1992a). Although trade publications recommend that the advertorial typeface be different from the rest of the magazine, and disclaimers be used that label the section as a "Special Advertising Section," there is no legal compulsion to do so. Some advertorials, like those appearing in the magazine *Electronic Gaming Monthly*, look exactly like regular articles and are not labeled as ads (Lipman, 1991). Similar camouflaged print ads can also be found in newspapers and even comic books.[4]

Television, though, has been the medium with the most visible camouflaged commercials. Television's obvious clutter problems and its zipping and zapping dilemmas have encouraged camouflaged commercials, as has deregulation. The conclusion of this section will discuss these incentives in more detail. TV commercials have copied many different program genres.[5] Six of these genres will be described in detail: sitcoms, soaps, sci-fi, sports, news and talk shows. After the six categories of camouflaged TV ads are described, this section will conclude with a discussion of the implications of camouflaged ads.

Ads as Sitcoms. Given that the situation comedy is increasingly the most common form of television program on the air and is a form of content that advertisers like, it makes sense that this is one of the most popular genres recombined with commercials. Ads may copy sitcoms at different levels: Some ads merely copy the narrative codes of sitcoms or use well-known sitcom performers in generic sitcom situations; others copy a specific sitcom.

An example of the more generalist sitcom-ad recombinant would be Domino's 1992 campaign that used *Perfect Strangers'* Bronson Pinchot. Aside from using a familiar sitcom face, the "plots" of these ads would usually be structured as mini-sitcoms (especially the type that one would expect Pinchot to appear in). One typical commercial in the series, for example, featured the actor being continually locked out of the house by mischievous kids. As one advertising executive said about the campaign, "We're taking the 23-minute sitcom and shrinking it down to a 30-second format" (Cortez, 1992b, p. 2). Ragu spaghetti sauce commercials in 1988 used the family sitcom format in their commercials, copying the elements of the genre—including a laugh track.

In an even more comprehensive attempt at the commercial-sitcom recombinant, Bell-Atlantic unveiled its mutant "sitcommercial," *The Ringers*. This 30-minute-long paid program had all of the surface elements of the sitcom: a focus on a family and its members' domestic and social situations, the 30-minute total length, the laugh track and even lame jokes. What it also had, beyond these elements, was an interweaving of advertising characteristics with sitcom icons. The plot was integrated with the product (speed-calling comes in very handy with teenager Ronnie Ringer's social life) and with internal sales pitches, as when the father of the family broke the fourth wall and spoke directly to viewers, telling them the advantages of such phone services.

Originally, the sitcommercial aired only in Baltimore, but with its perceived success it was later shown throughout Bell Atlantic's market area. The company has not ruled out further "episodes" of *The Ringers* (Loro, 1992).

Other commercials may not adapt the "problem-solution" format of the genre, but simply employ familiar faces in familiar personas. The use of endorsers in typecast television roles is a tried and true technique for advertisers. Robert Young, at the height of his Marcus Welby fame, paternalistically pitched coffee; Karl Malden, like his character Mike Stone on *The Streets of San Francisco,* commiserated with crime victims for American Express. Such endorsing is even more commonplace in the 1990s. Candice Bergen's Sprint commercials essentially have her act as Murphy Brown, sarcastic and smart-assed. The millions of *Cheers* fans recognized the nod to Lilith in Bebe Neuwirth's M&M commercial. When *Seinfeld* was the hip show, advertisers rushed to use these characterizations to make the show a referent system: Julia Louis-Dreyfus redoes her Elaine characterization on commercials for Nice 'n Easy hair treatments; Jerry Seinfeld makes observations worthy of his stand-up routine on American Express commercials; Jason Alexander is a George-like character on Rold Gold Pretzel commercials, and George's parents pitch the wonders of AT&T; Michael Richards maintains his Kramer persona in Pepsi commercials.

Other TV ads more exactly copy the sitcom by using the form, style *and* personnel of actual shows. *The Simpsons,* for instance, has appeared in TV commercials for several products. One product, in which a mini-*Simpsons* episode is recombined with the commercial function, is Butterfinger candy bars. The campaign uses the same drawing style, the same humor, the same cinematographic techniques, the same living room (including the same transformational couch), the same sound effects (like Maggie's pacifier sucking sound) and the same voices as the Fox show. A typical entry involves Homer's attempts to force Bart to give his dad a bite of a Butterfinger, with Bart responding by shoving Maggie's pacifier into Homer's mouth instead. There are two very short cartoon segments in this commercial at its beginning and end, with Bart tricking his dad in the first segment and Maggie grabbing the pacifier back in the second. In between is the hard sell for Butterfinger, showing the candy bar in luscious close-up as a narrator, a non-*Simpsons* intruder, describes it. This structure, then, makes the commercial essentially a *Simpsons* episode—with the mini-cartoon soft-sell portion even being interrupted by a hard-sell commercial. Commercials for major league baseball and the restaurant T.G.I. Friday's have used similar *Simpsons* iconography.

Another recombinant ad-sitcom strategy was used in commercials for Monsanto carpets. Monsanto used the cast of *Designing Women* to promote its wear-dated carpeting. Practically the entire cast (post-Delta Burke) appeared in the ads, in character. To accentuate the camouflage, the commercials often ran during the syndicated airings of the program. As one ad executive noted about the strategy, the innovation of the campaign was the ensemble approach: "An entire cast can merchandise a product far stronger than a single celebrity endorser" (Strauss & Reeves, 1992, p. B6). The use of the whole cast solidified the commercials' camouflaged effectiveness.

Ads as Soap Operas. Again, like many genres discussed here, it is not just during the 1990s that advertisers have thought to copy or incorporate soap operas and serials. The famous turn-of-the-century campaign for Sapolio soap had a serial quality to it. Each "installment" featured a different citizen of the Sapolio-dominated Spotless Town trying to build anticipation from week to week about each new advertising installment (Fox, 1984, pp. 45-46).

This tradition continues today, but with an even stronger association with the most dominant serialized form on television, the daytime drama. As with the sitcom, there are examples of commercials that copy specific soaps and characters and examples of commercials that copy the form of soaps.

One instance of the first category is a Konica commercial that tied into the ABC soap *All My Children*. A 30-second spot used to promote the contest, "Picture Yourself on *All My Children*," where the first prize was a guest appearance on the show, was produced in such a way as to take on the appearance of the soap opera. Shown during the ABC soap schedule (including *All My Children*), the commercial was set in a very legal looking set and featured actor Walt Willey, who plays a lawyer on the soap. The commercial was shot so that it took on the general appearance of a promo for the soap (Davis, 1993b).

Much more well known, however, is the highly successful series of commercials for Nestlé's Taster's Choice, which does not so much copy a specific soap as it captures the overall appeal and essence of soaps. These U.S. commercials were copied from an equally if not more successful ad campaign in Britain for Gold Blend instant coffee, also made by Nestlé. The U.S. version of these commercials began in 1990 and by the beginning of 1994 had at least eight installments. The series tells the unfolding story of a very yuppie couple, sometimes called Tony and Sharon (the actors' names) who have developed a relationship over Taster's Choice coffee. They initially meet when, as neighbors, she asks to borrow his coffee for a dinner party. The commercial serial has many thematic elements of soap operas. It focuses on affluent and attractive white people, material obsession (here an obsession with coffee, because it is a coffee commercial), sexual tension, interpersonal relationships and miscommunication about said relationships (the man mistakes the woman's brother for a rival suitor in one installment). Beyond these content elements, soaps also have a characteristic visual style and rhetoric (Timberg, 1982). The Taster's Choice ads captured these as well. The heavy use of "backstory," for example, to fill in viewers who may have missed the last installment about the story line, is found in every ad. Extreme close-ups, lingering reaction shots, unexpected entrances and cliffhanging endings similarly fill these commercials, just like soaps. It apparently has worked. Sales of the coffee have increased about 10% since the commercial soap began (Garfield, 1993).

Another 1994 campaign, MCI's Gramercy Press ads, also adopted a serialized, developing format, in this case around the lives of the employees of the fictional publishing house. The campaign, showing how the Gramercy employees have adapted to MCI's business computing system, even included "teaser ads" to spark interest in the commercial saga. The trade journal *Advertising Age* concluded about serialized ads in general that "Serial commercials seem to be the ad industry's strongest response so far to zapping" ("Zapping Zappers," 1994, p. 22).

Ads as Science Fiction. Given the popularity of the *Star Trek* phenomenon (including several movies and several TV series) and its entrenchment in popular culture, it is inevitable that advertising would grab hold. One ad for MCI's Friends and Family Calling Plan uses cast members from the original *Star Trek* and one member from *Star Trek: The Next Generation* to show the advantage of the plan. The ethos of the actors and their presumed relationship to each other come from the characters they play. Leonard Nimoy talks like Mr. Spock ("There seems to be some error," he says at one point when a *ST:TNG* character appears in the same ad with the original cast). Also in character, DeForest Kelley's Dr. McCoy shows open disdain for Mr. Spock in their MCI interactions. The commercial tries to maximize the credibility of the characters and the degree to which their credibility rubs off on the company. Kirk and company, for example, interact with the MCI representative on an affectionate, first name basis ("Anna [the rep] called me," Walter Koening/Chekov smiles to the viewer).

Much more deviously camouflaged, though, is an ad for Hallmark that disguised its ad origins by copying the tone of *Star Trek: The Next Generation*. The commercial opened with a shot of the *Enterprise*, its engines humming in the background. Then, when the shot moved to inside the ship, an actress, who occasionally played an Ensign on *ST:TNG*, appeared in her characteristic Star Trek uniform. Looking at a computer screen, she ordered, "Computer, access the new Keepsake Magic Ornament from Hallmark." Then Majel Barrett's voice (or a strong impression), who does the voice of the computer in *ST:TNG*, explained Hallmark's new *Enterprise* decoration. The *Enterprise's* computer, then, served as the narrator in this ad. The matchup of this commercial with *ST:TNG* was amazing. The sound effects were the same, including the beeps and pops of the computer, the zip of The Replicator when the crew member attempted to duplicate the ornament and the sound of the ship. The actors were the same. The visual effects, including the angle of the *Enterprise* as it approached in the opening shot and the diagrams around the ornament as the computer displayed it on the screen for the crew member (giving it a high-tech image) were the same. The sets and costumes were the same. Even the lighting and tone of the film were the same—the soft focus of the program makes the commercial stand out from other commercials that are videotaped or more harshly lighted. Indeed, the only elements that stuck out as un-*Star Trek*-like are the copyright notice at the beginning, in tiny print ("Star Trek © 1993 Paramount Pictures") and the Hallmark logo at the end of the commercial. Everything else, though, was designed to camouflage this commercial as a part of the *ST:TNG* the viewer just watched.

The placement of the ad accentuates its disguise. In local markets, during the syndicated first run and reruns of the series, this commercial was often shown *immediately* after the resolution of the episode, with scarcely a fade-to-black. The result was a seamless merge of the program with the program-disguised commercial. In one airing, the episode ended with a shot of the *Enterprise* and the hum of the ship in the background, and then the Hallmark commercial came up. The commercial's opening shot of the *Enterprise* was a mirror image of the closing shot of that episode. It was almost as if the commercial was just another scene in the episode.

Ads as Sports. Television advertising has nearly always attempted to link itself to the popularity of sports, mostly through the use of endorsements. In one commercial from the 1950s, for example, Cleveland Indians' Early Wynn, Bob Lemon and Mike Garcia explained to us why we should smoke Camels. Certainly this trend continues today: Michael Jordan is one of the top celebrity endorsers of the 1990s, in both his basketball and baseball versions. Shaquille O'Neal, Charles Barkley and Joe Montana are not far behind.

Ads as sports in the 1990s have added at least two levels of recombinant sophistication to the traditional sports personality endorsements. Both levels are designed to increase the similarity between the sports event and the sports commercial. One level involves the copying of a specific sports event, including the integration of key personnel in the event into the commercial. The other level involves attempting to copy the unpredictability of sports.

Football is a fertile arena for ads as sports. The National Football League, through its 1993 collective bargaining agreement, allows more NFL players, in their uniforms and with other NFL icons, to appear in product commercials than previously (Jensen, 1993b). Judging from the increase in sports event commercials since then, players are taking full advantage of their new commercial source of revenue.

The Super Bowl is a good example. The high-profile TV event of the year, the Super Bowl, has become as well known for the commercial spectacle as for the football spectacle. Advertisers during the Super Bowl want as much as they can get for their $1 million per 30-second slot (as of 1995). One way they maximize the effectiveness of the ad is to link their product as much as possible to the mega-event. Dana Stubblefield, Stan Humphries, Jerry Rice and Steve Young all appeared, in uniform, in a game situation, not just in the 1995 Super Bowl but also in a Doritos commercial aired immediately before the 1995 Super Bowl broadcast. Even more of a virtual Super Bowl was a commercial that aired the year before for Reebok. In this commercial, footage from earlier in that particular Super Bowl was edited into a 30-second commercial shown in the fourth quarter of the same game. In this commercial, completed in less than 30 minutes, scenes of Reebok's Instapump were intercut with scenes of Emmitt Smith's just-accomplished moves. The commercial ended with Smith's post-touchdown celebration from the third quarter. Final edits were finished with less than 1 minute to spare (McManus, 1994).

Even the announcers may get in the act. A 1993 commercial for Frito-Lay presents a bald Dan Dierdorf, Frank Gifford and Al Michaels introducing a mock version of ABC's *NFL Monday Night Football*. The announcers had supposedly lost a bet that they could only eat one Lay's potato chip. The camouflaged nature of the ad was accentuated when the ad was shown right before a *real* telecast of ABC's Monday night mainstay, featuring the same announcers (Mandese, 1993k). Another 1995 Super Bowl ad, for Rold Gold Pretzels, simulated actor Jason Alexander parachuting into the stadium during the game as the three ABC announcers express their astonishment. It was a two-part commercial, with the first part ending with Alexander jumping out of an airplane. Fade to black, fade in, and Al Michaels's voice is heard, "And welcome back to Miami where the Chargers . . . " According to *Advertising Age,* more than a dozen people telephoned the company after the spot aired, asking whether it was real or not (Wilke, 1995b).

It is not just the personalities of sports that make the genre so appealing; it is also the unpredictability. People often watch sports because they do not, and cannot, know what is going to happen. Consequently ads, aside from using sports figures, often try to recombine with sports by copying the suspense that sports brings.

Usually the suspense is manufactured, not really being the true suspense of sporting events. The annual Bud Bowl, paralleling the progression of the Super Bowl during which the series of commercials is aired, features a pseudo-contest between Bud and Bud Light. At an initial cost of $5 million to shoot the spots in 1989 (Bud Bowl I), Anheuser-Busch then forks out the significant media time costs to air the spots, only once, during the Super Bowl (Elliott, 1991). The Bud Bowl features lots of "in" jokes (such as parodies of sports announcers' styles and sports clichés) and often spotlights certain types of promotionally weak beer as the hero of the game (Bud Dry, for example, won Bud Bowl 3). The real sports element of the campaign is the unfolding nature of the series, trying to hook people in the Bud Bowl so that they will be interested in the final quarter. To achieve this end, Anheuser-Busch bought eight 30-second units in 1993 for Bud Bowl V ("Big Ads Back on Super Bowl," 1993).

But part of the appeal of sports for many fans is that *no one* knows what the outcome of the event will be, not even the participants. So the Bud Bowl campaign was an imperfect imitator of sports, because the resolution *was* known in advance (at least by the creators of the ads). A campaign that came closest to mimicking the unknown quality of the sports event was the "Dan Versus Dave" Reebok campaign of 1992. Like the Bud Bowl, advertisers tied this campaign to a real sports event: the Olympics. Unlike the Bud Bowl, however, Reebok as well as viewers did not know what would happen. In the highly visible campaign, the hook was to follow who would win the decathlon in the Olympics, with Reebok trying to establish fan support for *either* of its two endorsers, Dan O'Brien or Dave Johnson. Although the spots were lighthearted at first, they were calculated to create identification and spark competition between the two athletes, both of whom were predicted to make the U.S. Olympic team.

Unpredictability is dangerous in ads, however. Just as in real sports— sometimes the game can be a blowout, or a superstar can foul out or the high profile team might not make it to the finals—this sports gamble did not play out as Reebok would have hoped. After months of build-up, Dan O'Brien failed to make the U.S. Olympic team, let alone compete with Johnson in the Olympics. Reebok, though, rebounded well with an ad showing O'Brien's last failed attempt at qualification, Johnson's disbelief and the written copy, "Accountants are predictable. Bankers are cautious. Politicians are tentative. But athletes are glorious . . . life is short. Play hard." As it turns out, Reebok continued a humorous version of the campaign during the Olympics and ended up with millions of dollars in free publicity during sports and news programs with the resolution of their "ad as sports" (Sloan, 1992).

Ads as Talk Shows and Newscasts. Finally, two more genres with which advertising has attempted to merge are talk and news programs. These two forms are collapsed together into one section because of the role that infomercials have played in the development of these genres in television advertising.[6] As will be shown, however, certainly not all versions of these two recombinants have been via infomercials.

Infomercials, also called "long-form ads" and "paid commercial programming," are products of several factors. Increased technological and economic opportunity, such as cheap air time on cable channels and advanced 800- and 900-number phone technology, have encouraged their popularity with marketers. Decreased regulation of commercial time on broadcast outlets and the increased aggressiveness of advertising in general—caused by such factors as the need to break through clutter—have also been factors (Garfield, 1992). In the mid-1980s, infomercials became a mainstay of late night cable programming. Because ratings on national cable stations are low, especially late at night, and because infomercials take up an entire 30-minute block of time (thus saving the cable station the cost of providing paid-for programming during that block), companies with 30 minutes worth of selling could slip into these time slots for an incredibly cheap price. Advertisers, for example, could buy the 5:00 a.m. to 5:30 a.m. slot on the USA Network for about $2,500 in the early 1990s (Colford, 1992). Because of these factors, however, infomercials were often linked with somewhat sleazy companies (like those touting impotence cures).

Nevertheless, they have become a main source of revenue for many national cable stations. One study revealed that Lifetime in 1992 aired more than 43 hours of infomercials in 1 week, with The Nashville Network close behind at 42 hours (Winzenburg, 1993). By 1994, infomercials made up around one fourth of most cable systems' programming, with nearly 200 in release at any particular time (Steenhuysen, 1994). Infomercials have also proliferated in broadcast outlets as the government and self-regulatory bodies such as the National Association of Broadcasters have held broadcasters less accountable for the amount of commercial time. Sales from infomercials can be extremely lucrative: Gross sales from products went up from $300 million in 1987 to more than $900 million in 1993 (Levin, 1993b; Steenhuysen, 1994).

Infomercials are characterized by their length (30 minutes); their frequent use of 900 phone numbers to spark immediate, impulse consumption (although not all infomercials use 900 numbers); the appearance of celebrities (Kenny Rogers, Vanna White, Jane Seymour among many others); and their copying of other traditional program forms.

Much of the discourse about infomercials in the advertising and media industry trade journals focused on their entry into mainstream culture and advertising strategy (Cooper, 1993; Hinsberg, 1992; Levin, 1994b; Mandese, 1993b). Infomercials are not just for crackpot products anymore. With more established companies like Volvo and McDonald's exploring the use of infomercials, with their airing occurring more in broadcast as well as cable outlets and with their timeslots moving toward daytime and prime time as well as late-night fringe, it appears that advertisers will increasingly use the form. One example of an infomercial was discussed earlier in this chapter—the sitcommercial *The Ringers*. Infomercials, though, have copied other forms of television besides the sitcom.

One recombinant that has been exploited by infomercials is the talk show format. This is the format, in fact, that the infomercials have most frequently copied. Among the best-known infomercials is the *Amazing Discoveries* format hosted by Mike Levey, who is also the president of Positive Response Television, the infomercial company behind *Amazing Discoveries*. Because of his exposure on *Amazing Discoveries,* Levey is also the self-proclaimed "most watched man on television" (according to a trade ad appearing in *Adweek*). Promoting such products as flame-proof car wax, the program includes many elements of the talk show. The implication is that the infomercial is a weekly series (the connotation of *Amazing Discoveries* is that every week there will indeed be amazing discoveries discovered and profiled, as often happens in a real science program), and the infomercial includes a host, a "guest star" (often the marketer) and a studio audience.[7]

Many such infomercials have the formula for talk shows down (although sometimes the look or topic is quite amateurish, even if the routine is not). One infomercial talk show for Nu/hart Hair Clinics, hosted by Charlene Tilton, features the host along with the president and director of the clinic. The "host" and "guests" chat about the clinics. After about 10 minutes, the talk program then goes to a "commercial break" ("Stay tuned," the host tells us), where the information given throughout the program is boiled down to the more traditional 30-second commercial format. The rhetorical strategy of a 30-second spot within a 30-minute "program" strengthens the talk-show image of the infomercial.

Other infomercials have attempted to mimic news programs. In an infomercial that was eventually grounded by the Federal Trade Commission for overt deception, Nu-Day Enterprises promoted the "discovery" of a new weight loss program in a news-ad recombinant infomercial (Farhi, 1992, p. H1).

Short-form ads have also recombined with news. Because of the prevalence of local and national news "updates," designed to be short and concise (and, not coincidentally, the length of commercials), even the mundane 30-second spot ad can seem like a newscast.

The most infamous example of ads as morning news (i.e., the laid-back kind of news where everyone on the set has a cup of coffee) is the Linda Ellerbee/Willard Scott Maxwell House spots from 1989. Ellerbee, a former *Today Show* talent, appeared on a *Today Show*-like set and reported about the wonders of Maxwell House before sending it off to Scott, then the *Today Show* weather person, who interviewed friendly customers of Maxwell House, just as he interviews friendly people on *Today*. The ads were aired, not coincidentally, during *The*

Today Show (Alter, 1989). Likewise, Joan Lunden, in a series of ads airing through at least September 1993, capitalizes on her *Good Morning America* persona in Vaseline Intensive Care updates. In these ads, after an introductory musical riff that sounds just like a news update intro, she sits authoritatively behind a news desk and in front of over-the-shoulder graphics as she reports on the newsworthy things Vaseline can do. A series of 1994 ads produced for Disney's Buena Vista copy *Entertainment Tonight*-style news. "Movie News" is 60-seconds long and hosted by a John Tesh-like news anchor. It touts recent Disney movie releases using news packages with sound bites, movie footage and location shots. These commercials often aired during network morning news programs.

Implications of Camouflaged Ads

Creators of commercials in traditional media face a tough dilemma, a dilemma that has to do with the ethos of mass-mediated content. The dilemma is that commercials somehow have to deny their own image and purpose. Advertisers believe that the persuasive impact of a commercial is decreased when people *know* it is a commercial. They also believe that people tend to zap the commercial when they know it is a commercial. They also believe that the more that ads are non-ad-like, the more the ads will stick out in the clutter of advertising. They also believe that people tend to watch TV or read magazines for the non commercials—that is, the content. When all of these things are added together, one finds camouflaged ads.

Deception is at the heart of camouflaged ads. The premise is to fool us into thinking we are watching one thing when we are really watching another. For this reason camouflaged ads are antidemocratic: The practice is based upon lying. The advertiser wants viewers to believe that they are not watching a commercial, but they are watching a newscast called "Movie News," or the Super Bowl or an episode of *The Simpsons,* or a soap.

Are people fooled by camouflaged ads? The answer depends upon the particular camouflaged ad, and what one means by *fooled*. Do people who watch an infomercial or Joan Lunden for Vaseline believe, after the ad is over, that they have seen noncommercial media content? No. Most people are not fooled in this way. But, when a blurred commercial *first* comes on, are people at least fooled for a brief second, long enough to encourage them to look up, to pull the thumb off the remote? Probably. But no matter the magnitude of effect, the bottom line is that the intent of this attention-grabbing strategy is deception. Even if just for a second, the goal of camouflaged ads is to fool people.

In addition to their attention-grabbing function, camouflaged ads also serve the purpose of increasing the credibility of the product. With camouflaged ads, media content becomes a referent system. Does the credibility of the commercial go up when Bart Simpson is the spokes-character or when Dan Cortese pitches to MTV-watching Burger Kingers? Maybe. Again, as mentioned in Chapter 2, ads like to attach themselves to the socially desirable. This occurs at two levels. The first level is that in our society,

$$media\ content = entertainment/information/education,$$

$$advertising = selling.$$

So if advertising can shift this paradigm, so that people think

$$ads = entertainment$$

or

$$ads = information$$

(and the credibility that goes with information carriers), then they have enhanced their ethos. Camouflaged ads also plug into the credibility of specific programs. Young audiences value *Seinfeld,* so Rold Gold Pretzels take advantage of an association with this value; they attach themselves to the hipness and humor and good feelings of the program. The recombined strategy is even more effective when the desirable object is *right next* to the ad, when the camouflaged commercial airs during the program. Ads grab onto the credibility offered by the specific program copied, like the irreverence of Bart Simpson, or the authority of Joan Lunden or the ethos of the news and talk genres.

The enhanced credibility of camouflaged ads, like their attention-grabbing purpose, is also deceptive in origin. This deception marks an irony of infomercials. One justification that advertising people make for advertising is that it provides product information for the con-sumer. Now although print ads might (perhaps) be on somewhat firmer ground with the claim, it was really ridiculous to think that television and radio spots, lasting at most 60 seconds (with 15 seconds being the norm), could give us enough information to make an informed decision. At first, infomercials held promise in this light. Maybe the long length of infomercials would allow room for more detailed product information in an electronic form. The route that most infomercials have taken, however—deceiving us into thinking that the commercial is not a commercial but rather a talk show, newscast or sitcom—completely subverts that promise. One study of infomercial credibility found that viewers did have a propensity to consider info-mercials to be programs, and that in time this propensity would increase. As more time passed after seeing an infomercial, one would remember the host of an infomercial as more credible than when first viewed (Hallmark et al., 1993).

What makes this deception salient is that in blurred commercials, we do not get news or music videos or sports. We get Madison Avenue's unmitigated view of what media content should be. Advertising does not want perfect copies. Most of the descriptions of camouflaged ads here have focused on the similarities among the commercials and the copied programs. It is also enlightening to focus on their differences. This again brings up the issues involving advertising referent systems discussed in Chapter 2. In the case of camouflaged ads, the socially desirable referent system is media entertainment. Advertisements are linking themselves to media entertainment not simply by advertising in the entertainment, but by copying it. But when advertising engages in this social linkage process, it also changes the object to which it is linked. Advertising does not borrow meaning neutrally; it changes that meaning. Sometimes this change comes in the form of decontexualiza-tion, with the referent system being taken out of its social context when placed in an advertisement. Sometimes advertisements remove specific elements from the referent system, often elements that are critical of advertising or capitalism. Thus, when media content becomes the referent system, the content is altered.

We cannot trust advertising's version of media content, but the goal of such advertising is to prevent us from seeing advertising's guiding hand. *Star Trek* is not presented in the Hallmark commercial, but rather it is Hallmark's *version* of *Star Trek*. And this usually means that the media content is hollowed out: The innovative or resistant elements are removed, the content commercially gutted. Just as the Lucy in Philip Morris commercials is more domesticated and deferential than the Lucy in *I Love Lucy,* so are the modern versions of the blurred commercials more domesticated than the original content.

For example, going back to the Butterfinger's co-optation of *The Simpsons:* One big difference between the Program Simpsons and the Commercial Simpsons is the change in the object, degree and sophistication of Bart's ridicule. Certainly the nuclear family, especially as symbolized by Homer, is poked fun at in the program, as it is in the commercial. The program, however, aims more vicious criticism at religion (especially in the character of Reverend Lovejoy, who in one episode lies about the content of the Bible to Bart's sister Lisa); politics (after impressing his class with a show-and-tell of the Navy's "Neural Disruptor," Bart says "Don't thank me, thank an unprecedented eight-year military build-up"); big business (typified by the nuclear profiteer Mr. Burns and his yes-man Smithers); education (featuring teachers who are lost without their Instructor's Manuals); and even advertising, in the form of Krusty the Clown's shameless pitches. The advertising version of *The Simpsons* removes these elements. All that is left to ridicule, both because of time constraints and, more importantly, because advertisements strive to decontextualize and sanitize what they copy, is hapless Homer and his attempts to get Bart's candy. Although the wit is a bit sharper, these commercials are essentially little more than updated versions of Barney Rubble trying to get some of Fred's Fruity Pebbles. The look of *The Simpsons* is duplicated perfectly by the commercials, but the true innovations of the program—its critical essence and appeal—are removed.

Another example occurs in the *Star Trek*-Hallmark recombinant. In the program *Star Trek: The Next Generation,* the economics of the futuristic system was rarely discussed, but the implication was that technology and ethical advancement has eradicated the effects of capitalism, at least among the *Enterprise's* crew. Hunger and material want—extreme differences between the haves and the have nots—are not issues in the Federation. In the commercial version, the subtle socialism of the show is at best watered down by Hallmark's commodity *Enterprise* and at worst removed completely. The crew member in the commercial, after being duly impressed with the computer's description of the *Enterprise* ornament, orders The Replicator to duplicate the ornament but is sad when told by the computer, "Replications are copies—only Hallmark carries authentic keepsake ornament." When she asks how she can acquire the *real* ornament, the computer tells her that an 800 number will give her the information. Thus, in all the episodes of the *Star Trek* saga, the only problem completely unsolvable by its new technology and futuristic ingenuity is the gaining of an "authentic keepsake ornament." Becoming old-fashioned consumers, giving Hallmark some money, is the only way this problem can be solved. Want is reintroduced to utopia.

Such commercial transformations do not occur just in the fictional forms. The nonfictional recombinants are potentially even more destructive. By presenting themselves as "neutral" sources and then self-servingly distorting the information, they are being destructive to the democratic purpose of media. They undermine our ability to evaluate information. When "Movie News," by implication, claims to be an unbiased, if coy, news update, but then talks only about Disney products, it frustrates our ability to make informed decisions about these products. First of all, even if "Movie News" simply describes the availability of the Disney products, it would be deceptive. We might believe that an objective news organization is saying, "the availability of these Disney products is a significant and newsworthy item for you to know." Evaluative statements are even more problematic. "Movie News" in one edition claimed that Disney's *The Santa Clause* is "sure to be a holiday hit." We weigh such predictive or judgmental claims differently when we know the source is a self-serving one. Camouflaged ads want to keep that knowledge from us.

Can we turn to media content itself to inform us about the deceptiveness of camouflaged ads? Sometimes we can. "Movie News," for example, was the subject of a brief but disparaging article in the *Washington Post* (Farhi, 1994). But at other times media can participate in the deception. Sometimes this participation is fairly explicit. One disturbing element of *documercials,* infomercials designed to look like documentaries, is the extent to which they are treated as documentaries—not as commercials—by support materials or the television industry. To promote its documercial, Volvo included with their ads for the documercial the VCR Plus code to allow people easy recording of the ad (Horton & Serafin, 1992). Even more telling, the cable station Arts & Entertainment listed the Saturn infomercial as a "documentary" in its program guide: As one station executive argued, "As far as we're concerned, it's a program" (Serafin & Fahey, 1991, p. 58).

More subtle has been Nestlé's use of the media to reify, to make more real, its serialized Taster's Choice soap-ads. Certain ancillary activities and services have been created around the campaign. In many ways these activities have elevated the commercial serial to program serial status. At least four types of activities accompany successful soap operas and successful popular culture generally: advertising for the soaps, public relations activities, fan interest and merchandising activity. The Taster's Choice serialized campaign has received all four types.

Ads for the next installment of the campaign (an ad for an ad!) have appeared in *TV Guide* and in the ABC soap opera magazine, *Episodes* (Johnson & Mandese, 1992). The public relations efforts of the company have also been successful: ABC's morning news show *Good Morning America* has covered the commercial saga and has at least once "premiered" the spot free before the first paid media showing (Johnson, 1992b, p. 4). Segments of the public have responded to these efforts. Aside from the increase in sales, the company and its advertising agency get "bags of mail" about the couple—fan mail, just like the real soaps. Also, Nestlé felt confident enough in the popular support of the campaign to sponsor an essay-writing contest for fans to come up with their own resolutions to the story (Garfield, 1993). Finally, at least in the British version of the campaign, licensing and merchandising activity centering around the campaign has been successful. A novelization of the serial, *Love Over Gold,* was released in British bookstores in February 1992. Although the product itself does not appear on the cover, the logo of the company does, and there was "the odd mention of coffee in the novel," according to a Nestlé executive (Bowes, 1992). The book was a quick best seller in that country (Garfield, 1993).[8]

Finally, one last way that camouflaged ads may subvert the democratic purpose of media is in their effect upon non-advertising media content. Camouflaged ads can have at least two effects. The first involves the camouflaged ads' impact upon people's perceptions. Every time a commercial copies the documentary form or the news form, the credibility of that form decreases in people's minds. Thus, camouflaged ads increase the blurring of commercials as programs *and* programs as commercials, *both* sides of the equation. A study by Hallmark et al. (1993) found that if people are shown both an infomercial and a real program of the same genre back to back, then over time they mistakenly tend to remember the real program as a commercial. Such camouflaged commercials leech credibility, like a parasite, from the media content.

A second effect focuses on how camouflaged campaigns may sometimes intrude directly upon the content. Sometimes a camouflaged ad can integrate itself into the media content. One hint of how this might happen can be found in the 1994 Super Bowl, featuring the Dallas Cowboys against the Buffalo Bills. The section on "Ads as Sports" discussed the camouflaged Reebok Instapump commercial. Not mentioned was the impact that this commercial may have had on the game itself.

During the third quarter, Dallas was driving for what would turn out to be a key touchdown. Emmitt Smith, Reebok endorser, ran 16 yards for the score. After he scored the touchdown, the NBC announcers discussed the action as the replay of the touchdown and Smith's post-touchdown emotional celebration was on the screen. "And Smith," said one announcer during the replay, "his emotions driving him even after the touchdown." The other announcer responded with, "And you know that's unusual for Emmitt Smith. Normally very controlled." Such an exchange may have inadvertently revealed how the Reebok campaign intruded in the game. Was Smith, "normally very controlled," suddenly experiencing "driving emotions" because a camera, looking for commercial footage, was waiting for him in the end zone? Smith no doubt was informed about the planned commercial-to-be. This is a minor example of ad-to-content intrusion, but it may point to the dangers of such influence.

The Future of Camouflaged Ads

Certain evidence points to the increase in blurred ads, especially evidence revolving around television production. For example, the increase in first-run syndication may increase incentives for camouflaged commercials. Many producers of first-run syndicated programming sell advertising directly on their programs, using a system called *barter syndication*. Barter syndication offers advertisers "an identity with the program and an assured environment for commercials" (Fletcher, 1993, p. 302). One interpretation of this is that barter offers advertisers increased external and internal control. Because the producers may deal with advertisers directly, there may be incentives to strike deals with advertisers. Advertisers might shape the content of the program (external control) as they deal directly with producers. In addition, the content of the program might be available for advertisers to use in their ads (internal control). Using cast members, sets and production crews becomes easier. The *Star Trek*-Hallmark ad, for example, was probably the result of a barter deal.

Similar dynamics may be occurring in network television. One thing that may have prevented advertisers from using the cast, sets and other elements from network TV programs in their commercials has been the economic logistics of such maneuvers. In network television, three basic groups are involved in the financing of production: the program producers, the networks and the advertisers. This has been the case especially from the early 1970s to the mid 1990s, when the Federal Communications Commission forced the networks out of production. During this period, networks have traditionally acted as self-interested intermediaries between advertisers and program producers: Advertisers pay the networks, but the program producers pay the talent. This structure has always been an economic barrier to direct program-to-product plugging.

But all signs suggest that the link between producers and advertisers may become more direct on network television. The FCC-maintained Financial Interest and Syndication Rules, instituted in the early 1970s, prevented the networks from producing many of their shows. These rules expire in 1995. If the networks take on more of a television producer role, then the advertiser-talent link becomes closer and tighter. Before 1995, national advertisers paid the networks, not the producers of network programs. If the networks become producers, however, then advertisers will pay producers directly. Predictions are that the elimination of these rules will encourage the networks to produce, or at least coproduce, more of their own programs, and thus advertisers, because they pay networks, would have more direct access to producers. Thus, deals between advertisers and producers to use actual cast members or program elements will be made easier.

THE "LET'S HAVE OUR OWN CHANNEL" STRATEGY

With the addition of television, by which a picture of the product in colors will appear before the home radio audience, there is the probability that the department store counter will be radioed right into the home. It is conceivable, as someone has pointed out, that at a certain hour each morning a department store salesman will unroll bolts of fabrics or place other articles before a camera and with colored motion picture and microphone give a selling talk to several hundred thousand women who have seated themselves before the radio in their homes and tuned in for the daily store news.

—*Frank Presbrey, Advertising Historian,*
1929 (Presbrey, 1968, pp. 580-581).

TV Macy's will be a 24-hours-a-day, seven-days-a-week department store in your living room.

—*Myron Ullman III,*
Chair and CEO of Macy's,
announcing the creation of a cable television channel
for the fall of 1994 (cited in Schiller, 1993, p. 65).

So far three TV advertising strategies have been discussed: the use of words, of anticipation and of TV program characteristics. One last strategy involves the complete takeover by advertisers of an entire channel. All-advertising channels are becoming a reality in the television world. These channels are being created for many of the same reasons that infomercials have proliferated: the need to fill cable stations, especially with the talk of 150-500 cable stations; the advancement of marketing applicable phone technologies; and the incredible profit offered. All-commercial channels also offer advertisers the potential for more economic control than they would normally have: They become the only game in town. The two opposing quotes above illustrate the "progress" that television has made in this regard. Presbrey's prediction of a department store channel is becoming a reality for television. It is finally fulfilling its commercial potential.

Home shopping channels foreshadow such potential, where hosts and guests flack for items that viewers can dial in and order. If the callers are lucky, they can even become part of the commercial message by being allowed to talk with the host on the air: Ads as call-in shows! Barry Diller, the creator of Fox Television, legitimized the future of this format with his two-channel format. QVC network is meant to be the upscale all-selling channel. The Q2 network is designed for younger buyers and covers topics like entertainment and exercise (Donaton, 1993f). During Diller's tenure, such name-brand manufacturers as Calvin Klein and Donna Karan entered the home shopping arena (Underwood, 1993b). In addition to these two channels, there is the Home Shopping Network (HSN), which is more of a Wal-Mart commercial station ("Pleased to Be TV's Wal-Mart," 1993). As a whole, the home shopping channels brought in $2 billion in sales in 1992 (Underwood, 1993a). The Big Three broadcast networks have experimented with the format and are expected to become further involved with such "transactional" selling (Mandese, 1992j). Home shopping may be a preview of selling on the information superhighway, as a later chapter will explore.

The control offered by owning an entire channel is practically limitless. Control over promotional timing gains Swiss-watch precision. If VCR time shifting took the control over daypart placement away from advertisers, home shopping channels give control back with a vengeance. For example, sellers can exactly time specific pitches to match symbiotic events. One QVC executive bragged that, "Ten seconds after the [1993] Super Bowl was over we were on the air with Dallas Cowboy products" (Underwood, 1993b, p. 28).

Of course, ownership allows complete control over the length of advertising time—it essentially goes on forever—and the symbolic environment that surrounds the ads. Home shopping channels are for loyal viewers very dependable (never going off the air), friendly and glamorous, all at the same time. One major goal of home shopping is to lull that thumb away from the remote control. Because of the successful symbolic manipulation QVC and HSN have established, many people apparently experience home shopping channels as entertainment programming. Program hosts receive hundreds of viewer letters a week. One writer notes that the on-screen shopping personalities "are followed with soap opera-like devotion" (Underwood, 1993b, p. 24). Viewers will watch home shopping channels long before they buy a product from them, sometimes for months (Underwood, 1993b). With phone and credit card sales making home shopping so accessible, a friendly or glamorous host can move tremendous amounts of merchandise. A visit by Ivana Trump on HSN in April 1993 garnered $10,000 worth of orders in a one-minute period several times (Underwood, 1993b).

Also part of this mix are all-infomercial channels that have been created or are planned. On Labor Day 1991, the Home Shopping Network Inc. launched Infonet, the 24-hour infomercial channel, airing other companies' infomercials as well as its own produced long-form ads ("Infomercial Network Launched," 1991). Similarly, debuting in December 1994 was CRN, the Consumer Resource Network. With Ford and State Farm Insurance among its charter advertisers, this network was "being positioned as 'informational' programming sponsored by corporate marketers to distance it from more typical hard-sell infomercials" (Levin & Mandese, 1994, p. 64).

In the fall of 1993, one of the biggest media stories in the news was the corporate fight over motion picture producer and distributor Paramount. In one corner of the acquisition ring was the friendly investor, Viacom, the parent company of MTV and Nickelodeon. But in the hostile corner was Barry Diller's QVC. Given the promotional control over content that all-shopping channels offer, QVC's attempt at a hostile takeover of Paramount became very interesting. Although the hostile bid failed, it encourages one to ask, "What level of economic and symbolic control would be achieved when a company whose focus is on the advertising and direct merchandising of products acquires an entertainment programming company?" Predictions are that such mega-companies will be best positioned to take economic advantage of the predicted expansion to 500-channel television systems. Home shopping and advertising channels are being groomed as important elements of this expansion. Such channels widen the amount of media content devoted solely to promotion and selling. Would their control over the symbols in the ads and around the ads be complete with control over major media corporations as well as media outlets like cable channels?

Advertising's control over television may have just begun.

Notes

1. National television advertising's inexperience with the written word sometimes shows in embarrassing ways. For example, a commercial for HBO, shown during ABC's *Monday Night Football*, asks the grammatically dubious question, "Has Saturday Night Lost It's Magic?" Also, in a promo for *Seaquest DSV* shown during a fall 1993 episode of *Seinfeld*, one of the names linked with the show is "Steven Speilberg"; *Entertainment Weekly* felt compelled to tell the staff of the program, "It's *i* before *e*" (quoted in Shaw, 1993, p. 12). In fact, exactly the same mistake also appeared in newspaper inserts for the "Kellogg's & NBC Present Breakfast Around the World" cross promotion.

2. The unique selling proposition (USP) is the strategic idea that advertisers should look for something unusual about the product that advertisements can promote, a concept defined by advertising giant Rosser Reeves. As Reeves saw the term, the USP can really apply only to products that do, indeed, have something materially different about them (Schudson, 1986).

3. Many vintage camouflaged ads mentioned here are available from Video Resources New York Inc. The cigarette advertisements mentioned in this section, for example, are found in *Classic Cigarette Commercials from the 50's and 60's, The Collector's Edition, Volume One.*

4. One example of a camouflaged newspaper ad appeared in an early 1994 issue of the *Roanoke Times and World News*. The ad looks just like a short news item, with the headline "Weight Loss Amazes Researcher," and a dateline of "Washington." It is not much different from the "reading notices" at the turn of the century.

One example of a blurred comic book/advertisement is found in a 1989 issue of *Archie*. Archie Comic Publications had struck a deal with the toy company Kyosho to promote Kyosho's motorized cars, planes and boats. In this issue, as part of the deal, the comic book story itself had promotional elements and the advertisements for the company had comic book elements. The plot of the comic book story centered on Archie and other Riverdale characters involved in a remote-control car race, with Archie's team being sponsored by Kyosho. To solidify this connection visually, Archie and his pals wore Kyosho clothing in the story. The story, then, was essentially an advertorial (in this case an Archie-torial) for the remote controlled toys. Also, an ad for the Kyosho catalog appeared in the same issue, with Archie himself endorsing the product in the ad, communicating via word balloon his enthusiasm for the toy company: "Outrageous! Now you can join the R/C fun, too!!!" (Lipman, 1989, p. B6). That last "too!!!" is key to the blurring effect. It explicitly connected the ad to the comic book story: They had become part of the same narrative thread.

5. The complete list of copied TV genres in advertisements could go on and on. Here are some samples. *Ads as Dramas:* In 1993, the exercise machine company SLM aired a "storymercial," a 30-minute commercial featuring a dramatized plot about training for a championship, complete with a love story subplot (Lasek, 1994). New England Telephone aired a series of commercials in 1988 featuring a developing plot about a troubled family brought together by the miracle of the telephone (Morreale & Buzzard, 1992). *Ads as MTV:* This would include ads that copy specific music videos, like Crystal Pepsi's version of Van Halen's *Right Now* music video; ads that copy programs on MTV, like Burger King's "BK Tee Vee" campaign featuring *MTV Sports'* host Dan Cortese; and ads that copy the overall quick-cut and image-oriented style of MTV videos, like one 1993 commercial for Ray-Ban sunglasses that featured 46 different shots in its 30-second screen life. *Ads as Cartoons:* Since the beginning of TV, ads have used animation to appeal to children. Some ads, though, use specific TV characters in their ads. Fred and Barney still promote the various Pebbles cereals; Wile E. Coyote tries to power down the Energizer Bunny; scenes from *Batman: The Animated Series* (with sound track) are shown at the beginning of a Batman toy commercial; Rocky and Bullwinkle appear in Taco Bell ads; Bugs Bunny starred with Michael Jordan in Nike commercials; Garfield sparred with the Honey Nut Bee in Honey Nut Cheerios ads. *Ads as Reality-Based Shows:* As programs like *America's Funniest Home Videos* and *Cops* became popular on television, advertising jumped on the bandwagon. Viewers supposedly sent in their own home-video versions of Surf detergent commercials in 1988 (Wolff, 1991); we get to see, live on tape, a couple find out if the woman is pregnant via the miracle of Warner-Lambert Co.'s e.p.t. home pregnancy tests. *Ads as Documentaries:* An infomercial for Saturn automobiles, titled "Spring, in Spring Hill," aired nationally in 1992. Labeled by the industry as a "documercial," the 30-minute long paid commercial centered on the creation of the company and included "folksy" footage from Saturn's Tennessee facility located in Spring Hill. *Ads as Public Service Announcements:* Commercials for the Incredible Crash Dummies toy line tied into the PSAs (public service announcements) that made Vince and Larry memorable and commodifiable. Reminding kids, "Don't *you* be a dummy; buckle your safety belt!", these toy commercials celebrated the carnage that could happen if the kids did not buckle. In the commercial version, the dummies are little figures that fit into toy cars that would smash apart when aimed at hard objects.

6. Although to a lesser degree than TV, radio has also flirted with infomercials. The National Infomercial Marketing Association was still developing guidelines as of 1993, but the fit of infomercials with talk radio seems to be a natural (Miles, 1993).

7. The Fox program *In Living Color* has parodied infomercials like *Amazing Discoveries*. At one point the impossibly smiling host, played by David Allen Grier, asks the audience,

"Are you as happy as I'm paid to be?!" and the audience replies in unison, "We're getting paid, too!"

8. About the only differences between the Taster's Choice commercials and a real soap opera are the spin offs that soap operas generate and the fact that soaps are listed in *TV Guide*. The British version of the Nestlé product has corrected these discrepancies, however. A "sequel" to the Gold Blend ad-as-serial began airing in Britain in November 1993, after their Tony and Sharon story line had been resolved. Many newspapers in that country listing the airing times of the first installment (Wentz, 1993).

5

CROSS PROMOTION
Control Through Cooperation

BUSINESS, especially big business, abhors competition. When businesses face competitive situations, they face potential economic instability; organizations fight for the same dollars and some might get more than others. If the situation is really competitive, it might even mean bankruptcy. In competitive situations, economic predictability becomes uncommon for industry. This is why businesses, if permitted, strive to eliminate competition through such means as vertical and horizontal integration, where they can control at least large sectors of the market, if not the entire market.

Advertising also abhors competition. Businesses will try to use advertising to create monopolies, at least artificial monopolies, and undermine any competitive thread. Advertising emphasizes brand image so much in part because a brand is a way to install a virtual monopoly (Preston, 1994). If a product can establish a definite brand image through its referent system linkages that is different from other products, then it can claim a unique symbolic space. Although there may be a hundred soft drinks, there is only one that can "Provide the Power of Dew." There is only one that impresses male twenty-something thrill seekers who have "Done That; Seen That." In this way, Mountain Dew attempts to create a monopoly of meaning over other soft drinks. Obviously, some brand monopolies are more successful than others. Also, when some brand monopolies become successful, they often are not monopolies for long: Other products may attempt to establish a very similar brand system to get a piece of the market pie the original brand monopoly carved out.

Besides branding, another promotional technique used to decrease competition and to increase monopolistic control is the huge, blitzing, mega-campaign.

Advertising rewards the big. Breaking through the clutter or keeping audiences from zapping or reaching hard to find audiences can often be achieved by ubiquitous advertising campaigns. The bigger the better. Big, flashy and pervasive campaigns may completely overwhelm smaller efforts by the competition. Such efforts, though, are necessarily expensive, which is why only the very big can afford such campaigns, and then only infrequently.

There is one way to cut down on the expense, a way that the modern advertising environment has cultivated. This tactic does not necessarily create "monopoly advertising," but perhaps does encourage "oligopoly advertising." Two or more companies seeking to reach the same audiences, but finding their own individual promotional efforts lacking, have with increasing regularity pooled resources (both economic and symbolic) and have developed joint promotional campaigns to reach these audiences. So we see advertising campaigns featuring the marriage of CBS and Kmart, McDonald's and United Airlines, Barbie and Reebok, *The Lion King* and Burger King, to name just a few. Paying lip service to the God of Competition, one advertising executive described this trend by noting, "An atmosphere of competitive cooperation is establishing the worldwide environment of the '90s" (Danna, 1992, p. 18). But make no mistake, the emphasis is on *cooperation*. As an ad for CBS appearing in a November 1992 issue of *Adweek* argues, "If two heads are better than one, aren't two companies better than one as well?"

This strategy, called *cross promotion,* encouraged by the social and cultural dynamics of the 1980s, is increasing in frequency, visibility and sophistication and has even spawned new genres of promotional techniques. This chapter will explore cross promotion, first discussing the specific reasons why cross promotion is the strategy of choice for many companies, what specific new functions cross promotion serves for advertisers, what the future may hold for this promotional tactic, and how it contributes to or detracts from the media's democratic purpose.

The Reasons for Cross Promoting

Cross promotion has been called by a trade journal writer, "one of the hottest ideas in marketing these days" (Warner, 1994, p. 16). The frequency of corporate alliances throughout the world grows about 40% each year (Spethmann & Benezra, 1994). Many factors discussed in Chapter 1—clutter, zipping, advertising-free premium cable channels—have contributed to the cultivation of this strategy. Other factors not yet discussed have also specifically encouraged companies to "cooperate competitively." Overall, seven additional explanations for the popularity of cross promotion can be delineated.

THE DRIVE TOWARD COMMERCIAL EFFICIENCY

The rising cost of advertising seems always to have been an issue for advertisers since the creation of advertising. The recession of the early 1990s hit advertising especially hard and increased the acceptability of cross-promotional activity (Fahey & Hume, 1991a). Rough economic times encouraged companies to maximize the efficiency of their campaigns, which meant getting the most advertising exposure—and impact—for their advertising dollar. Often, the cost efficiency of such efforts encouraged the cross promotion to continue after the recession had passed. Cross promotion helps companies meet their efficiency imperative in tough economic times, and the appeal of that efficiency may carry over to not-so-tough times.

Cross promotion allows the participants to increase the reach and/or frequency of their ad messages without increasing their budget. Essentially, a company gets two (or more) advertisements for the price of one. When the soft drink Shasta cross promoted with the producers of the 1993 movie *The Beverly Hillbillies,* Shasta received double-dip advertising. Not only did Shasta advertise its new soft drink flavor,

"Moon Mist"—featuring the likeness of Granny Clampett on the can—in free-standing inserts (FSIs) in newspapers, but Shasta also appeared in the movie as a product placement (Lefton, 1993). Shasta thus got double the value for its dollar. True, Shasta had to share promotional time in its own ads and point of purchase displays with *The Beverly Hillbillies*. This, though, is a small price to pay for the increased reach via the product placement, and Shasta can even market the movie tie-in as a "value added" benefit to the consumer. A later section will explain the "value added" characteristic of cross promotion.

This sort of "two for the price of one" advertising strategy can add up to millions of dollars in free advertising. And the efficiency incentive of cross promotion especially rewards the big, as the resulting amount of "free" advertising a company gets depends upon how big they are and what they can offer other companies. The benefits of cross promoting increase geometrically as the sizes of the cooperating companies increase. For example, rising advertising costs have encouraged many big movie marketers to increase their cross-promotional activity, using the blockbuster potential of their movies to bloat promotion to mammoth levels (Brown, 1990). The 1992 movie *Batman Returns* spent millions on advertising its movie, but received the equivalent of a much larger advertising budget—$65 million—through cross-promotional publicity supplied by such organizations as McDonald's and Choice Hotels in *their* tie-in ads with the movie (Magiera, 1992c).

Large advertisers know that cross promotions with other large advertisers make for huge campaigns, increasing the effectiveness and efficiency of the ad efforts. As *Advertising Age* noted about the "huge joins huge" strategy, "big fish swimming together can make big waves" (Fahey & Hume, 1991a). In fact, the goal of *Fortune* 500 cross promotions often is to create not just big waves, but tsunamis that engulf entire continents. Cross promotion, then, allows advertisers to have a voice that can deafen nations. For example, Disneyland Paris (formerly Euro Disney), in promoting its 1992 opening, used deals with promotional partners as one of its main strategies to garner blanket publicity. In the Netherlands a cross-promotional contest between Disney and Nestlé involved 2,500 grocery stores, or about 90% of grocery sales in that country. Nestlé boasted that this effort was the largest single promotion in the history of the Netherlands (Browning, 1992). Given such efforts, it does not seem much of a hype when CBS puffed in a 1992 trade ad appearing in *Adweek,* "When we merged the merchandise marketing power of Nabisco with the entertainment marketing power of CBS, the leveraging of dollars and muscle combined to reach consumers where they live, where they shop, everywhere!" Although this 1984-ish scenario is desirable for CBS and Nabisco, the image of all-reaching advertising is not a comforting one.

THE DEVELOPMENT OF THE "COMMODITY REFERENT"

As noted throughout this book, advertisers love to use symbols of the good and desirable as referent systems. If advertisers (through their research or intuition) believe that their markets admire the Grand Canyon and believe the Grand Canyon has a consensus of connotations that their product needs, then they will link their product to it. In late capitalism, though, such "natural" referent systems often present a long-term problem for advertisers. Referent systems may have a limited shelf life. A natural referent system might not be as effective after many advertisers exploit it. Advertisers have to be concerned that they can "use up" or "burn out" referent systems.

Elaborating on this, advertisers know that they have to grab potential consumers' attention. If something is used too often in advertisements, then it will no longer be an effective attention grabber. The familiar is boring, especially when used repeatedly in the same selling context. After a while, the Grand Canyon becomes uninteresting to commercial watchers and thus becomes a promotional liability. Worse, though, if advertisers use a referent system too much, then the referent system can become promotionally contaminated. Viewers of the ad may become cynical about the Grand Canyon's use in advertising. After a while, consumers might see how advertisers have decontextualized the Canyon for advertisers' selling purposes, and then its usefulness as a referent system is diminished. Advertisers obviously want to avoid these dangers. They are always looking for new referent systems.

So they turn to other, newer, hipper, but also universally shared referent systems. Here, the effectiveness of product advertising in society plays a crucial role. Through previously successful ad campaigns of the past, many products and companies have such a positive and coherent symbolic image that they, too, can be used as a referent system for *other* products. As R. Goldman (1992) argues, when the usefulness of natural referent systems declines, "advertising begins to cannibalize itself, feeding on the recycling and recombining of previous advertising styles and signs, in the quest for new twists on old meanings" (p. 226).

Cross promotion is one version of this recycling. Modern advertising has led to the creation of a new type of referent system: the *commodity referent system,* where a manufactured commodity becomes a referent system for other commodities. As late capitalism has matured, the inventory of available commodity referents has grown formidable. Because advertising is so pervasive and so strategic, the commodity referent often has a more coherent and accepted image than natural referents. The meaning of "Pepsi" might be more widely shared throughout the population than the meaning of "Grand Canyon." Pepsi, after all, has a larger advertising budget.

Cross promotion exploits this trend. Cross promotion has proliferated in part because it allows one company to piggyback on the successful image of another company (or both companies to ride on each other). Advertiser X can exploit the established and positive meaning of "Pepsi," carefully shaped through decades of advertising, when it cross promotes with Pepsi.[1]

United Airlines joined with McDonald's to include "Happy Meal" choices in a market test in mid-1992. Advertising for United promoted the Happy Meal availability, which included a toy United 747 piloted by Ronald McDonald (Teinowitz, 1992). It was not the quality of the food that led United to cross promote with McDonald's. It was the quality of McDonald's as a commodity referent. United no doubt hoped to plug into not only the popularity of McDonald's food, but also their "Food, Folks and Fun" family image.

But there is more to cross promotion's use of the commodity referent. A cross-promotional campaign feeds back into the commodity referent and strengthens its social status. Cross promotion legitimatizes and even celebrates the commodity referent. Advertiser X implies, through its cross promotion with Pepsi, "Here is the image of Pepsi! My product acknowledges this image, likes this image and wants to be a part of this image!" This has a certain degree of irony to it. Normally, advertisements devalue their referent systems. Every time the Grand Canyon is used in an ad, the meaning of the Grand Canyon is cheapened just a little bit by its subordination to a promotional goal. The commodity referent is different, however. The commodity referent's very purpose is tied into promotion and selling. Pepsi cannot be cheapened by a promotional goal because it would not exist, in any form, without that goal. The commodity referent's use in ads for other products may elevate its status. Advertiser X so believes in the legitimacy of the commodity referent—the image of Pepsi—that it will use it in its own ads, too. When you are asked to be an endorser for a product, you know you have made it big. You have social legitimacy. This includes Pepsi as well as the celebrity flavor of the week. Advertiser X wants to exploit Pepsi's image. But Pepsi benefits, too. By mentioning Pepsi in its ads, Advertiser X grants a certain degree of cultural authority to Pepsi's image.

Viewed in this way, cross-promotional ads are intertextual: They are dependent upon the audience's acquired knowledge about commercial symbols. The campaign is not effective without this knowledge. Because cross promotion is intertextual, it is similar to the Energizer Bunny commercials discussed in Chapter 4. In fact, one could argue that the Bunny is a twisted version of cross promotion, in that the Bunny pops up in other (pretend) products' commercials. Yet there is a very significant difference between official cross promotion and the make-believe cross promotion of the parody-centered Energizer Bunny ads. The Energizer Bunny winks at the audience, encouraging the viewer to understand and even poke fun at the conventions of advertising (at one point the Bunny knocks over a plastic mug of ale with a styrofoam head in a fake beer commercial). Cross promotion, on the other hand, removes even this mild form of critical awareness by asking the audience to embrace completely the previously established meanings of advertising. The intertextual nature of cross promotion is played straight in a way that celebrates and legitimizes the referent meanings of both products. Rather than revealing the meanings embedded in commercialism, it solidifies them.

THE INCREASED NEED
FOR ENTERTAINMENT PROMOTION

Entertainment cross promotion is hot, and movies and network television are among the biggest sparks. The promotional dimensions of entertainment have contributed to the rise of cross promotion. Robert Pittman, the chair of Six Flags after Time Warner acquired the amusement park chain, has said, "entertainment and marketing are merging" ("MTV's Pittman Gets 'Physical' With Six Flags," 1992, p. 42). One manifestation of this is the cross-promotional deals between entertainment companies and other manufacturers. The economic zeitgeist of the 1990s has forced entertainment conglomerates to make this strategy a necessary part of their promotional arsenal.

The movie studios routinely plan for cross-promotional deals as a way to increase their marketing reach. Movie studios have embraced cross promotion especially because of the tactic's ability to reach youthful consumers. The strategy encourages them to link with other youth marketers who can reach young people in different social places, like fast-food restaurants or grocery stores.

Fast-food chains and retailers might seek out cross promotions with motion pictures because of the glamour connotations offered by Hollywood, and because grocery and drug retailers are becoming an important venue for video sales. The motion picture industry is a prime source for commodity referents for such businesses.

Let's focus on the incentive for companies to create tie-ins with movie companies because of the allure that Hollywood-produced commodity referents bring. Wasko, Phillips and Purdie (1993) note that cross-promotional deals with movie studios give the non-movie marketers' "essentially dull products (in terms of image) the chance to be thought of as part and parcel of a world of mystery and wonder" (p. 279). If the specific movie has *already* proven its popularity with an audience (as in the new release of the video version of a hit movie), then the commodity referent system becomes even more desirable because of this track record. One Pizza Hut executive specifically pointed to the value of symbolic linkage with proven Hollywood products when discussing that company's cross-promotional deal with the video release of Disney's *Beauty and the Beast*: "Kids don't just like *Beauty and the Beast,* they love it. And a lot of adults feel the same way, so it provides us with a little emotional bonding, which hopefully holds over to our stores" (Grimm, 1992c, p. 32). Pizza Hut thus links itself to a referent system, *Beauty and the Beast,* which in many ways was as desirable for kids as more traditional referents like Santa Claus.

Cross promotion even allows access to Hollywood referents that advertisers would not otherwise receive. If a marketer makes a cross-promotional deal with an upcoming film, the studio may allow the marketer to use clips from the film in product commercials. This is especially valuable if the stars of the film are advertising virgins. Advertisers practically salivate over untouched but popular Hollywood referent systems. Steve Martin, at the height of his popularity in 1987, appeared in Diet Coke commercials. How could this be when, according to a Hollywood producer, Steve Martin has "never done a commercial and never will"? It occurred because Martin did not appear as himself, but rather appeared in the commercials as the Cyrano de Bergerac-ian character, C. D. Bales, from his hit movie *Roxanne*. The studio allowed Diet Coke to use scenes from the movie in their commercials (Savan, 1994, pp. 279-281). Cross promotions open access to such symbolically pure resources.

Cross promotion is thus an expected part of certain mainstream genres like action movies (*Batman Forever* and Kellogg's), children's movies (*Casper* and Pizza Hut) and comedies (*The Coneheads* and Subway). The summer of 1995 featured an "unprecedented" increase in the number of cross-promoted blockbusters, at least five (*Casper, Congo, Batman Forever, Pocahontas,* and *Mighty Morphin Power Rangers*), showing the attractiveness of the strategy to Hollywood and its partners (Goldman, 1995, p. 1). Even whole studios have successfully attempted cross promotion. Paramount's "Passport to Summer Entertainment" contests in 1991 and 1992, using several promotional partners, were designed to promote several films under that studio's umbrella.

An even stronger incentive for cross promotion comes from the three broadcast networks, or at least NBC and CBS (ABC has lagged behind in such efforts, at least before Disney purchased it in summer 1995). The Big Three networks are facing an erosion of both audiences and advertisers because of competition from cable, VCRs and other networks. The exodus of both groups has encouraged cross promotion.

Audience erosion causes a promotional dilemma for the webs. When the three networks as a whole reached 93% of the television-viewing public, they could get away with simply promoting their shows on their own networks. Often using flashy fall campaigns (like NBC's "The Place To Be"), the networks would often feel that the reach of such self-promotion was sufficient. This is no longer true. The promotional dilemma of the modern television network is this: If ratings are eroding, then how effective is it to promote a network's own shows *on* the network? Put another way, they face the same frustration with their advertising effectiveness as *any* advertiser does. Thus, the networks have a strong reason for exploring alternate ways of promoting their own shows (including touring college campuses, as discussed below).

The networks' problems have created some bizarre alliances, including examples of "sleeping with the [network] enemies," cable and video. Both NBC and CBS have formed cross-promotional deals with the cable network Comedy Central, in which their own network sitcoms are pitched to cable lurkers, especially at the start of the fall seasons (Burgi, 1992; Mandese, 1992i). CBS had struck a deal with Blockbuster Video to promote the network's programs in the *Hot Pix* video magazine distributed at Blockbuster in 1993, hoping to reach "light network viewers" (Mandese, 1993d, p. 8).

The networks are not partnering just with other TV outlets, however. They are also joining with retailers. A large part of the reason for this is, again, the desire to reach potential viewers of network TV with a promotional vehicle *other than* network TV. One study found that network cross-promotional efforts using free-standing inserts in newspapers, like CBS's partnership with Kmart, were the second most effective way to generate awareness of new shows (after network promos) (Mandese, 1992c). In addition, when the cross-promotional partner creates point-of-purchase displays that feature network programs (as in Target's agreement to promote the NBC program *Blossom* in their stores), then that also becomes a unique way to promote television away from television.

There is another reason for the networks' interest in cross-promotional deals, a reason that has more to do with advertisers than with audiences. As network audiences decline, so does advertiser interest in the medium, at least compared to the past. Striking up cross-promotional deals with advertisers can be a sly way to force these advertisers to increase their ad spending on the network. The 1991-1992 "CBS College Tour" is an example of this seduction. Both CBS and NBC have organized college tours featuring games and displays to promote their programs, and their advertisers, to advertiser-desirable students. To become a cross-promotional partner in the 1991-1992 CBS College Tour, a company had to agree to boost advertising spending on CBS or to shift a larger percentage of their ad budget to CBS. In fact, those who participated in the tour increased ad spending on the network by an average of 40% (Mandese, 1992f).

MANEUVERING IN A COMPETITIVE RETAIL ENVIRONMENT

Changes in retail outlets in the 1980s have encouraged manufacturers to build up their industrial clout through cross-promotional efforts. These changes include the growth of powerful retail chains, the increased competition for shelf space and the sales of videotapes in traditional retail outlets.

Retail has been one sector of the economy, like many others, that has seen the growth of industrial giants. It is no longer the case that large brand manufacturers like Coca-Cola can push their retailers around. Now, it is often the retailer who does the bullying. As Mayer

(1991) points out, in 1989 five chains controlled about one half of the U.S. sales for nondurable, nonfood consumer goods (p. 7). The explosive growth of Wal-Mart illustrates this trend: Wal-Mart was the No. 3 retailer in 1989, but by the next year was No. 1, with sales of more than $32 billion (Fisher, 1991). Wal-Mart is often *the* dominant retail outlet in a community; sometimes it is the dominant social *space,* retail or otherwise. With this degree of retail clout, brands must somehow prove their worthiness for prime shelf space. If two brands can speak with one promotional voice, then the retailer might be more likely to listen. And if a manufacturer can swing a cross-promotional deal *with* a retailer, as Kodak has with Kmart, then the chances of royal treatment increase even more (Cortez, 1992a).[2]

Besides the strength of large retail chains, what makes the fight for display attention even more difficult is the increased competition for retail shelf space and consumer notice in a "cluttered" environment, especially in the large retailers. Concentrating on supermarkets: In 1982 the average supermarket carried between 12,000 and 15,000 items: 10 years later, that figure had tripled (Ourusoff, 1992).

The big retail chains have added to this retail clutter. Many retailers have created *private labels,* like Wal-Mart's "Sam's Choice," to compete with the national brands. And when a retailer creates a private label, it is not for the manufacturing and selling of only one or two products. Kroger, for example, manufactures around 4,000 products in its Kroger line. Private labels accounted for 15% of food store sales in 1994, up 3% from a year earlier (Sloan, 1995). Logically enough, because the retailer receives a higher percentage of the sales, the companies might privilege their own labels with preferred shelf space over the national brands. What make matters worse for branded manufacturers is that consumer preferences may be leaning toward private labels. One study found that nearly 80% of shoppers who were surveyed said they had switched to private labels in some capacity (Warner, 1994). Cross promotion is one way to grab the retailer's, and consumer's, attention by combining economic and symbolic promotional resources. Manufacturers hope that both groups' heads will be turned at the point of purchase, when in-store displays and ad campaigns that combine well-known products are made available.

The development of large-scale video sales and rentals in retail outlets like supermarkets and drug stores has also encouraged cross promotion. In 1991, supermarket video business (including rentals and "sell through") was a $1.35 billion enterprise, with revenues expected to increase, especially in video sales (McCullaugh, 1992a). Many retail products have joined video titles in cross-promotional efforts. The previous section described the appeal that Hollywood has for nonentertainment brands: Hollywood gives the brand a glamorous referent system. Having a miniposter for a movie like *Hook* hanging from a bottle of Ocean Spray (in the form of a "necker," as they call it in the ad biz) gets the Ocean Spray bottles noticed by both the grocery store manager and the customers (McCullaugh, 1992a). Then when customers buy the videotape, they often find a coupon for the Ocean Spray-like partner shrink-wrapped with the tape. The makers of the videotape also take advantage of the cross promotion. Because grocery stores and drugstores sell tapes, videotape titles are encouraged to find "supermarket-friendly" partners so that when customers buy a bottle of Ocean Spray, they are reminded of the video they can rent or buy by the coupon attached to the bottle. Impulse buying (or renting), then, is now a prime motivation of video-consumer product cross promotion (Alaimo, 1992). One product becomes a form of place-based advertising for the other product. Also, such cross promotions frequently come with point-of-purchase displays or endcaps that hold the videotapes, thus encouraging the retailer to privilege the tape display with prime "home video real estate" (McCullaugh, 1992a, p. 55).

THE DEVELOPMENT OF CORPORATE SYNERGY

One hassle with cross promotion that companies find unpleasant is having to deal with other companies. Negotiations for the activity take up corporate time and resources, and often the results of these negotiations lead to each company making at least symbolic concessions if not economic concessions to their promotional partners. But if a conglomerate owns several different organizations, each of which can develop cross-promotional campaigns with the other satellite organizations, then all the concessions stay in-house. The driving force of organizational "synergy," where the whole of the corporation is greater than the sum of its parts, has influenced corporate growth. With a synergistic philosophy, corporations will acquire other businesses not because of these businesses' profit margins, but because these businesses contribute to the goals and character of the parent corporation. This is especially true in the promotional sector. Conglomerates may acquire companies that will help them promote and merchandise their products. The growth of synergistic corporate growth in retail, manu-facturing and especially entertainment conglomerates have made cross promotions and general merchandising activity logistically easier and allowed maximum benefits.

The entertainment conglomerate Time Warner is a good example of how corporate synergy leads to in-house cross promotion. When the movie *Batman Forever* looked to establish a cross promotion with a book company, either for the book adaptation of the movie (the "novelization") or for a "The Making of *Batman Forever*" book, then Warner Books was a logical choice. Time Warner owns both Warner Bros., the studio for *Batman Forever,* and Warner Books. When Warner Bros. wanted to strike a deal with a comic book company for a comic adaptation of the movie, then DC Comics, another satellite company, came to mind. For the sound track, then, Warner Records, or Atlantic Records or Elektra Records were logical choices. If they wanted to establish a "Batman" ride or stunt show in an amusement park (which they did for *Batman Returns*), then the Time Warner-owned Six Flags would get the nod. When they wanted to generate publicity for the movie, through media interviews or Sneak Preview features, then Time Warner vehicles HBO, Cinemax, *People, Time,* and *Entertainment Weekly* could lend a hand. When they looked to coordinate licensing activity, they went to their in-house merchandiser, The Licensing Corporation of America. All of these different outlets, under one corporation, can be used for licensing and cross-promotional purposes. Although Time Warner found it advantageous to deal with other companies for promotional benefits, the incentive is still to grow and keep everything under one corporate umbrella.[3]

Similarly, Disney could promote its hockey team The Mighty Ducks with stadium promotions featuring trips to Disneyland and *The Mighty Ducks* home video (J. Jensen, 1994b). Or it could promote the 1994 theatrical release of *The Mighty Ducks 2* with a publicity appearance by the actors in the stadium during an actual game, attracting more than 200 movie reporters (Magiera, 1994). With the networks, NBC's cross-promotional contest with General Electric, "Win with GE and Be on NBC," is made more attractive by the fact that GE is the parent corporation for NBC. Cross-promotional possibilities—and the desire to control such possibilities—have been one of the reasons for corpo-rate growth, especially in the entertainment industry, and one of the reasons for increased cross-promotional activity has been the increase in such growth.

RESOLVING REFERENT SYSTEM CONFLICTS

When advertising as a whole senses that desirable audiences love or admire a particular icon, a feeding frenzy often develops. Several advertisers want to use that referent system in their ads. When that icon is a completely manufactured cultural text, like Simba in *The Lion King,* then the creator of that movie can coordinate the different advertisers who want to link the movie with their products. Simba does not care who the advertisers are. Simba also will not venture out on his own to sign other deals without the studio's consent. When it is a real human being who is the hot symbol, however, problems can arise.

In the multimarketed example of Michael Jordan, Nike became most publicly upset with the former basketball franchise not because of his gambling or because of his flip-flopping from basketball to baseball to basketball, but rather because of his association with other marketers, particularly Hanes. Nike had worked hard at shaping and controlling the particular Nike image of Jordan, and Nike felt that TV commercials that displayed Michael in his underwear, or joking about his underwear, undermined that image. Conflict between the marketers over their referent system resulted. And from the endorsers' point of view, if they simply take *all* offers to appear in advertising, they may find that they have a short promotional shelf life because of an overexposed and fragmented image.

Smart agents of hot human referent systems can prevent such teeth gnashing by building in cross-promotional deals *among* different marketers, with the endorser as the common link. "Why fight," the agent may ask, "when we can all benefit from a coordinated campaign featuring my client (and I can get a percentage of both endorsement deals)?"

Such has been the case with two hot sports endorsers, Shaquille O'Neal and Emmitt Smith. O'Neal was the common link in a 1993 national promotion between Pepsi and Reebok, in which Pepsi drinkers who sent in a certain amount of bottle caps from Pepsi products could receive a discount on Reebok products. Smith took it upon himself to form a company, Emmitt Inc., to coordinate and integrate his endorsement contracts (Jensen, 1994a). The company attempts to join unrelated product campaigns to maximize the coherency of Smith's image and thereby sustain his promotional endurance. Hot advertising properties like O'Neal and Smith are logical linking pins for cross-promotional deals. Such alliances are more likely to sustain a unified image of the endorser (thus providing long-term flack potential) and prevent marketer conflicts over the endorser.

CROSS PROMOTION WORKS

A final reason for the increase in cross promotion is the mounting evidence that cross promotion is effective as a marketing strategy. Much of this evidence points to cross promotions' success not just in raising awareness, but also in increasing sales or boosting the revenues of the companies involved. Marketers perceive that cross promotion positively affects the bottom line, even if it may have other less socially desirable effects.

So, for example, *Advertising Age* credits Mattel's 1990 cross promotion with Coca-Cola for Mattel's 19% sales increase (Fahey & Hume, 1991a). Both CBS and Kmart have reported increases in their customers' attention after a 1990 alliance, with CBS winning the premiere week in the fall of that year for the first time in 6 years and Kmart noticing increased store traffic (Mandese, 1991a). CBS's competitor, NBC, similarly attributed a rise in ratings, at least in part, to its 1992 cross promotion with Kellogg's (Mandese, 1994a). Choice Hotels credited its cross promotion with *Batman Returns* for its increased business in the summer of 1992, with their jointly sponsored contest generating more than 100,000 entries (Magiera, 1992d). Supermarkets have noted dramatic increases in sales of *both* supermarket-friendly products like Tide detergent *and* videos like *Hook* when cross-promotional in-store displays are added (Alaimo, 1992).

Even when one promotional partner does not live up to its side of the deal (a movie bombs), the other partner might still achieve its goals with the promotion (increase sales or awareness for relatively small costs). Trade journals made much of the Barq's Root Beer tie-in with the disappointing box office performer, *Cool World*. Despite the movie's nosedive, the cross-promotional contest with the movie helped the soft drink win retail outlet display space normally reserved for Pepsi and Coke products (Magiera, 1992d; Tyrer, 1992). Similarly, a Pizza Hut executive called that company's tie-in with *Rocketeer* "a very successful promotion," even though the executive also described this movie as "not by anybody's measuring stick a Hollywood blockbuster" (Brown, 1991, p. 6).

The Development of
Cross-Promotional Commercial Functions

The above section surveyed the different reasons why cross-promotional activity has increased in the 1990s. The story does not stop there. Many cross-promotional incentives have encouraged cross promotions to take peculiar forms or to emphasize certain unusual techniques. Because of cross promotions' corporate dualism, and because of the specific problems that many cross-promotional partners have faced, the strategy has developed idiosyncratic *types* of advertising. These types are designed to increase both the breadth and depth of advertising.

A biological metaphor may help clarify the effect of cross promotion upon advertising. If changes in biological organisms can be attributed to the organisms' adjustments to new environments, then the manifestations of cross promotion can be explained in the same way. With the changes in the promotional environment in recent times, cross-promotional activities have mutated advertising to help it adjust. As a result, the new environment has led to new commercialistic organisms. These new forms serve different functions of promotion: functions that cross-promotional strategies are particularly good at fulfilling.

The three functions of cross-promotional advertising, and the forms that fulfill these functions, are the microcommercial, the multilevel commercial and the multi-placed commercial. Although these three forms merge in actual practice, analytically they serve separate purposes.

THE MICROCOMMERCIAL FUNCTION
IN CROSS PROMOTION

The *microcommercial* function that cross promotion sometimes takes refers to the "big fish make big waves" element. Recall CBS's gushing quote about being able to reach people "everywhere!" because of marketing partnerships; the microcommercial may come close to achieving this goal. Big national advertisers want to develop techniques for reaching *everybody* (or, at least, everybody with a minimal level of disposable income). In a previous environment, network television was the reliable vehicle for reaching the entire nation, but no longer. In a new cluttered and zapped environment, advertisers have had to become creative, and cross-promotional strategies, including microcommercials, have fostered their creativity.

What are microcommercials, and how do they work? They focus on the concept of "impressions." Rather than thinking in terms of ratings, it is more in vogue for advertisers to measure impressions. Impressions are the potential number of times consumers can be exposed to your message or logo. The more impressions you can garner with your cross-promotional deals, the more pervasive will be your campaign. Two points are especially relevant to the idea of "impressions": (a) The threshold of needed impressions is increasing—advertisers are proud when they can earn impressions in the billions, not just in the millions; and (b) *anything* can carry an impression. This latter point is especially important for understanding the microcommercial and its role in cross promotion. If, as a marketer, you are looking into the possibilities of cross promotion, a potential partner may be especially valuable if that partner can offer a unique and effective advertising "vehicle." Does the partner offer some message carrier that is unique, striking and especially ubiquitous? The microcommercial, then, is an advertising vehicle that can be practically anything as long as it meets these criteria. Anything that can carry a message is a potential microcommercial. Microcommercials thus allow advertising to blanket consumers in a promotional cloth. The sections below discuss the microcommercial use of food, toys and cards.

Food as Microcommercials

When your cross-promotional partner manufactures food and agrees to place your product on the food (or, more exactly, on the label for the food), that means that potentially everyone who walks into the grocery store will see your product logo; that means that consumers who buy the food will see the logo; and that means that the people who cook and consume the food will see your logo. If you can turn food into a commercial, you are guaranteed both quantity of impressions and quality of impressions. Sometimes the food microcommercial can even deliver a "captive" audience, force-feeding symbols to consumers along with their meal. A few examples will illustrate these commercial benefits.

Cereal is an archetypal example of the microcommercial. In a deal designed to grab loyal viewers' attention and promote the then down-on-its-luck network, NBC and Kellogg's joined in a cross-promotional deal that featured the placement of NBC series personalities on cereal boxes. Characters from *Seinfeld* appeared on the demographically matched Low-Fat Granola, *Blossom* on Corn Flakes and so forth. NBC saw this as a way to promote their shows outside of TV's own admittedly flawed promotional arena, *and* they could do it with a microcommercial that was pervasive and a part of every loyal breakfast eater's morning routine. People read cereal boxes as they eat, and NBC knew this. One NBC executive noted that, "We think of them [the cereal boxes] as 100 million mini-billboards that will be in the most uncluttered environment—people's homes" (Mandese, 1993f, p. 32). Actually, the figure was closer to 125 million boxes, and the campaign itself generated around 3.6 billion total impressions (Mandese, 1994a). When Paramount likewise struck a deal with Kellogg's to promote the *Star Trek VI* video on the boxes of Frosted Mini-Wheats, a Paramount executive concluded with glee,

> We're getting 5 million-6 million impressions with this promotion. It also gives people something extra to talk about. And cereal boxes may be one of the few last frontiers where people sit down at the breakfast table and actually read what's on the box. (McCullaugh, 1992a, p. 55)

If what is on the box is an ad, then mission accomplished. The audience, in this sense, becomes captive—if they are captive to the stereotypical breakfast routine. Better still (for advertisers) if the cereal itself is an ad, then the promotional message becomes even clearer. Hence the value of *Batman Returns* or *Addams Family* cereals timed to the release of their licensing partners. In order to promote the then-named Euro Disney, that company arranged a deal with Nestlé and General Mills to launch Trio, a cereal featuring Donald Duck's nephews, Huey, Dewey and Louie, on the box, starting in Euro Disney's home country, France (Crumley & Wentz, 1992).

Cereal, though, is not the only food that cross promoters can use as a microcommercial. Besides the examples mentioned earlier ("neckers" on Ocean Spray; Shasta's *Beverly Hillbillies* soda), Paramount was hoping to "generate about 1 billion consumer impressions in the US alone" for the 1992 video *Wayne's World* on Hostess, Doritos, O'Ryans, Fritos and Butterfinger products (McCullaugh, 1992b, p. 47). Cross promoters have also used fast-food collector's cups, fast-food paper placemats and fast-food paper bags as microcommercials.

Toys as Microcommercials

Product licensers know that toys can serve as promotion for their licensed commodities: A T-Rex toy can serve as a great ad for *Jurassic Park*—the theatrical movie or the video—and Mattel's Happy Meal Snack Maker Set may inculcate kids into the McDonald's mentality. Cross promoters know this as well, but they have certain advantages over the licenser. Licensers arrange for the creation of new toys (a *Jurassic Park* T-Rex doll). Cross promotion links with already established and popular toys. Partners have found that linking up with well-known toys guarantees retail space. The toy, after all, has already proven to be a sales hit. It is therefore a great way to reach kids. It also has another important advantage: Cross promoters who make deals with branded toys associate their product with something kids like. If they can successfully solidify the association in kids' minds by making their product *a part of* the beloved toy itself, they hope to establish "brand loyalty" for their product at a very early age. They hope there will be a symbolic leakage between the toy and the toy's promotional partner and that kids will remember their fondness for both products when they grow up. There is an incentive, then, to try to turn established toys into microcommercials.

One microcommercial that has grabbed the attention of several marketers is the Barbie doll. Created in 1959, Barbie has become an immensely powerful economic and symbolic commodity. Barbie as a brand name is estimated to be worth $2.2 billion to its parent company Mattel and generated nearly $840 million in revenues in 1991 (P. Brown, 1992).

What makes Barbie so lucrative? For one thing, the sheer numbers involved with Barbie sales: In the late 1980s, about 30 million Barbie dolls were sold in more than 100 countries (Michalowska, 1990); this was in addition to the outfits and accessories sold separately for the dolls—more than 100 new Barbie outfits are released each year (Stewart, 1989). According to Mattel executives, 95% of girls between the ages of 3 and 11 have at least one Barbie ("Mattel Planning Barbie Expansion," 1991).

Also, Barbie generates her share of income by licensing her name out to other companies for merchandised products. For example, the Barbie Carrying Case, first manufactured in the early 1960s by a non-Mattel company, has been called "probably the first time a character created as a toy served as a licensing vehicle" (Simons, 1985, p. 20).

Aside from the coloring books, the Marvel comic books, bedding, paper dolls and puzzles, another notable example was the Breakfast With Barbie cereal, released in 1989 and backed with a $10 million ad campaign from Ralston Purina (Sanchez, 1989).

One thing that makes Barbie so valuable as a merchandising partner is the ego-involvement and intensity that (mostly) little girls experience with Barbie. Advertising for Barbie dolls, with such slogans as the squealing, "I'm *so* into Barbie," accentuate this. The official Barbie Fan Club had 650,000 members who received *Barbie* magazine in 1989; the magazine gives its members updated information about the latest Barbie fashions (Gellene, 1989).

Most relevant for this discussion is how cross promoters have used Barbie as an advertisement for other products. Because of Barbie's ubiquitousness (10 million sold each year; millions more ogled over in stores) and her attraction to kids (as shown by the Barbie fan club and merchandising), she is a very valuable cross-promotional partner. By showing Barbie to be a consumer of a certain well-known product, the manufacturers of this product hope that little girls who play with Barbie will become inculcated into that product's promises as well. If Barbie is a role model of consumption, then why not use this role model as a referent system—and a microcommercial—for real-world commodities?

McDonald's, once again promotionally ahead of its time, was one of the first companies to realize Barbie's partnering potential. In 1983, one Barbie outfit was a McDonald's waitress uniform, thus getting little girls ready for their first fast-food job (Gellene, 1989). Benetton, the "hip" fashion line, signed Mattel as a promotional partner in 1990. In this deal, originally introduced in Europe, Mattel created five new Barbie dolls under the name "United Colors of Benetton Barbies," with complete Benetton brand name wardrobes available for the dolls (Michalowska, 1990). Likewise, one might also have bought Barbies that used Reebok products, Dep hair products (which came with the Totally Hair Barbie), Bongo fashions, mini-Celeste Pizza for One boxes in the Barbie Grocery Set, Rollerblade Barbies and Troll Barbies (the relentlessly cute little dolls with Don King hair). Finally, in a deal that could set feminism back 25 years, one can now also buy a *Baywatch* Barbie.

A TV commercial for the Troll Barbie reveals the micromentality of the strategy. It illustrates how Barbie's consumption lifestyle becomes a valuable symbolic referent system to link with the product *and* how the physical doll itself can be a microcommercial for the product. The

Troll Barbie is not just a Barbie with a troll haircut (although the Troll Barbie does have a rather punkish 'do). What *really* distinguishes the Troll Barbie is the doll's immersion in troll product consumption. As the TV commercial jingle for the Troll Barbie harps, "She's got trolls on her earrings; trolls from head to toe; a troll on her necklace; she's really in con-troll." Actually, of course, the jingle lies. Both senses of that last word are lies: The Barbie doll is very much pro-troll; and she is symbolically out of control, in as far as the doll's immersion in troll consumption. Essence of troll surrounds this manifestation of Barbie. Indeed, the Troll Barbie teaches a little girl how to truly spend her money on troll commodities: The doll's clothes have a troll print pattern, trolls are on her jewelry and Barbie comes with her own little troll toy. The Troll Barbie's effectiveness as a selling tool is accentuated by the fact that the Troll Barbie may be on sale in a toy store right across the aisle from more "pure" troll merchandise. A child can instantly model Barbie's consumption right there in the toy store.

The Troll Barbie, as with all the cross-promotional Barbies, does more than simply promote consumerism, the focus of many of Barbie's critics (Motz, 1983). These Barbies promote a *specific* consumerism— they become ads for other products aimed at an audience that manu-facturers want to reach. Brand loyalty, the notion goes, begins early in a consumer's life. What better way, then, to reach a young consumer than by association with a toy that sells in the tens of millions, that stresses the value of conspicuous consumption and that is beloved by the young? With Barbie, the goal is more than to encourage the consumer to spend money immediately on the cross-promotional partner (although this may be, as in the case of Troll Barbie). The goal is also to stick the partner's image in the girl's head so that, when she reaches the disposable-incomed teen years, she will remember Barbie as a McDonald's employee or as a user of Dep, Benetton and Reebok products. Barbie becomes a promotional investment. She becomes Brand-Loyalty Barbie.

Cards as Microcommercials

One problem with food and toys as microcommercials is that the consumer will interact with them only during certain activities (eating and playing, respectively). Promoters, though, would like to link with partners who can somehow guarantee that the microcommercial would be with the consumer *always,* so that the promotional impact would be at its greatest. Cards, especially credit cards, when used as a cross-promotional device, help to fulfill this desire.

A major development in credit cards in the 1990s is the *co-branded card,* in which one company, like General Motors, will sign an agreement with a credit card company, at first mainly MasterCard, to create a jointly sponsored credit card. Usually, such cards offer a "value-added" bonus to the consumer (like credit toward GM products every time the card is used). The card itself also prominently features the name of both co-branders. Companies who have co-branded credit cards include GM and also General Electric, GTE, AT&T, Ford, Shell,[4] and even *Star Trek.* Both the credit card company and the co-brander benefit from the cooperative deal. MasterCard was the leader in this strategy. Because of its status as a perennial also-ran behind Visa, co-branding allowed MasterCard to distinguish itself from the industry leader. It also allowed MasterCard to disassociate itself from the negative referent systems of banks (especially during the savings and loan scandals) by associating itself with the positive, service-oriented referent systems of other companies (Lefton, 1992a, 1992b). Master-Card attributed 70% of its card growth in 1993 to co-branded cards (Levin, 1994a).

The co-branding partner also receives benefits from the card. First, of course, co-branded credit cards encourage the purchase of commodities from the co-branded partner, especially when the customer earns "credit" discounts on the co-branded products. Another big advantage for the co-branding partner is the microcommercial advantages that the credit card offers. The logo and name of the co-brander often cover the credit card. For example, the GM card carries the logo of the car company and the name "The GM Card." In addition, the background of the card features a repeating pattern of the names of the six GM car brands associated with the card. As one credit card industry analyst points out, "it's like having millions of tiny billboards" in consumers' wallets (Lefton, 1992b, p. 18).

It is also like having billions of dollars in consumer debt. Charge card volume in 1994 was more than $470 billion, and rising (Spethmann & Benezra, 1994). With credit cards now persuading consumers to spend via plastic promotional messages on the cards themselves, one wonders to what extent this strategy has contributed to the increased debt. Savan (1994) argues that even value-added cards, in which purchases on the card build up credit for the branded item, is often a sham. The credit earned often has a definite ceiling, and once that ceiling is reached no more credit toward a desired item can be earned. In addition, the high interest rates of such cards may more than counteract the funny money built up through overconsumption.

Such is the pervasive nature of cross promotion through the microcommercial function. As the above discussion shows, one big advantage of the microcommercial function of cross promotion is its ability to be a pervasive and obtrusive form of advertising, sometimes literally following consumers wherever they go: on the breakfast table, in the playroom, even hanging at your side or connected to your butt (where you find co-branded cards). Other commercial forms encouraged by cross promotion stress different advantages. The multilevel commercial function is equally as valuable for cross-promotional advertisers.

THE MULTILEVEL COMMERCIAL FUNCTION IN CROSS PROMOTION

The reader may recall that one reason for the increase in cross promotion is its commercial efficiency: Cross promotion allows two advertisers to share a commercial space for the price of one. "Multilevel" commercials strike at the heart of this promotional advantage. These allow one commercial space to become a promotional vehicle for more than one commodity—indeed, sometimes for three or more commodities at several different levels, as will be seen. This, again, points to the cooperative nature of cross promotion. Instead of the philosophy of "This town ain't big enough for the two of us," it is more like "This commercial is too big for the one of me."

The cross-promotional philosophy encourages *all* commercial time and space to be used to its full promotional advantage, and that includes piling one pitch upon another. One commercial selling just one product is viewed as "dead air," at least promotionally. Every potential line of text, every potential blank space becomes fair game in the multilevel ad. Although the multilevel commercial might seem to contribute to the clutter problem of advertising vehicles, if done correctly the strategic matching of referent systems to promotional messages can serve to increase the impact of the multilevel commercial. Multilevel cross-promotional commercials will pile on cross-promotional partners, with not just two companies promoted—three or more are becoming increasingly common. Multilevel commercials can be found in both print and electronic media.

Multilevel Print and Electronic Commercials

Print ads for more than one product can take a variety of forms, but a common one is the free-standing insert (FSI) in newspapers. For example, the 1993 Kmart-CBS "Premiere Party Open House!" was promoted with a 10.5" by 12" glossy FSI placed in mid-September newspapers, right around the debut of the new network television season. According to a trade ad in a June 1993 issue of *Advertising Age,* newspapers distributed 140 million of the FSIs. The insert as a whole promoted both Kmart and CBS equally. On the front cover of the insert, Kmart's name/logo can be found six times, CBS's three times. At the top of the cover are pictures and names of four CBS programs, however—all of them the white-bread family programs that are the most advertising friendly, like *Evening Shade* and *Dave's World.* The only two programs *not* mentioned in the entire insert are *Murder, She Wrote,* which skews old, and the extremely popular but also extremely serious and somewhat advertising hostile *Sixty Minutes.* On the front of this cover appears a picture of The Big Red Boat (the cruise is a prize in the Open House contest, again fitting in with the family theme of Kmart and the CBS programs) and two bottles of Crystal Pepsi. When you open the insert to the double-paged promotion of the contest, Kmart's name/logo is found 12 times and CBS's 15 times.

Of course, as the insert points out, the contest itself encourages the viewer *both* to watch CBS and to shop at Kmart. It is a two-part contest: The viewer watches CBS to match numbers on "special CBS announcements" and goes to Kmart to match other numbers to "WIN A $100 KMART GIFT CERTIFICATE!" (But participants should beware of becoming a referent system themselves: The fine print informs the sharp-eyed that "By participating, winners agree to use of their names/voices/likenesses in publicity and advertising without additional compensation").

This cross promotion also featured a television counterpart. The television ads that plugged the tie-in were also multilevel in nature. As a CBS trade ad boasts, tools to promote the partnership included "Kmart/CBS seamless 'promercials,' which thematically combine a promotional announcement and a Kmart commercial enhancing the power of the message." In the promercial, the CBS spokesperson, Mark McEwen, chats with the Kmart representative, Jaclyn Smith, to emphasize the seamless quality of the hybrid form (Mandese, 1993k).

Another televisual example was found in Blockbuster Entertainment outlets in 1993. When customers rented a video at the regular price, they received in their Blockbuster bag the short "video magazine" *Hot Pix,* which came out every month. *Hot Pix* was the product of a cross-promotional effort among Blockbuster and several partners, but especially between Blockbuster and CBS. The tape was coproduced by CBS and hosted by (as he introduces himself) "Mark McEwen of CBS," who is also the voice of CBS Entertainment, often doing voice-overs at the ends of programs to preview upcoming programs. McEwen introduced the 10-minute tape as "your 10-minute ticket to the best in movies, music, television, and home videos." This, of course, was a lie. It was not a highlight of the best in those forms of entertainment; it was a highlight of the best *cross-promotional* deals that Blockbuster and CBS could put together. *Every* promotional second was centered on Blockbuster and CBS in this video, and we would *not* see "the best in movies, music, television, and home videos" if they did not somehow have a prearranged economic arrangement with the two organizations.

For example, the video began with a highlight of the theatrical release of *Beethoven's 2nd,* which at first seemed *not* to be tied into those two organizations. But then immediately following the trailer, McEwen ordered us, "After the movie, use your *Beethoven's 2nd* movie ticket stub, and the rebate form on your *Hot Pix* cassette box for great savings on the purchase of the original *Beethoven* home video [at Blockbuster, of course]." Then a trailer for the home video came on. Then appeared trailers for CBS programs, including *Return to Lonesome Dove* and *Picket Fences,* and trailers for other home videos sold at Blockbuster, like *Home Alone 2: Lost in New York*. Finally, the video promoted a tie-in contest, with prizes including a Chevy truck and B.U.M. fashion wear (at one point B.U.M. products were shown in a Chevy truck). Then, ending the *Hot Pix* video (and fulfilling, one supposes, the opening promise to give us the "best" in music), McEwen introduced a "video from B.U.M." that was nothing more than an MTV-like commercial for B.U.M. Although the participants ended the *Hot Pix* distribution in January 1994, it nevertheless pointed to the multilayered possibilities of videotape.

The multilayered function of cross promotion is disturbing for two reasons. One has to do with the goal of the ad. Not all advertisements work, obviously. It is logical to believe, though, that some ads do work. Advertisers spend billions on the premise that some ads work. This book is based on that premise, too. Some ads can be very persuasive for some audiences. When we see a pizza ad that grabs our attention, makes us laugh and makes the pizza look good, it is a short step to the sale. What if the effective ad, then, asks us not just to do one thing, but two things or more? The cross-promotion campaign is not successful unless it satisfies *all* partners. It pushes up the stakes. Watching CBS is not enough; one must also shop at Kmart. We can obviously choose to do neither of these. The fact that the ad has doubled its selling goals, though, stacks the deck against those viewers who are especially persuadable.

Another disturbing element of cross promotion is the recombinant advertising form that it creates. Both CBS examples point to how cross promotion can melt the boundaries between advertising and media content. In the networks' desperation for advertising dollars, they are willing to make special deals with advertisers, often creating content that appears to be one thing but is really another. Is this 30-second spot a promo for a CBS program or a commercial for Kmart? It is both. And the fact that two of the spokespersons for these companies, Mark McEwen and Jaclyn Smith, actually interact in the promercial ties CBS in with its advertisers even more directly. Is the *Hot Pix* video an entertainment video, like just about everything else in Blockbuster, or is it just a video commercial? It has the technique and retail environment of a video but the substance (or lack thereof) of a commercial. The video is a multilayered ad, but it tries to hide some of the levels. Cross promotion between a media organization and an advertiser encourages such confusing forms. Like camouflaged commercials, the multilayered ad makes it difficult for media citizens to determine the origin of the message. Our ability to evaluate the message may therefore be frustrated.

The Synergistic Multilevel Commercial

Multilevel commercials are also increasingly used with media conglomerates that encourage internal cross promotion among their holdings. With increased media conglomeration and the emphasis on licensing in entertainment media, sometimes the multilevel cross-promotional commercial can reach a level of synergistic sophistication that is astounding. One such example warranting special discussion is the cross-promotional efforts of *Batman Returns,* the 1992 theatrical hit. The cross-promotional deals established with Choice Hotels, as well as the corporate tie-ins with other Time Warner holdings, inspired the promoters of the movie to explore the promotional possibilities of a multilevel commercial.

For example, unlike the first *Batman,* the parent company exploited its television production unit to a large degree for the promotion of the sequel. Warner TV was able to invade prime-time network television with a cross promotion that served not only to promote the movie but also the movie's cross-promotional partners and Time Warner's corporate holdings. The week before the movie's theatrical debut, the half-hour *CBS Special Presentation,* "The Bat, The Cat and The Penguin," aired. This program was essentially a *network* infomercial. The company with something to promote (Time Warner) contributed to the making of the special (via Warner Bros. Television), combining both internal and external control. Hosted by TV mainstay Robert Urich (who at times looked really bored), the infomercial was designed to promote the movie through the liberal use of movie clips, behind-the-scenes action, star and crew interviews and tours of the set.

The interesting thing about this special was the multilevel commercialism that defined it. Because "The Bat, The Cat and The Penguin" had the image of a network television special, it had to have commercials inserted into it to maintain this image. But all the commercials, with the exception of the network promo and one Nytol commercial, served to promote Time Warner's interests. In fact, the Nytol commercial and the network promo, because they did not fit in with the corporate promotional synergy, were probably the most *non*commercial things about the whole "special."

Near the beginning of the CBS special, for example, the announcer of the infomercial informs us that, "This special presentation of 'The Bat, The Cat and The Penguin' is brought to you by Choice Hotels International." Choice Hotels was a cross-promotional partner for *Batman Returns,* and the commercials for Choice Hotels shown during the special promoted their movie tie-in, using special effects techniques and the sound track right out of the movie. These commercials were multilayered in the most complex connotations of that word; the levels of commercialism were layered on each other like an onion, with each layer reinforcing the other. At the first layer was the special itself, an infomercial for *Batman Returns;* at a deeper level was the commercial for Choice Hotels, which appeared in the infomercial for the movie; then at the deepest level was the commercial for *Batman Returns* that appeared *in* the commercials for Choice Hotels that appeared *in* the infomercial.

The special, then, featured commercials within commercials within commercials.

Yet the commercials for Choice Hotels were not the only promotional advantage Time Warner received from this special. Time Warner inserted other, even more synergistic commercials in the special. Ads appeared during the special for Time Warner video releases (like *JFK*); for Time Warner theatrical releases (like *Lethal Weapon 3*); and for Six Flags Amusement Parks—all of these items pitched in commercials within commercials.

Conglomerates love the multilevel commercial. It allows them to "take over" a message system, even if just for a small time. One argument for spot advertisements as a funding system in media is that the system provides some measure of diversity. Different advertisers, at least, will be found on network TV or in newspapers at any given time. They may all be trying to sell us things, but at least they are different sellers for different things. When conglomerates cross promote, even this mild, limited diversity is removed. Time Warner essentially took over an entire half hour of network time. They controlled the program *and* the spot commercials in the program. Time Warner had complete internal control. The *Batman Returns* referent system was duplicated perfectly in the images and tone of the commercials for the cross-promotional partner, Choice Hotels. And Time Warner had external control. The upbeat, celebrity-oriented movie preview was a perfect environment for advertising and in addition promoted their movie and their comic books. One voice dominated a half hour of television, internally and externally. This is bad enough, but CBS's little tag before the Time Warner infomercial, telling us that the following program is a "CBS Special Presentation," again denied viewers the knowledge that a multilayered but one-voiced commercial was really to follow.

THE MULTI-PLACED COMMERCIAL FUNCTION IN CROSS PROMOTION

A final function of cross-promotional forms is to increase the possibility that one campaign can reach markets in more than one advertising place. Often, *place* might refer to different promotional places: This simply means that one product will be mentioned in another product's commercials and vice versa. *Place* also might mean different physical places, thus tying in the cross-promotional strategy with place-based advertising—especially those examples found in entertainment and retail places. The coordinated multi-placed ad becomes a tag-team ad. A potential consumer is exposed to the commercial message in traditional media (like an ad on television), then is exposed to the commercial message in the home domain of one product partner, and then goes to the home domain of the other product partner (or partners) and is exposed to an ad there. And often the different advertisement locations will refer to each other: A promotional ad in one place encourages you to go to another place, where a promotional ad refers you back to the first (or a third) place. The best multi-placed ads are the ones that match market "places": where one partner will choose another partner based upon its home domain, with a desirable market likely to go to *both* places. Unlike place-based advertising discussed earlier, though, in cross promotion the ads are coordinated for even more symbolic effectiveness. Cross promotion creates tag-team ads to hit the consumer with a one-two punch. There are increasingly fewer places where one can duck for cover.

Multi-placed ads provide yet another reason why movie studios can be such attractive cross-promotional partners. The movie theater is a great place to reach young people. So movie studios, as mentioned earlier, link with partners who can likewise deliver young, potentially moviegoing markets.

In keeping with the multi-placed goal, product placement in movies is becoming valuable as a multi-placed resource. Using plain old scenes from movies in product commercials, like Diet Coke did with the 1987 Steve Martin vehicle *Roxanne,* is not enough. Product placements can provide both barrels of a double-barreled marketing strategy because of their prevalence in movies and their ever-increasing utility for home-based advertising. It is not just that products get exposure in a movie with the placement, and the movie companies get monetary compensation or the use of free props. The movie company and its cross-promotional partner are strategically using the product placement to maximize the commercial benefits of the activity. As an example of this, scenes from a movie with a product placement have appeared in television ads for both the movie and the product. In this sense, the original product placement and the television advertising featuring the product placement serve as a multi-placed ad, reaching people in the movie theater *and* in the home.

For example, an ad for the "original" *The Addams Family* featured a scene in which the creepy little girl Wednesday, selling lemonade at an outside stand, is talking to a Girl Scout who is selling her perennial cookies. "Is your lemonade made with real lemons?," the Girl Scout asks Wednesday. "Are your cookies made with real Girl Scouts?" Wednesday deadpans back. In the background of this scene is a billboard for Tombstone pizza, one of the few cross-promotional partners for the dark comedy. The product placement gave the pizza company a double promotional benefit. The image of Tombstone pizza appears in both the original movie and the movie's television ads.

Much more elaborately, another movie scene with a product placement has also appeared in a product commercial, in this case giving the movie the double promotional benefit. The movie *Demolition Man*, released in the fall of 1993, cross promoted with Taco Bell in a way that made the movie, commercials for the movie and commercials for Taco Bell practically identical and, of course, multi-placed. The Sylvester Stallone vehicle was different from a movie such as *Total Recall*, which stressed quantity in its 28 brand-name mentions (Wasko et al., 1993, p. 276), or *MAC and Me*, which was a B-movie rip-off. *Demolition Man* was a mainstream, big-named, blockbuster-designed release contrived to maximize the promotional *quality* of its product placement strategy.

Taco Bell in the 1990s has successfully targeted itself to the young, especially those between 18 and 30. The "value-oriented" fast-food chain positioned itself to budget-conscious high school and college students with its 59-cent (or less) value deals; its expanded restaurant hours (with some outlets being open 24 hours); and its "hip" commercials (such as the ones featuring MTV artist Bill Plympton). Such tactics have reflected its ad agency's year-long research into the consumer mind of 18- to 30-year-olds. As one market researcher noted about Taco Bell's pervasive youth-oriented strategy, "They're trying to leave no daypart uncovered. They're looking for every last little place they can sell a taco in and every time of day they can do it" (Cortez, 1993, p. 46).

Movie theaters have become one such "little place," especially movie theaters that feature youth-oriented action movies like *Demolition Man*. Given these matching demographics, a link-up between Taco Bell and the Stallone movie was a natural. What was promotionally "innovative" about the deal, however, was the intertwining of the advertising world with the motion picture world. Peggy Charren, founder of Action for Children's Television, has argued that product placements encourage movies to be set in the present, to maximize scenes with modern commodities (cited in Wasko et al., 1993, p. 274). Yet Hollywood is getting around this constraint by recreating the past or envisioning the future with current products. For example, what would fast-food restaurants look like in the future?[5] *Demolition Man,* with its fast-food promotional partner, was very happy to show us. In this futuristic movie the Stallone character, John Spartan, is a man from the past who is thawed from suspended animation. He is startled by the fact that the only fast-food restaurant left standing is Taco Bell, which is symbolized by a futuristic chrome version of its current logo. The dialogue of the movie integrates Taco Bell several times. "Now all restaurants are Taco Bell," says Stallone's romantic interest played by Sandra Bullock, Officer "Huxley" (with a name coming out of the Let's-Hit-Them-Over-the-Head-With-Obvious-Literary-References school of character symbolism). "I would like you to accompany me to Taco Bell," the leader of the future says to Spartan. "You're the guy outside Taco Bell," Spartan says to a rebel leader. Similarly, the scenes of the movie (the Taco Bell logo appears prominently on buildings and vehicles); the plot of the movie (a key scene takes place in and around a future Taco Bell); and even the film's credits (several actors are listed as "Taco Bell Patrons" at the end of the movie) reveal the intertwining of movie with restaurant.

Also, it is interesting how advantageous the movie's symbolic environment was for Taco Bell. Although the movie ridiculed many aspects of the future, other characteristics of this future world are quite desirable, including the emphasis on health (unhealthy foods, like salt, are illegal, for example) and cleanliness. Thus, in this ultra-healthy world where people only eat the right things and everything is dirt-free, the restaurant chain wanted us to believe that, as one character describes it, "Taco Bell is the only franchise to survive the fast-food wars." The movie provided a very desirable semiotic wrapping for Taco Bell.[6]

The degree to which Taco Bell accepted the symbolic advantages of the cross promotion was driven home by its own commercials tying in with *Demolition Man.* Taco Bell's ad, which served as a multilayered commercial as well as a multi-placed commercial, was designed to blur the boundary between the cross-promotional partners even further than the movie did. The movie was symbolically separated from contemporary Taco Bells because the movie at least had the premise of talking about the Taco Bells of the future, not the present. Taco Bell commercials for the cross promotion removed even this minor separation. In the Taco Bell ads, there were subtle hints at the beginning of the 30-second TV spot that this was a commercial for Taco Bell: The audience may have heard the taco bell ringing in the background and may have seen the corporate symbol (the futuristic version) in the bottom-right corner. But these were subtle hints: Clearly the commercial was designed to mask its true source and to fool the casual viewer into thinking this was an ad for *Demolition Man*.

Action scenes from the movie were the first thing shown in the commercial—in other words, a lot of quick cuts between chase scenes and things getting blown up. In the background, the sound track of the movie played while an authoritarian narrator intoned, "The year, 2032 . . . the city, Los Angeles . . . the movie, *Demolition Man* . . . " At this point, the ad *was*, in essence, an ad for the movie (although an inaccurate ad: The setting of the movie was not Los Angeles, but the fictional San Angeles). Then the commercial exploited its multilayered and multi-placed nature. The narrator announced, "the restaurant . . . ," and, in a collapsing of the two promotional texts, a character from the movie, Officer Huxley, in a clip from the movie, completed the Taco Bell narrator's sentence for him: "All restaurants are Taco Bell," while intercutting scenes from the movie that featured the futuristic Taco Bell restaurants and logo.

The Taco Bell commercial, though, presented *its* version of the future, rather than the "pure" *Demolition Man* version. Why are all restaurants Taco Bell? Not because of the vague and mysterious "franchise wars," but rather, as the narrator specifically informed us, "The reason . . . delicious tacos, burritos and nachos." Then the multilayered nature of the commercial was emphasized further by the dialogue that the narrator continues with the characters from the movie. Is the quality of the "delicious tacos" the *real* reason Taco Bell is the only franchise in our crystal ball? "Exactimundo," answered Wesley Snipes's Simon Phoenix; how are we supposed to react to the narrator's summary of Taco Bell's low prices? Stallone's John Spartan mumbled the proper response: "I'm impressed."

The commercial then ended with a summary of one of the biggest advantages of this cross-promotional campaign for the restaurant: the glamour of the movie as a referent system. The narrator finalized the tie-in between the two partners with, "The action . . . the adventure . . . the excitement . . . is now playing at a Taco Bell restaurant near you," and, indeed, the viewer was not sure if the narrator, when beginning this sentence, was referring to the movie or the fast-food joint.

Three especially illustrative elements can be pulled from the Taco Bell-*Demolition Man* cross promotion. First, this campaign, unlike other similar Hollywood-fast-food tie-ins, had an almost "gratuitous" (for lack of a better term) nature to it. The *Batman Returns*-McDonald's tie-in offered consumers the Batman cups and the Batman Happy Meals; the *Jurassic Park*-McDonald's tie-in and *The Lion King*-Burger King tie-in both offered their consumers microcommercial cups. These premiums, then, served as a kind of "excuse" for the cross promotion, a beneficial reason for the promotion's cooperative existence. The Taco Bell-*Demolition Man* tie-in, though, was seemingly done just for the hell of it. The consumer received *no* benefit (however superficial) from the collaboration: All the benefits were the textual and promotional ones received by the two companies.

The second "lesson" one can learn from this example involves the role of product placement. The tie-in could highlight to advertisers the increased benefits they could receive from product placements, allowing this strategy to become even more integral to cross-promotional deals with Hollywood. Product placement becomes material for more traditional product commercials. It saves on production expenses. Because the movie mentioned and showed Taco Bell so much, the commercial producers could simply edit scenes from the movie with voice-over narration. At the same time, the product placement very firmly linked the product with the movie referent system in the ad.

Finally, the movie *Demolition Man* served as a multi-placed commercial at several points. First, the product placement scene was itself a multi-placed commercial for Taco Bell when it appeared in the movie theater as part of the movie and when it appeared in the home as part of the TV commercial. And the campaign as a whole became a multi-placed strategy in the Taco Bell restaurants because point-of-purchase promotional displays added to the mix. Taco Bell, for example, created special bags to highlight the tie-in. One side of a bag displayed the futuristic Taco Bell logo from the movie and the logo for *Demolition Man*. The other side featured text to draw the connections between the two partners tighter: "THE FUTURE IS HERE," reads the headline of the bag. The rest of the copy notes, "IT'S 2032 A.D. THE DEMO-LITION MAN'S BEEN JOLTED FROM A 40-YEAR DEEP FREEZE CRYOSENTENCE. HE'S TIRED. HE'S HUNGRY. AND HE'S AFTER HIS DEADLIEST ENEMY. BUT THINGS ARE LOOKING UP. TACO BELL IS STILL HERE." In *this* version of the *Demolition Man* narrative, the crassest of all, Taco Bell actually helped the protagonist solve his problems. But the larger point here is that the campaign becomes a triple-placed strategy: in theaters, in the home and in Taco Bell.[7]

Conclusion: Cross Promotion
and the Commercialized Voice

Cross promotion solves many different promotional problems and fulfills many different promotional functions. Like most of the other advertising phenomena discussed here, however, cross promotion, in trying to solve advertisers' problems, often has implications beyond advertising. Specifically, the increased control that cross promotion offers to advertisers may subvert democratic information and diversity.

One thing that democracy depends upon is diversity of information, sources, social positions and viewpoints. Without such diversity, the decisions that democratic participants make will not be the best-informed decisions. An ideal democracy, then, has a balance and availability in its diversity that citizens may access.

Cross promotion throws available and accessible information out of balance. It allows advertisers to speak with a more imposing "voice" than noncommercial sources. The voice metaphor, in fact, may be helpful here. Cross promotion extends the social reach of the commercial voice in at least four ways: amplified voices, impersonated voices, controlled voices and nonstop voices. The danger here is that such characteristics may make it difficult for citizens to hear over commercial speech.

AMPLIFIED VOICES

Cross promotion allows each of the participants to speak with a louder voice than they would alone. It allows the partners to sing in unison, to make sure that no ear is deaf to their song. If network television can no longer deliver the audience numbers, the "product poundage" that it used to, do not abandon it. Simply add to it.

Through the microcommercial, virtually anything can carry an advertising message. If a cross-promotional partner sells food, or toys or cards, then these items can be used to amplify your commercial message. Through cross promotion, retailers can hear the partners' voices and grant them more attention. The multi-placed commercial could reach audiences everywhere, including the home. The micro-ad can be coordinated with multi-placed partnerships so that everyone is in the same key.

Those institutions that do not offer the economic and promotional advantages of such commercial entities as Coke or McDonald's cannot wire into the amplification system. Cross promotion, then, becomes a spiral: The big may roar even louder than before, with the small becoming ever smaller by comparison. Noncommercial institutions and sectors of society might find themselves ignored. Chapter 6, on sponsorship, will discuss a ramification of this: Often those with the smaller voices, to maintain their social place, are forced to sing the same songs as those with the amplifiers. To switch metaphors briefly, if big fish make big waves, they also eat up more and more resources (and even, occasionally, other smaller fish).

IMPERSONATED VOICES

Cross promotion also allows corporations to speak with the voices of others. When a promotional partner can provide a vehicle that does not quite look like a commercial, it may disguise the commercial purpose. This is a value, for advertisers, of the multilevel function of cross promotion. Symbolic vehicles can carry more than one selling message or more than one symbolic function. The multilevel ad can carry more entertainment or information than the traditional ad, but it still has a strong selling component that defines its essence. The problem is that the other levels may mask this essence.

So, Kmart is able to impersonate a CBS promotion in "promercials." A commercial for B.U.M. designer clothes is able to impersonate a music video when it is placed in the symbolic environment of a Blockbuster-distributed *Hot Pix* video. Ads for Six Flags, Warner Videos and Warner Bros. theatrical releases are able to impersonate autonomous companies when they appear as spot ads in the Warner preview "The Bat, The Cat and The Penguin." This, again, could confuse viewers who wish to use their knowledge of a message's source to evaluate that message.

In this sense, cross promotion is similar to camouflaged ads like a talk show-formatted infomercial. In both cases, an advertisement impersonates another media form. There is a significant difference between the two, however. In the talk show deception, *real* talk shows may object. They may realize that every time an infomercial impersonates a talk show, the credibility of talk shows in general declines. The relationship between the infomercial and the talk show is antagonistic. But in the case of cross promotion, the impersonation is welcomed by both the impersonator and the impersonated. In fact, the impersonated may have initiated the process. CBS is proud to be able to offer "promercials" to cross-promotional partners. Impersonation may not be the sincerest form of flattery, but it definitely is a seductive one.

CONTROLLED VOICES

Corporations involved in cross-promotional deals want to make sure that their partners are the best economically and symbolically for the corporation. They want to maximize the partner's effectiveness as an economic force and the partner's "fit" as an appropriate and favorable referent system. For many products, such measures of economic and symbolic quality are easily determined by the products' track records in both realms. Everyone knows what Barbie's monetary value and social connotations are. Mattel has successfully established Barbie as both a commodity and a commodity referent. But there are times when the efficacy of a cross-promotional partner is less known and more risky. Such instances illustrate the cross-promotional drive for control. In this case, corporations want to control the voice of their promotional partner.

For example, Hollywood cross promotions like product placement and merchandising favor certain *types* of movies over others. As Wasko et al. (1993) point out, movies that stress economic predictability and symbolic safety become the most promotionally attractive.

Cross promoters arrange deals *before* a movie is released in a theater—before the promoters can determine the movie's economic success and semiotic acceptance. This being the case, cross-promotional partners want some sort of guarantee that the movie will be an effective tie-in, both economically (that it will be a hit) and symbolically (that it will fit in with the partner's image and will not involve the partner in controversy). Both the economic and the symbolic realms create incentives for the creation of certain types of movies and not others.

Cross promotions further encourage a "blockbuster" approach to moviemaking (Wasko et al., 1993). Often, companies that tie in with Hollywood find that the cross-promotional campaign was a success for the company even when the movie bombed. Yet companies nevertheless want to arrange tie-ins with successful movies. Given that participants ink a contract before the movie hits the box office, cross promotion as a stream of monetary and promotional resources for motion pictures gravitates toward certain types of motion pictures: those that fall into a blockbuster formula. Movies with big stars, with an action or comedy orientation, with lots of special effects and with happy endings are especially valuable for cross-promotional partners. Many factors of big-time moviemaking (bank financing, corporate owner-ship, product placement, licensing deals, teen audiences) encourage such a blockbuster approach to movies, but cross promotion is becom-ing an increasingly important and institutionalized part of the incen-tives package. Movies that fit the blockbuster formula will be eligible for cross-promotional dollars and publicity; those that do not fit the formula will not be eligible.

Similarly, movies that are "safe" in content are valuable not just for their economic predictability, but also for their symbolic friendliness. This lesson was brought home to Hollywood in 1992 by the highly publicized controversy over *Batman Returns*. The watchdog Dove Foundation publicly attacked the movie's cross-promotional strategy, receiving print coverage in the *Chicago Tribune,* the *New York Times, Entertainment Weekly* and *Advertising Age*. Perhaps most visibly, NBC's daytime program, *A Closer Look,* hosted by Faith Daniels, also covered the controversy and devoted an entire half-hour show to the issue. The Foundation and much of the media coverage criticized especially the "dark" tone and themes of the PG-13 movie, and the inappropriateness of the movie's relationship with McDonald's. The publicity focused on the excessive violence, the plot of The Penguin to kidnap and kill children, and the sado-masochistic overtones of the Batman-Catwoman relationship. The moviemakers intended these themes for an older audience, but McDonald's distributed Happy Meals with Batman toys intended for a younger audience (Daly, 1992; Millman, 1992; Magiera, 1993a). Although McDonald's did not shorten its promotion, the publicized event may have encouraged a more long-term effect: cross-promotional partners linking with "safer" symbols (and thus financing these safer symbols). Pizza Hut, for example, felt more comfortable tying in with the cartoon movie *We're Back* than the blockbuster *Jurassic Park* because the former is a "softer, sweeter" dinosaur movie (Grimm, 1993, p. 12).

Although the curtailing of excessive violence is perhaps a noble goal, one possible effect could be to encourage mainstream, blander Hollywood material. The fact that both *Batman* and *Batman Returns,* two movies about a comic book hero who is triumphant in the end, were considered "dark" movies suggests a watering down of the definition of what is, in fact, considered an acceptably downbeat movie. As Prince (1992) explains,

That *Batman,* the major blockbuster of 1989, seemed so initially different from the optimistic fantasies of Spielberg or Lucas and could have been discussed as a grim and dark film reflecting the era of crack epidemics, homelessness, and relentless corporate acquisition reflects the general absence of an authentically critical filmmaking in our time. (pp. 22-23)

After the *Batman Returns* controversy, even this superficial level of "blockbuster grimness" may be too much for the commercial imperative of film. Pop filter *Entertainment Weekly* (owned by Time Warner) predicts that Warner Bros. in the future "intend to make sure that *Batman 3* and its progeny showcase a much less dark Dark Knight—kind of a *Batman Lite*" (Daly, 1992, p. 35).

As Wasko et al. (1993) argue, cross-promotional partners may want more guarantees, possibly beyond the point of script access to the point of script involvement, that the movies will not be unacceptably dark and risky. As one writer concludes about the motion picture industry's view of the *Batman*-McDonald's controversy, "McDonald's committed to the deal before its management knew enough about the film's content" (Millman, 1992, p. 1). It could be that cross-promotional partners will increase their ability to "know enough."

The issue of control also becomes salient when a cross-promotional partner for a particular movie has other cross-promotional partners. The partner may "suggest" that the film also include its other partners—and remove competitors. Such was the case with the National Football League's participation in the 1994 movie *Little Giants,* essentially *The Bad News Bears* in shoulder pads. Amblin Entertainment, the maker of the film, approached the NFL about providing equipment. The football league eventually provided the equipment, marketing support and "creative direction," but for a price. Products by NFL sponsors fill this movie. In addition, if a sponsor declined to contribute equipment, the moviemakers could not use a competitor's equipment. The moviemakers even changed the script to accommodate the cross-promotional partner. The small football players in the movie originally played in the Pee-Wee league. This was changed to Pop Warner, which had a previously established marketing relationship with the NFL (J. Jensen, 1994c, p. 16).

The attractiveness of popular video releases for tie-in partners also illustrates the issue of control in cross promotion. Cross-promotional marketers are crazy about videotape tie-ins. Many products may insert coupons in a video cassette box, help promote the video in their own media advertisements or point-of-purchase materials, or insert an advertisement before the movie on the tape. Home videos have become popular tie-in partners for those who do not wish to gamble on a film's economic and symbolic success. They provide a built-in track record measure (the box-office sum at the theaters). But cross-promoting on videos also provides another level of control that cross-promoting on first-run movies does not: The artists involved in the original movie are more likely to be removed from the decision-making process in home video, either because of legal issues (their contract did not extend to video promotional decisions) or because of logistic issues (the artists have moved on to other projects they care more about). As one entertainment marketing coordinator complained, "We've run into problems with creative approval on lots of movie projects—with Spielberg and with Tim Burton on *Batman* where he had to approve everything" (Tyrer, 1992, p. 52). In preparing cross promotions at the video stage, such control problems are much less likely.[8]

NONSTOP VOICES

Many indicators point to the increased used of cross promotion as an advertising strategy. Three factors suggest that cross promotion will expand: the long-term investment needed for such a strategy, the increased institutionalization of the strategy and the increased diversification of media conglomerates. These may lead to cross-promotional voices that simply will not shut up.

Cross promotions have an incentive to repeat. Often, when tie-in partners agree to a cross promotion, it is with the understanding that the same cross promotion will occur year after year, with perhaps a few stylistic changes, unless the promotion just bombs (Petersen, 1991). Especially for seasonal promotions, it is important for cross promoters to try to build audience anticipation *about* the promotion. Also, because several companies are involved (at least two manufacturers and usually a retailer), the first attempt at cross promotion is used to "get the bugs out." As one industry analyst describes the long-term incentive, "There's a need to involve a sales force, distributors, retailers or franchisees. The first run can serve as a dress rehearsal for a better version on the second go-round" (Petersen, 1991, p. 20). So CBS and Kmart cross-promote not just for 1 year, but for several; Paramount continued its "Passport to Summer Entertainment" for 3 years; Holiday Inn and Procter &

Gamble tied in together for several years in a campaign. In a similar vein, signing long-term promotional deals with movie companies may allow a cross-promotional partner to have first say about whether to tie in to any sequels spawned by a hit movie.

Cross promotion is also increasingly an institutionalized activity. For example, in 1992 NBC created a new department, NBC Marketing, designed to developing cross-promotional deals with advertisers (Tyrer, 1992). Similarly, the cartoon company Hanna-Barbera created a marketing department in 1989 to likewise encourage such deals (Magiera, 1991). Some advertising and marketing companies make a living on cross promotions. They act as matchmakers for potential cross-promotional partners. Companies like Deare Marketing, Co-Op Promotions and Co-Options help to coordinate campaigns and bring partners together (Fitzgerald, 1994b).

With the increase in media organization conglomeration, the incentives to cross-promote in-house also increase. Mergers like Turner Broadcasting and Hanna-Barbera; Viacom, Paramount and Blockbuster Entertainment; Disney's ownership of the Mighty Ducks hockey team and the ABC TV network; and Marvel Comics buying Fleer Trading Cards, to name just a few, point to a continued emphasis on the activity.

It is perhaps the beginning of the new age of competitive cooperation, with consumers having more than their share of crosses to bear.

Notes

1. Sometimes a marketer will have such a successful commodity image that "renegade" cross promotion is a danger, where a competitor uses the image in its ads. Comparative ads, for example, use commodity referents in a kind of "anti-cross promotion," where the ad negatively mentions competing products. One TV commercial for Nissan's Altima, for example, features a voice-over that notes, "It has a highly advanced multiple link suspension system, but it's *not* a BMW." The commercial then goes on to point out Altima's cheaper price compared to the referent BMW. Altima is thus able to exploit BMW as an elite, but expensive, referent. Perhaps a more interesting example involved Mattel, the maker of Barbie, in 1991. A Swedish toy company, a competitor of Mattel, attempted to use the commodity image of Barbie in the TV ads for their doll, "Petra." A proposed Petra commercial informed little girl viewers about Petra: "She came from Europe to play with your Barbie doll. I hope they'll be good friends." Because Mattel received no symbolic or economic advantage from this effort, they successfully argued for a restraining order against the advertisement (Sharkey, 1991, p. 16).

2. Sometimes a cross-promotional deal between a retailer and a manufacturer is the way to go. Such an arrangement can successfully counteract cross-promotional deals that

the manufacturer's competitor has established with other manufacturers. Pepsi's cross-promotional deal with the video release of *Home Alone,* for example, in which Pepsi placed a $5 rebate coupon in the tape, was overshadowed by Coca-Cola. The retailer Phar-Mor, in a deal with Coke, slapped a $6 rebate on the cassette for the purchase of Coke products at Phar-Mor ("Nothing Simpler Than a Movie Tie-in. Not," 1991).

3. Of course, as Meehan notes (1991), 1989's *Batman* used the same synergistic strategy as its sequel, but with even greater success. This success came despite the fact that at the time the parent corporation was not yet Time Warner, but a relatively scrawny Warner Communications Inc. One interesting external cross-promotional and licensing partner for both the original *Batman* and for *Batman Returns* was Ralston Purina. This company produced two cereals (the Batman and Batman Returns cereals) based on the movies. Batman Returns cereal is, as far as I know, the first sequel cereal.

4. Shell traditionally had offered "proprietary" credit cards that were usable *only* at Shell stations, but industry analysts predict that many such cards may expand to full service credit cards, usable anywhere (Lefton, 1992b).

5. The 1994 live-action movie *The Flintstones* has shown us the product placement possibilities for "historical" movies: McDonald's Golden Arches have their genesis in mastodon tusks, according to MCA Universal's vision.

6. The relationship of culture to commercialism in general—as portrayed in *Demolition Man* and as enacted with the movie's promotional strategies—is an interesting one. In the movie's version of the future, the hottest radio station plays nothing but commercials: The most popular hit "single" is the Armour Hot Dogs jingle, with which people joyfully sing along. Although this is presented ironically, the degree to which *Demolition Man* accepts commercial invasion through cross promotion and product placement shows that maybe such a world is not so unlikely, nor so undesirable, to the producers of the movie after all.

7. If one factors in the promotional deals made with General Motors, then *Demolition Man* gets exposure in two other places as well. The movie features both futuristic GM cars and a 1970 Oldsmobile (over which characters Spartan and Huxley practically have an orgasm), and one scene takes place in an Oldsmobile showroom. Mattel manufactured small toy versions of the GM-*Demolition Man* vehicles, which GM dealers placed on display, and sold the toys at retail outlets (Petersen, 1993).

8. Even in cases where the artist does complain about cross-promotional deals involving the video release of a movie, money may help ease artistic indignation. For example, in discussing Kevin Costner's reaction to a plan to distribute inexpensive taped copies of *Dances With Wolves* at McDonald's, *Brandweek* reported that at first Costner "railed at the idea of his Western epic being commoditized with burgers and fries. But Big Mac . . . considerably sweetened the deal for the star, one source said" (Grimm, 1992e, p. 2).

6

SPONSORSHIP

Control Behind a Philanthropic Facade

WHAT does it mean to be a "socially responsible" corporation? Many may feel that such a term is an oxymoron. Employees of corporations, though, would like to feel that they work for a socially responsible organization that gives something back to the communities from which it profits. But what does it mean to "give something back?" When corporations give money, who benefits?

Those interested in these questions may place possible answers along a continuum. One end of the continuum centers on the public good: The corporation decides to spend its money for a cause that provides a community with something that the community needs but does not yet have. Corporations at this extreme end of the spending continuum are good "corporate citizens." They become philanthropic, or patrons of the public good. The most extreme version of this patron form of spending, which corporations in all likelihood rarely ever do, would be anonymous giving. Here a hospital or a half-way home or a cultural festival receives the money with absolutely no operational or symbolic strings attached. Yet the connotations of *patronage* imply just such a charitable act. When Andrew Mellon donated the National Gallery of Art, he insisted that his patronage be kept out of the museum's name ("Bossy Sponsors," 1994). Accordingly, Simkins defines *patronage* in regards to for-profit organizations as "financial or material assistance given *without* the expectation of any return even in the form of publicity" (Simkins, 1986, p. 8).[1]

The other end of the continuum, though, is firmly pointed toward that expectation. The corporation spends the money for purely self-serving, promotional ends. Here, instead of money being spent to feed the hungry, it is spent to advertise on, for example, *Lifestyles of the Rich and Famous*. Advertising, then, in its most obvious, no-holds-barred promotional form, belongs squarely at this end of the continuum. The relationship between the corporation and the recipient becomes that of a buyer and a seller rather than that of a patron and a beneficiary.

Between these two extremes, theoretically, is sponsorship. *Sponsorship* is a corporate activity that stresses both the philanthropic goals of corporate giving and its promotional goals. As defined here, sponsorship is the act of corporate giving to some activity—sometimes for-profit, sometimes not—in an attempt to capitalize on the philanthropic ethos of patronage as well as the promotional functions of advertising. The dualistic nature of sponsorship explains why the word often has multiple meanings. The definition of sponsorship can emphasize its philanthropic elements: A "sponsor" is often someone or some organization who donates to, and takes responsibility for, the public good. Interestingly enough, according to *The American Heritage Dictionary,* one definition of *sponsor* is "a god parent." The term *sponsorship* can also mean just another form of media advertising, however. Often, in this realm, sponsorship is used as a contrast to spot advertising: Sponsorship involves ONE promoter giving all the funding to, and getting all the promotional time from, a media program. Spot advertising, conversely, involves several advertisers sharing the total advertising time. Early television programs like the *Colgate Comedy Hour* and *Philco TV Playhouse* were examples of sponsorship, with a more recent well-known example being the *Hallmark Hall of Fame.*

As discussed here, the differences among sponsorship and both patronage and advertising are crucial, helping to explain sponsorship's usefulness to corporate promoters. It is easy to see how sponsorship differs from patronage: The promotional function of the giving becomes much more salient in sponsorship than in philanthropy. Anonymous giving is not an option in sponsorship.

The differences between sponsorship and advertising, however, are more subtle but equally defining. The odd example of the 1994 World Cup soccer broadcasts on ESPN illustrates one of the most crucial differences between sponsorship and advertising. At the beginning of each World Cup soccer match broadcast, ESPN claimed to give viewers these broadcasts "commercial free." This is wonderful; sports as the result of patronage. Not quite. When one actually watched the broadcasts, one would notice that, in fact, the commercial messages never left the screen! In the upper-right corner of the soccer broadcasts would be a continual graphic for Canon, Snickers or some other World Cup soccer sponsor. The rotating logo system guaranteed 18 minutes of screen time for each sponsor (Sandomir, 1994). Taken as a whole, commercialistic promotion was a part of literally every minute of the games. So how could ESPN claim to give viewers the broadcast "commercial free," when more commercial time was shown on the soccer broadcasts than any other of its sports broadcasts?

The World Cup example points to an unusual contradiction of sponsorship when compared with traditional advertising. Sponsorship, as manifested in the 1980s and 1990s, is at the same time *less* obtrusive and *more* obtrusive than traditional spot advertising. Both sides of the equation offer potential benefits to sponsors.

Sponsorship is less obtrusive than advertising for several reasons. For one thing, even when the "cause" is one that is obviously for profit and would exist anyway, with or without the sponsor, the use of the word *sponsor* instead of *advertiser* invokes the philanthropist. A sponsor is someone special. As one marketer argues about the positive connotations of sponsorship, "Sponsors don't want consumers to know that [the sponsorship] is purchased. They want people to think it's awarded— like the Nobel Prize" (Horovitz, 1994, p. D6). Another reason sponsorship is less obtrusive than traditional advertising is that, especially in sponsoring a live event, the company can promote its name without obvious 30-second spot commercials. Sponsorship can be more subtle than spot advertising if it needs to be.

Cigarette promotion illustrates this advantage. When the government banned cigarette advertising from U.S. television beginning in 1971, cigarette companies switched to print advertising, outdoor advertising and sponsorship. The International Motor Sports Association's Camel GT Series, for example, began in the early 1970s, and the Virginia Slims Tennis Tournament likewise was created around that time. In 1993, cigarette companies spent $80 million on event sponsorship, of which three fourths went to sports (Whalen, 1993). The conglomerate Philip Morris, which owns cigarette companies as well as other product manufacturers, spent more money on events sponsorship, by far, than any other organization. The company spent more than $90 million, with RJR Nabisco spending more than $35 million (Levin, 1993c). In 1991, RJR Nabisco sponsored some 2,500 sporting events (Hilts, 1991). Events sponsorship, with this promotional form's unobtrusive nature, allowed cigarette companies to maintain a foothold in television despite the ban. By sponsoring such televised events as the Nascar Winston Cup, RJR Nabisco still managed to place its product on television but in a less blatant and more legal way than outright product advertisements.[2]

Sponsorship, however, is often *more* obtrusive than traditional advertising. Sponsorship is a funding strategy that is often designed to link the sponsor strongly with the sponsored. With sponsorship, one sponsor can dominate promotional time. In sponsored events, the sponsor's name usually appears throughout the event, sometimes from beginning to end, sometimes in the background and foreground. In the World Cup, Snickers received more screen time than Tony Meola. Illustrating the ubiquitousness of sponsorship, in Great Britain in the mid-1980s, cigarette companies so heavily sponsored televised snooker tournaments that studies showed that many children believed that cigarettes *were* advertised on television, despite a long-time ban on such advertising (Simkins, 1986).

That fact that sponsorship can be both less intrusive and more intrusive than traditional advertising explains much of its attractiveness as a modern promotional strategy. The rest of this chapter will explore the recent increase in sponsorship activity by corporations and its peculiar nature. Ultimately, the chapter will focus on the implications of sponsorship for a participatory citizenship.

The Increase in Sponsorship and Its Promotional Nature

Sponsorship as a promotional activity is not new. The first instance of the company sponsorship of an event occurred at least as far back as

1887, when the French magazine *Velocipede* sponsored an early automobile race (Lucas, 1992). Texaco began sponsoring radio broadcasts of the Metropolitan Opera in 1940 and Philip Morris sponsored museum exhibitions in 1965 (Lubell, 1990). Sponsorship dominated broadcasting from its beginnings until the early 1960s.

Several factors have led to a significant increase in sponsorship beginning in the 1980s. To briefly preview later arguments, many factors discussed earlier—zipping, zapping, clutter, deregulation—have encouraged the activity. Another factor in the increase is the rising cost of traditional advertising slots in media (McCarthy, 1991). Promoters view the sponsorship of large and small events as a way to stretch the traditional advertising dollar, especially through free publicity, as a later section will detail.

More specifically, cable television has encouraged more sponsorship. Cable has allowed many more events, especially sporting events, to be aired on television. This makes such events more attractive to sponsors by pushing up their promotional value ("Advertising Everywhere!", 1992). Another way cable has encouraged sponsorship is the increase in the number of cable stations, especially economically unestablished cable stations. Many new cable stations, operating on less than broadcast network-level funding, see sponsorship deals as a way to bring in revenue quickly and develop a friendly reputation with advertisers.

Many events, organizations and charities have increasingly come to depend upon sponsorship. Public funds for many nonprofit organizations have declined due to deregulation. This has been coupled with a late-eighties recession that cut down on private donations both in this country and in Great Britain during the Thatcher administration (Shaw, 1990). The economic costs of advertising and promoting not-for-profit events and charities have increased. Such organizations have found that, in the hyper-promotional 1990s, simple announcements shown on late-night fringe TV can no longer compete with flashy product advertising (Roan, 1994). Such factors have left public media, the arts and other organizations in dire straits. Not-for-profits, then, need sponsors' money or resources. Needy organizations approach corporations for several types of resources. They might simply wish to receive sponsored money. The nonprofits might also approach sponsors for shared advertising space and time (Lublin, 1990); or for things to be bartered, like greatly discounted hotel rooms for the nonprofit's use if travel is involved (Sebastian, 1992).

Since the 1980s, then, sponsorship activity has increased, and it has increased in several ways. First, the amount of dollars promoters have allocated to sponsorship has increased. In 1985, total sponsorship spending approached $850 million ("Entertainment Marketing," 1992). By 1993, this figure had reached $3.7 billion, more than quadrupling in that 7-year period (Levin, 1993c). Similarly, the number of companies that sponsored events had also increased, from 1,600 sponsoring companies in 1985 to 4,500 sponsoring companies in 1992 ("Entertainment Marketing," 1992). Sponsorship for the arts has increased from a mere $22 million in 1967 (Lubell, 1990) to more than 10 times that amount, $245 million, in 1993 (Levin, 1993c). Sports, especially, has captured the fancy of potential sponsors over the past few years. Sponsorship for sports greatly increased between 1985 and 1993, going from less than $1.3 billion to $2.4 billion ("Entertainment Marketing," 1992; Levin, 1993c). Christopher Whittle, who admittedly had a self-interest in nontraditional forms of promotion, has argued that event sponsorship will continue to grow until it overcomes traditional media advertising placement as the primary category for advertising spending (Hume, 1992a).

Perhaps more important, sponsorship has "increased" in another way since the 1980s: The intensity of its promotional function has increased. Many corporations have increased their sponsorship activity in response to the rising costs of traditional advertising spots. Accordingly, some companies are shifting money from their traditional media buys to sponsorships (Brunelli, 1993). Given this, in referring to the philanthropy-promotion continuum, sponsorship has been pushed to emphasize the promotional side rather than the philanthropic side. As a result, sponsorship has begun to affect the expectations of both the sponsors and the sponsored about what sponsorship's role is. With many sponsorship activities in the 1990s, the relationship between the sponsor and the sponsored has become more that of the buyer to the seller, rather than the patron to the beneficiary.

Sponsorship *is* advertising.

Several marketing executives and analysts have stressed that sponsorship, before the 1990s, was often initiated at the "whim of the CEO": When that corporate executive favored tennis, the company would sponsor tennis events. The increase in the amount of money involved in sponsorship, however, has altered the approach of sponsors. "With companies spending millions of dollars, the days of doing a corporate sponsorship just because the CEO likes it are over," according to one marketing consultant (McCarthy, 1991, p. B1). Systematic promotional goals often drive sponsorship decisions. "Philanthropy and patron-of-the-sport days are gone," said another consultant, "We wanted the recognition" (McCarthy, 1991, p. B5). Sponsorship has become just like any other advertising buy. Sponsorship becomes valuable when it fulfills a company's marketing needs, especially when it can be tied specifically to sales increases. As a writer for *Advertising Age* concludes, "Many marketers evaluating where to begin or renew a [sponsorship] deal now look to the bottom line—not the boss's back nine—for answers" (Levin, 1993c, p. S1).

The relatively new obsession corporations have with measuring the effectiveness of sponsorship as a sales tool illustrates the new attitude toward sponsorship. Specialty companies like D&F Consulting will track a sponsorship's effectiveness as a publicity getter or a sales booster (McCarthy, 1991). Other companies try to measure how profitable a sponsorship deal was for them through very elaborate sales-tracking techniques. Here is how a trade journal described Colgate-Palmolive's evaluation of its sponsorship of the Starlight Foundation, a cause similar to the Make a Wish Foundation, using coupons placed in free-standing inserts as a tracking device:

> Using supermarket scanner sales data, Colgate compares product sales in the three weeks following a coupon drop with average sales for the six months preceding it. The difference is then multiplied by the brand's net profit margin and the event's cost on a per-unit basis is subtracted to find the true incremental profit. (Levin, 1993c, p. S1)

Such mathematical complexity gives nuclear physics a run for its money. It illustrates, however, the seriousness with which corporations treat their ability to evaluate the promotional benefits of sponsorship.

For the sponsor, the promotional goal of the sponsored activity begins to overwhelm the goal of contributing a social good. Instead of sponsoring a cultural form that would not exist otherwise, corporations instead might sponsor things that would exist anyway with or without sponsorship money, but that would most contribute to their promotional goals. Money that might go to a cultural fair could instead go to a major college football game. Increasingly, it may even go to a fragmented part of that game, like the halftime report or the instant replay. A later section will argue that such a bottom-line perspective influences the corporation's view of what to expect from sponsorship and how much control they demand from the sponsored activity.

Similarly, as the sponsors are viewing the sponsorship more as a promotional advertising commodity, with themselves as the buyers, the sponsored have begun marketing themselves more as a seller of a commodity. Often, with for-profit institutions like professional sports, this simply means marketing themselves to corporations more efficiently than in the past. Such has been the case with the National Basketball Association during the tenure of Commissioner David Stern, whom observers have described as fostering a "sponsorship friendly attitude" (Levin, 1992c, p. 3). Professional sports teams increasingly depend upon sponsorship income: Some pro baseball teams receive around one third of their revenue from sponsorship (Winski, 1992); they are very sensitive to the bottom-line needs of the sponsors.

For many not-for-profit organizations, the new stance toward sponsorship-as-promotion involves not just inviting the commercial goal into their home, but offering to make it the landlord as well. Not-for-profits have been forced to become more aggressive in their search for sponsored dollars, perhaps to the point of institutionalizing the willingness to shill.[3] In the current sponsorship environment, the sponsored themselves often must show potential sponsors the promotional benefits of the sponsored. Sometimes, this takes the form of beefing up their promotional value. In 1991, the Smithsonian began acknowledging the contributions of sponsors in their public exhibitions, changing a long-standing prohibition against such promotions ("Advertising Everywhere!" 1992). Other sponsored organizations offer more than just increased linkages between the sponsored and the sponsor. Some sponsored activities, like the Quebec-based circus Cirque du Soleil, routinely survey their audiences for demographic information that potential sponsors might find valuable (Sebastian, 1992). The Boy Scouts of America itself paid for a test-run of a joint ad with American Airlines to entice the corporation to contribute to the ads regularly (Lublin, 1990). Often, the valuable time of not-for-profit personnel goes toward collecting such research, schmoozing with the sponsors and providing them with ancillary marketing services. WGBH-TV, a member station of the Public Broadcasting System and one of its biggest producers, helped Holiday Inn and Toyota coordinate the promotional campaigns associated with their cosponsorship of *Where in the World Is Carmen Sandiego?* (Goerne, 1992).

To summarize, the cycle of promotion that surrounds corporate giving can become a vicious one very easily. Sponsors increasingly emphasize the promotional value of the sponsorship. Other revenue streams, like charity giving and government funding, dry up for the nonprofit organization. The percentage of sponsored revenue compared to other sources increases for the needy organization. Its dependency upon sponsorship also increases. The sponsored organization increases its own marketing research and promotional attractiveness. Suddenly, the supposedly noncommercialized not-for-profit organization becomes, in essence, a commercial entity. Once the sponsorship gate is open, the commercial flood rushes in. Sponsorship becomes a very powerful form of advertising.

The Olympic Games are a good example. Two major events led to the commercialization, at a grand level, of the Olympics. First, in 1981, the "pure amateur code" of the Olympics began to be dismantled, which triggered what John Lucas (1992) calls the birth of "modern Olympic entrepreneurship" (p. 74). The second event was Peter Ueberroth's role as the president of the Los Angeles Olympic Organizing Committee and his marketing gusto toward the 1984 Los Angeles Games. The 1976 Montreal Olympic Games experienced a deficit of $1 billion (Gelman, 1984). How could Ueberroth turn this around? The strategy here was to limit the number of official Olympic sponsors, but to increase the depth of these organizations' visibility and linkage with the Olympics (Gelman, 1984). Such a marketing tactic signaled to potential mega-sponsors the value of the Olympics as a mega-promotional vehicle. The L.A. Olympics turned a profit of $215 million (Manning, 1987), but pointed the Games in a promotional direction that may be permanent. The commercialistic momentum begun in Los Angeles led to unbelievable levels for the 1992 Barcelona games. Nicknamed "The Olympi-Ad," the biggest story of the 1992 Olympics, according to columnist Rob Buchanan (1992), was "how the Olympics have transformed themselves from a nationalist sports festival to an international marketing event in just eight years" (p. 20). Sponsorship has fundamentally altered both the symbols and the economics of the Olympics. One simply could not watch the 1992 Olympics without being exposed to corporate promotional messages. Earlier in the history of the modern Olympics, approximately 95% of the International Olympic Committee's income came from television rights; now the figure is closer to 50-50 between television and sponsorship (Lucas, 1992).

Given these trends of sponsorship, how has that funding strategy specifically manifested itself? Because of the impact the current advertising environment has had upon the sponsored-sponsor relationship and the advantages that sponsorship as a promotional activity offers advertisers, several observations about modern sponsorship can be generated. These observations, as promotionally enacted, further increase sponsorship as a major mechanism for the commercialization of American life.

Observation One: Sponsorship Strives for External Economic Control

Earlier chapters discussed how advertising often seeks to control, economically, the mediated environment that surrounds the advertising message. Of the different promotional phenomena discussed in this book, sponsorship is the one that offers the promoter the greatest economic control. Because sponsorship involves one organization giving money to another organization for services (in this case, promotional services), the sponsor often tries to influence, economically, the sponsored as much as possible.

The early history of broadcasting illustrates how sponsorship can increase the external control of media messages by advertisers. Originally, before the 1920s, the funding of radio was wide open, with the advertising option often discussed with disdain or not at all (Barnouw, 1966). But as radio became more popular, as the cost of using telephone lines for network connections increased and as radio talent began to demand payment, the pressure for a financial system increased. Public funds were deemed not an option, and the one-way transmission nature of broadcast radio made "subscription radio" impossible to enforce. Thus, by 1922, promotional messages began to be broadcast as part of the funding structure. Radio advertisers, though, did not use "spot" advertising, which was what newspapers and magazines used. Instead, a system was chosen that accentuated the control of radio content by powerful advertising companies: sponsorship.

Most media historians who discuss the development of sponsorship in radio argue that this form was chosen because of advertisers' caution regarding radio's social image. Specifically, there was concern about radio's intrusive nature: its beaming of strange voices and music directly into one's living room. This intrusiveness might turn people away from the crassly commercialistic advertisement (Barnouw, 1966; Fox, 1984). Radio broadcasters were concerned about this problem, as well. Sponsorship therefore developed, where one advertiser would fund an entire program and where (at least at first) the name of the advertiser and the product would be discreetly mentioned before and after the program. Because sponsorship is less obtrusive than spot ads, advertisers decided it was more appropriate for the early radio environment.

Another, complementary, explanation for the development of sponsorship in radio, and advertising's subsequent entrenchment in broadcasting forever, has to do more obviously with the issue of control. Radio was live and transitory, which made it different from practically every other advertising medium at the time. These qualities made advertisers nervous for several reasons, all focusing on the issue of advertiser control.

One reason for the concern was that, although advertisers could approve the scripts for commercials and programs in advance, the live nature of early radio meant that advertisers could *not* approve in advance the final form of the broadcast. Even if the talent stuck to the script for a commercial or program, their timing or tone of voice could undermine the verbal message. The final version of a magazine ad could be checked before it appeared before the public; not so with live radio commercials. Also, the ephemeral nature of radio made confirmation of the commercial airing difficult. Did the commercial air as promised, and in the manner promised? Paranoia regarding deception over unaired ads prompted some extreme behavior by advertisers. George Washington Hill, the notoriously tyrannical executive of the American Tobacco Company, kept radios in every room of his home to check continuously that stations aired his company's cigarette commercials correctly (Fox, 1984). Finally, unlike the print media, early radio organizations and personnel were untested with, and not socialized into, the commercial imperative that advertising demanded. Advertisers could not trust many of the radio companies to be properly deferential to advertising. In fact, even as late as 1924, William Sarnoff, the NBC pioneer and budding mogul, argued against advertiser-oriented radio (Leiss et al., 1990).

So, at least in part because of the problems of control, advertisers made sponsorship the primary funding system of radio from the mid-1920s until the mid-1950s. Advertisers took steps to maximize the control that sponsorship offered. Advertisers and their agencies did not just provide the funding for radio shows, they produced them as well. Most large advertising agencies developed radio departments that would coordinate the production of their client's sponsored shows (Barnouw, 1966). "Sponsorship booths," which housed the sponsor's representative, were a part of many major radio broadcasting facilities.

At first the messages about the sponsors and their products in the programs were discreet, mirroring advertisers' fear of radio's intrusion. But by the early 1930s, as listeners became used to advertising on radio, commercialism on radio ran rampant. The time devoted to advertising on radio surpassed that of news and education in just a few short years (Barnouw, 1966), and some programs were grotesquely plug-oriented. Sponsorship's obtrusive nature began to dominate. Fox (1984) relates how the radio program *The Sir Walter Raleigh Revue* included 70 references to the show's sponsor (Sir Walter Raleigh tobacco products) in 1 hour.

From these early days of radio until late-1950s television, individual advertisers were at their most powerful in broadcasting. As the current CEO of Procter & Gamble observed about this period, "we, the advertising industry, took over our environment" (Artzt, 1994, p. 42). Sponsorship delivered both long-term allocative control and day-to-day operational control into the hands of advertising. Because they produced the shows themselves, and because the networks were dependent upon advertisers for *both* programming and financing, advertisers could define the financial structure of broadcasting. They defined the commercial imperative that still drives the system. They could also supervise and control the routine operation of individual programs. In addition, for large sponsors, the individual influence often went beyond the shows they produced. For example, Bayer Aspirin and its advertising agency were able to negotiate the reduction of a competitor's comparison ads by threatening to pull Bayer's show off NBC and jump to another network (Fox, 1984). And, of course, advertising's allocative control affected the *type* of programs and the *tone* of the programs.

One might wonder whether this is all a moot point now, merely an interesting historical "tsk-tsk," given that sponsorship was practically eliminated in electronic media (at least, until recently). In the late 1950s, the quiz show scandals severely embarrassed the involved sponsors. In addition, production costs of prime-time programs began rising. For these reasons, individual advertisers were persuaded to give up their day-to-day operational control (sponsorship) for more diffuse involvement. Broadcasting, then, switched to spot or "magazine style" advertising. Did this not undermine the control that advertising had over broadcasting?

On the surface, yes; advertisers did give up operational control. It is, however, incorrect to think that television removed a layer of commercialism when it eradicated sponsorship. One could argue that the reason the networks moved to kill sponsorship was that as a form of financing it was not commercial *enough*. Because operational control remained in the hands of individual advertisers and advertising agencies, they tended to be myopic in their view and promoted only *their* company's program and commercial interests. This tended to fragment television's content. This undermined the ability of the networks as a whole to manipulate such elements as schedule coherence, holistic programming strategy and audience flow for maximum ratings. So at least one reason spot advertising became the dominant form for broadcasting was that it helped increase its overall commercial imperative. It made television more efficient as a commercial vehicle, and, of course, made more money for the networks and stations. As Barnouw (1978) concludes about the loss of operational control, advertising no longer needed it: The institution of broadcasting was already solidly centered on the needs of advertisers by the time sponsorship faded away. The more obtrusive form of control was eliminated, but the more effective and subtle allocative control was strengthened. Make no mistake, however: Sponsorship helped to define the development of broadcasting as a supreme advertising carrier. As a system for external control, it was nearly absolute.

To shift back to the present: Most sponsorship deals do not grant this high degree of economic control to the sponsors. Nevertheless, with the buyer-seller mentality surrounding many sponsorship agreements since the 1980s, the sponsors are increasingly expecting a significant amount of financial influence over the sponsored. As an AT&T marketing executive bluntly stated about AT&T's sponsorship role, "This is not and has never pretended to be a philanthropic organization, this is marketing. We are buying something. We are cutting a deal. And we expect to have our hands in the projects we become involved with" (Raffio, 1990, p. 112).

The desire for economic control by sponsors is clearly seen in the motivations behind the "return of 'the sponsor,'" in television and other mediated programming, as *Forbes* described it (Fanning, 1989, p. 136). Both domestically and abroad, both in cable and broadcast, there seems to be a return to the early, "Golden" years of television in which sponsors had both allocative and operational control over television content.

Domestically, cable stations, often desperate for advertising dollars, are very willing to construct sponsorship arrangements for individual programs. Channels like Bravo, Lifetime and The Discovery Channel have created single-sponsor deals with advertisers, but Comedy Central has been especially aggressive in this area (Bryant, 1993; Moshavi, 1993; Stern, 1993). Comedy Central in 1993 signed an agreement with PepsiCo for the sponsorship of *A-List:* Part of the deal was to change the name to *Pepsi's A-List*. It also arranged single-sponsorship deals with AT&T for a news program and with Certs for their *Comedy Central's Boot Camp*.

Similarly, sponsorship is returning to the broadcast arena. Sponsorship is fostered because the networks seek to stroke advertisers in the more competitive environment, and advertisers look to gain as much advantage as they can. Advertisers have become more aggressive in their sponsorship of broadcast productions. An advertiser coalition formed in 1993 to finance prime-time programming development illustrates this promotional aggression. The coalition, Television Program Partners (TPP), consists of such major marketers as General Motors and Procter & Gamble. Essentially a TV production "studio," the organization looks to reduce the cost of advertisers by making their financial role in program production and development more direct and efficient (Mandese, 1993e, 1993i). TPP has produced such award shows as "The World Music Awards" ("Safe (and Dull) at TPP," 1994).

Other signs point to increased advertiser sponsorship of broadcast programming. Similarly to TPP, Chrysler has investigated forming a syndicate to sponsor made-for-TV sporting events that lend themselves to marketing and promotion (Jensen, 1995). In 1994, the greeting card company Hallmark acquired RHI Entertainment, a TV program developer, making Hallmark "the leading independent producer of long-format network TV programs" (Fitzgerald, 1994a). Advertising agencies are also flirting with direct control over TV production. In 1994, Grey Advertising established a subsidiary to produce children's television programming; a bit earlier Grey's competitor, D'Arcy Masius Benton & Bowles formed a similar unit, Tele-Vest, for TV movies (Goldman, 1994b).

In the same vein, the global television market seems more receptive to advertiser-sponsored (or even -produced) material. The barter system of program financing is relevant here. Barter is the system in which the producer charges a television station less money for the rights to air a program. In return, the producer receives a percentage of commercial time that the producer can sell directly to advertisers (or use to promote its own interests). Deregulation is relevant as well. The deregulation of many European broadcast systems has created a demand for flashy and advertising-receptive commercial programming. In response to both factors, advertisers like Procter & Gamble and advertising agencies like the Japanese Dentsu have explored the possibilities of sponsored production (Fanning, 1989; Mattelart, 1991). About the need for syndicated programming in Europe, one advertising executive concluded that "ad agencies in Europe will play a large role in helping to create a situation analogous to the U.S. in the 1950s" (Fanning, 1989, p. 136).

Why would advertisers and advertising agencies want to become involved in the financing of, or even the direct production of, television programming? One explanation spotlights money management and the attempt to reduce costs (Mandese, 1993e). Another focuses on the increased ease of cross-promotional and merchandising deals when advertisers control the licensing rights to programs (Goldman, 1994a). A final explanation, though, highlights the increased economic influence over television content that such a funding system would allow. Such sponsors occasionally acknowledge this directly: "Producing our own shows gives us a better chance to showcase our brands and also have control over the program" (Fanning, 1989, p. 136).

Television may not mind relinquishing control, if the price is right. About its sponsorship deals with advertisers such as Bristol-Myers and Procter & Gamble, one Lifetime cable network executive notes that advertisers prefer sponsorship deals because they allow the sponsor "to have editorial control of the environment" of their ads. This executive went on to describe the station's willingness to help sponsors meet this control goal. The executive announced that, "We're ready and willing to talk to advertisers about dramas, series, movies, what have you. There are no limits, no rules" (Moshavi, 1993, p. 42).

Television is not the only medium experiencing a wave of sponsorship financing. "Custom publishing," where one sponsor creates a magazine that potentially carries only that sponsor's ads, was a publishing trend of 1993. These magazines look just like spot ad magazines and are sold at newsstands. Jenny Craig sponsors *Body Health,* Mary Kay Cosmetics sponsors *Beauty,* and the sponsor of *Sony Style* is obvious. *Advertising Age* began a story about custom publishing with the lead, "If you're looking for that perfect magazine buy, the right editorial environment without ad clutter, then do it yourself" (Steenhuysen, 1993, p. S24).

The economic control by the sponsor over the sponsored is the fuel that runs the current sponsorship engine. It is the explanation for why organizations seeking sponsorship have allowed many antidemocratic trends, discussed later, to foster. The buyer-seller attitude and the accompanying control expected to go with it have sometimes allowed sponsors to exert explicit control over the sponsoreds' content. Herb Schmertz of Mobil Oil, for example, would choose the programs shown on *Masterpiece Theater,* and Exxon executives would decide which programs appeared on *Great Performances* (Aufderheide, 1991; Wicklein, 1989). In reality, of course, rarely does a sponsor need to exert such explicit control. More likely, the payer of the piper does not have to call the tune: The piper knows exactly what the payer wants to hear. The economic control embedded in modern sponsorship has led to unintentional control. It has socialized the sponsored to alter their "product" for what they believe sponsors want.

Observation Two: Sponsorship Reaches Hidden or Reluctant Demographics

Going back to an earlier point—if the media sell audiences to advertisers, one characteristic of this "product" that is especially desirable is "product purity." Advertisers want audiences that have demographic characteristics that lend themselves to spending and to a susceptibility to the selling message. Reaching the most desirable demographics through traditional media is often difficult for advertisers, however, especially given the mobility of these groups. Affluent markets or markets willing to part with their money are active. They go to social events. Sponsorship allows marketers to reach these groups. Sponsorship can reach desirable audiences by going to the events that these audiences frequent. The decision about whether to sponsor a particular event or not often comes down to the demographics that the event may deliver. Also, because of its philanthropic connotations, sponsorship may provide a way for marketers to "sneak into" people's consciousness without the obtrusiveness of traditional advertising.

Sponsorship opportunities can offer up many different types of "demogenic" audiences for promoters. For example, sponsors view certain events as valuable in reaching some of the *most* desirable audiences, including those discussed below.

THE WELL-TO-DO AUDIENCE

The high arts and other elite cultural events are especially valuable in targeting the rich, who are desirable for marketers because of their ability to purchase high mark-up items and for their ability to influence financial and political opinion. Mercedes-Benz's sponsorship of the Chicago Symphony Orchestra in 1992 illustrates the first goal ("Call It Classic-Aid," 1992). The car company hoped that its sponsorship of the "high-art" event would be sufficiently impressive and marketable. For such events, sponsors often expect to receive any customer mailing lists that the event's coordinator might have that would grant access to elite names and addresses. The sponsors might also expect to schmooze with the elite audiences at private receptions (Judson, 1994). The value in sponsoring (or "underwriting") the Public Broadcasting Service is an example of the second goal of reaching elite-events audiences. Groups such as Mobil have linked with PBS programming to influence society's influencers and to market their wares. Sometimes conservative foundations with really no overt product to "sell," such as the John M. Olin Foundation, will underwrite PBS programming ("The Right-Wing Agenda: Buying Media Clout," 1992) with such a goal in mind. Their perspectives can receive not only airtime, but can receive airtime with the potential opinion leaders of business and industry. Such sponsorship becomes a subtle investment in future public policy.

GENERATION X

Corporate sponsorship also seeks to reach the post-baby boomer generation. In fact, corporate sponsorship may be one of the most applicable promotional strategies for this market. R. Goldman (1992) has argued that as audiences have grown up with television, and with the ads that accompany television programs, they have become more advertising literate. Recent generations more willingly ridicule and scorn inept advertising messages. The post-1960s, post-baby boomers are perhaps the clearest example of this resistance, as by this time the spot advertising format of television and other media was completely normalized for audiences. Also advertising resistant are many Generation Xers; instead of growing up during the countercultural sixties, they grew up during the Reagan eighties when corporate intrusion was a routine part of life. Given these two influences (resistance to blatant ad messages; tolerance of commercialization in general), sponsorship seems a perfect choice for this market. A marketing executive concludes about this market, without a trace of irony, that, "With their social concerns, media acumen and demands for authenticity [!], Generation

X members are prime candidates for event and lifestyle marketing. They won't resent your corporate presence as boomers did" (Schreiber, 1993, p. S3).

Accordingly, then, marketers have looked for appropriately "authentic" sponsorship vehicles for post-boomers—events that might be relatively small but have X-centric demographics. Coors Light, using a huge inflatable beer can, has sponsored women's beach volleyball (Brunelli, 1993). Busch, applying a similar strategy, has sponsored the Professional Surfing Association of America's Bud U.S. Pro Surfing Tour (Barker, 1991). Sponsoring events such as these allow corporations like AT&T to reach these audiences as they are forming their brand preferences: Those in their twenties are a "vulnerable audience for us," according to an AT&T executive (Schlossberg, 1992, p. 7). The adjective choice is telling: Generation X audiences are desirable because they are perceived as especially susceptible to sponsorship efforts.

Woodstock '94 illustrates the desirability to sponsors of those born post-1960. As *Variety* described the event, it "was conceived from Day One as something that would sell to a specific demographic long after the event itself" (Robins, 1994c). The Marketing Corporation of America, an organization that earned its reputation through the promotion of packaged goods rather than entertainment events, helped shape the event for maximum demographic purity. Research studies on the desirability of particular bands and focus groups with Gen-Xers helped to determine the musical direction of the event (DeNitto, 1994b). And when corporate logos were found everywhere during Woodstock '94, marketers believed that, with this particular audience, it did not matter. "Young people today are used to attending concerts deluged with T-shirts and sponsors—and they don't care," according to one Woodstock executive (DeNitto, 1994b, p. 14). Sponsors care, though: That is what makes this market so attractive.

TEENS (AND YOUNGER)

Speaking of vulnerable audiences, a winter 1993 episode of *60 Minutes* detailed the corporate intrusion of advertising into schools. And about time. The focus of the program was Channel One, a source that disdains traditional media advertising, including television, which makes one wonder if this was part of the *60 Minutes* green light for this topic. Another major source of corporate influence in schools, however, is sponsored materials. *60 Minutes* did touch on sponsored materials, but the corporate foothold allowed by this avenue is larger than the program presented. Corporations attempt to reach the school-age audience primarily through two versions of school sponsorship: the sponsorship of curriculum or supplementary learning materials and the sponsorship of high school sports.

Corporate-provided, self-serving learning materials, like many trends discussed here, are not new: Ewen (1976) discusses the "tooth brush drills" and "cocoa production demonstrations" conducted in schools as early as the 1920s (p. 90). Such trends continue today with cuts in government funding and with some school systems looking for cheap but flashy audiovisual and reading materials to grab the interest of the bored 12-year-old. Given these factors, many corporations and government bodies are happy to supply such materials. Many materials seem designed for planting the seeds of long-term brand loyalty, or even recruiting future employees. United Parcel Service distributes a free film called *We Are the Parcel People;* Oscar Mayer offers the more vacuously titled *Pride on Parade,* about their company (Bates, 1989).

Harty (1989) argues that such corporate materials are at their core anti-intellectual. They are anti-intellectual for several reasons. One is the material's one-sided nature. Such materials want to present the corporate perspective, and that is it. One rarely finds dialectical thinking in corporate-produced pedagogy. Also, the sources of many of these materials are at best implicit, and often hidden, which further discourages critical analysis. Finally, besides their obviously one-sided nature, they reinforce the idea of public and private schools as primarily trade schools designed to train people for employment rather than as educational sites for critically aware citizens (Harty, 1989). The anti-intellectual nature of sponsored materials is accentuated by the fact that they are distributed in an environment that, by definition, is meant to be intellectual.

If corporations want to reach high school students outside the classroom, there are increasingly available opportunities for the sponsorship of extra-curricular activities. This is especially true in the realm of high school sports. As *Advertising Age* discusses the marketing possibilities of the high school sports market,

> The potential audience is significant: 11 million high school students who spend $60 billion annually and parents who spend $250 billion. High

school football and basketball attract more than 400 million paying spectators each year, several times the audience of professional baseball, basketball, and football combined. (Hume, 1992c, p. 32)

Budget cuts again influence the acceptance of sponsored activity in the public domain. Many schools have been forced to charge fees to those students wanting to participate in high school sports. Because marketers can justify the invasion of high school sports with the promise of eliminating "pay to play" requirements (Jensen, 1993c), sponsorship of such events is increasing.

The National High School Coaches Association, for example, has aggressively sought corporate sponsors for its national championship events in several sports. One sponsor incentive is access to a couponing programming that could specifically target four million high school students and access to a database of 19,000 secondary schools (Jensen, 1993c). The sponsorship of state-level high school sports has been institutionalized: School Properties USA will arrange such deals for states for a large cut of the sponsorship revenue. This organization helped to arrange the California Interscholastic Federation/Reebok State Championships, for example, with Reebok getting on-site signage and their name on tickets (Hume, 1992c). Other states, like Indiana, have simply arranged their own corporate sponsorship deals (Millman, 1991).

THE PLANET

The reach of capitalism has greatly increased since the mid-1980s, and not just because of the unraveling of the Iron Curtain. The current world economy finds the existence of global advertisers (like McDonald's), global advertising agencies (like WPP Group, the world's biggest) and global media (like CNN or MTV, which broadcast to scores of different countries). It is no wonder, then, that global companies search for global promotional strategies to reach the new global markets. As opposed to a multinational strategy, which seeks to shape different advertising campaigns for different cultures, a global strategy applies one monolithic campaign that will strike the same promotional chord with different countries and cultures. A global strategy, for global marketers, is much more cost-efficient than a multinational strategy in that one idea can stretch to so many different locations (Leiss et al., 1990).

Sponsorship, with the increased reach of global media coverage, is one way to implement a global strategy to a global market. Sports events are increasingly valuable for this goal, especially events with international appeal (like soccer and the Olympics). MasterCard premised its $75 million sponsorship of the 1994 World Cup soccer matches (at least $15 million for the rights, up to $60 million for promotional support) on the company's movement into the new capitalistic world marketplace. According to one MasterCard executive, "As the Iron Curtain falls and the world gets smaller, everyday people are now worldwide travelers, [and] we want to say MasterCard is universal money" (Fahey, 1991, p. 45).

Likewise, the Olympics offer tremendous global advantages, both in terms of reach and in terms of universal appeal. Coca-Cola, which earns 64% of its sales outside the United States, did its best to monopolize the 1992 Summer Olympic sponsorship completely—which is difficult and expensive to do (Sharkey & Battaglio, 1992). The Olympics typically have a worldwide television audience of around 2.5 billion people (Fannin, 1988). To make global marketing easier for the Olympics, organizers have considered creating "package" deals with major sponsors, which would combine traditional sponsorship deals with global television coverage arrangements (Martin & Mandese, 1993). As a 3M executive concludes about the advantages of the Olympics as a global (rather than multinational) advertising strategy, "The Olympic theme has universal appeal and it is something we can use regardless of where we are to show that we are speaking with one voice" ("3M's Global Hope," 1988, p. 66).

Coca-Cola participates in more than 900 sponsorships domestically and internationally (Horovitz, 1994). If Coke is speaking "with one voice," the message is no longer "We'd like to teach the world to sing," but instead, "We'd like to teach the world to spend."

Observation Three: Sponsorship Links the Corporate to the Culturally Good and Desirable

A large benefit that corporations receive from sponsorship is the link between the corporation and the corporation's product and a noble referent system. In traditional spot advertising, the connection between the advertiser and the program is diffused. Many advertisers connect only disjointedly to the media content. Sponsorship creates a much stronger tie between sponsor and sponsored, both because sponsorship often means *sole* sponsorship and because the sponsored text itself stresses the tie between the sponsor and the sponsored, sometimes to minutely pervasive levels (as the next section observes). The sponsor's name may appear in the event, or depictions of the event may appear in the sponsor's own commercials. Often, then, a corporation's decision to sponsor something will come down to how advantageous the sponsored's image is for the corporation, regardless of reach or audience.

Take underwriting on PBS for example: What many sponsors hope for is a semiotic blending of the "high-culture" programming of the public television system and their corporate name. As a PBS executive noted, compared to traditional advertising, "PBS is a different way for the companies to get into the mind of the consumer" ("More Companies Tune In to PBS," 1991, p. 17). So when Mobil underwrites the elite-sounding *Masterpiece Theater,* the company hopes that the high-culture association will raise their social (and economic) standing as well. AT&T successfully demanded that the MacNeil/Lehrer newscast on PBS expand to a full hour, despite most public television station managers' objections, "because American Telephone and Telegraph wanted credit for providing the first hourlong 'network news program' " (Wicklein, 1989, p. H35).

Ironically, though, much of PBS's value to advertising is its image of being advertising-free. First, advertising-free media is especially valuable to advertisers, when they can get to it, because it helps solve their clutter problem. As a member station executive notes about PBS's high-culture (read, "commercial-free") air, "PBS still has a refined image. It's uncluttered air. [Sponsors] are associated with the show in a much stronger way than they can be on network TV" (Goerne, 1992, p. 16).[4] A Mobil executive especially was taken with the "halo effect" that comes with being associated with PBS programs. Besides raising the image of the company in some nebulous public arena, the association with PBS also helps with very "bottom-line" problems like corporate recruitment of future employees ("More Companies Tune in to PBS," 1991).

Another key benefit of using sponsored events as a referent system, referring to a point made earlier, is the connotation, true or not, of philanthropy. It is not just that a sponsoring company is associated with opera. It is also that a sponsoring company is providing, is donating, opera. This is a strategy similar to the product-as-generator strategy in advertising. In this strategy, the product claims to provide the desired referent system. A BMW leads to social respect. Sponsorship often has a similar symbolic advantage. "Here is the social good provided by our company," sponsorship may imply.

This strategy, in many instances, is based upon deceit. Marketers can use high culture for promotion and then benefit from the image that comes from *not* doing such commercialistically vulgar activities. For example, a 1992 article in *Marketing News* (see Goerne, 1992) discussed the benefits of PBS underwriting for advertisers. At one point in the article, a public television station executive highlights the advantages of the patron-image that PBS offers: "They're [the corporate under-writers] perceived as good corporate citizens. It's not inferred that they're doing it for commercial reasons." But, of course, most (if not all) *are* doing it for commercial reasons. The article, a few paragraphs later, points out that one of public television's "biggest problem is convincing corporations that it's all right to market a product through public TV" (Goerne, 1992, p. 16). PBS's image as a forum free from commercial exploitation is the very reason why commercial interests should try to exploit it, this quotation implies.

At least one study suggests that the incorrect "inference" of sponsorship = philanthropy bleeds over into the sports world as well. Advertising agency research has found that more than half the respondents to a survey about Olympics sponsors "felt that they were making a contribution to the Olympics when buying sponsors' brands" (Fannin, 1988). A Visa ad informed card holders about how they could help the 1992 Olympic Team simply by being a good consumer. "Using Visa Is All It Takes To Support The U.S. Olympic Team," a headline in the ad noted. Every time the consumer used the Visa card, "Visa will make a donation to the 1992 U.S. Olympic Team." Of course, the ad does not mention the benefits Visa also receives from the increased consumer debt incurred through such card usage.

One twist on the sponsor-as-high-culture-generator strategy is that corporations will occasionally use sponsorships to help counteract the corporation's negative image on certain issues. With the philanthropic connotations, corporations hope to "cleanse" the picture that relevant publics have of the corporation. Virginia Slims, a women's cigarette, links itself with an athletic endeavor, a women's tennis tournament (where, presumably, few of the participants use their products' sponsor). Thus, a company that sells a product profoundly antihealth can associate itself with a celebration of healthy exercise. Similarly, Schiller (1989) points out that in 1987 Philip Morris sponsored an exhibition of African American art in a museum in Harlem while at the same time targeting blacks in cigarette ads, perhaps hoping to counterbalance the decrease in cigarette smoking in middle-class whites.[5] Many companies that have sponsored environmentally friendly nature programs on PBS often turn out to be anything but environmentally friendly. For example, BASF, "one of Western Europe's most energetic toxic dumpers," has sponsored *Adventure;* Waste Management, the "most penalized hazardous-waste company in EPA history" was a sponsor of *Conserving America: Only One Earth* ("Acts of Contrition," 1991, p. 40).

Sponsored events can be of symbolic benefit to a sponsor in other ways besides exploiting the connotation of an elite, commercial-free culture. An event is a potentially beneficial referent system if the event simply is beloved by a desirable market, even if that event is part of the stereotypical "mass culture." An executive of Coke says this explicitly: "We want to be places where people are having fun. That way we become part of the fun" (Horovitz, 1994, p. D6). The sponsor hopes that, even after the sponsorship is over, this association continues. Whenever the audience sees or hears about the sponsored item, even without the sponsor, marketers hope the symbolic bleeding continues. As an executive for *Rolling Stone* magazine observed about Michelob's sponsorship of a Genesis rock tour, the sponsorship created "a musical association so strong that every time you hear a Phil Collins song you think of Michelob" (Savan, 1994, p. 286). Michelob thus becomes permanently associated with the "fun" of Genesis. Long after the sponsorship was over, Phil Collins was pocked with Michelob's symbolic infection.

Observation Four: Sponsorship Offers Ubiquitous Promotion During Sponsored Events

The use of sponsored events as referent systems, as implied above, depends upon how firm the link is between the corporation and the sponsored event. Corporations not only want to solidify the association between sponsor and sponsored, however; they also want to maximize the "frequency" of their sponsorship. They want to get every possible promotional moment out of their sponsorship efforts. Like the strategy of the cross promotion, sponsors want to achieve the optimum number of "impressions," or the times people see their corporate name, logo or product. In fact, sponsorship has a big advantage over traditional media advertising—especially electronic media advertising—in terms of impressions. Viewers cannot zap sponsorship-oriented promotion when done "correctly" (i.e., with marketing utility as the imperative). In its most imperialistic form, sponsorship intrudes on every moment of the sponsored event. The product logo is visually merged with the event. The only way to zap the promotion is to zap the event itself. Tape recording the program only delays the impression: Fast-forwarding through the commercials becomes impossible when the commercials are in the program itself. With sophisticated marketing strategies and the economic leverage that sponsors hold, sponsored events often become one big, multilayered promotional vehicle. During events, sponsors may promote their participation in a variety of ways.

THE NAME OF THE EVENT/PLACE/TEAM

Sponsors may feel that a subtle "funding for this event provided by . . . " message is not sufficient. They will often demand that the name of the event reflects their participation. Such a strategy helps to decrease clutter (they are clearly the major promotional force of the event) and helps to increase free publicity surrounding the event. Sometimes, when an event is first created, the sponsor will establish the connection right away. The Virginia Slims Tennis Tournament, created by the sponsor, is a good example of this. New leagues, teams and places are often especially vulnerable to a sponsor's demands that the name reflect the sponsor's contributions. Other times, though, the sponsor will demand that the name be added to the original, nonsponsored name. College football bowls illustrate this. In 1985, the Fiesta Bowl became the Sunkist Fiesta Bowl. Later, Sunkist dropped its sponsorship, and it became the IBM OS/2 Fiesta Bowl. What was once the Orange Bowl is now the Federal Express Orange Bowl, the Sugar Bowl is the USF&G Sugar Bowl and the Gator Bowl is the Outback Steakhouse Gator Bowl. At other times, sponsors throw decorum out altogether and demand that their name be substituted for the original name. John Hancock in 1989 renegotiated its sponsorship of the Sun Bowl, so that the pesky *Sun* was removed from the name for the purely promotional moniker, the John Hancock Bowl (McCarthy, 1991). The CarQuest Bowl, similarly, goes for the commercial gusto in its bowl sponsorship.

The locations that host events, and even whole sports teams, are also fair game for names. The Hoosier Dome, for the next 20 years, will be the RCA Dome. The first all-women's baseball team, sponsored by Coors, is the promotionally named Silver Bullets.

When this occurs, the logos of the event/place/team feature prominently the name of the sponsor. This comes in handy before and after commercial breaks on televised sponsored events, when a graphic informs viewers what they are watching and, with sports, updates the score. Also, when announcers during the event say the name, it is often impossible to avoid the sponsor's name, especially in such cases as the John Hancock and CarQuest Bowls. Although there were controversy and cynicism in 1989 about John Hancock's name demand (McCarthy, 1991), one marketing study claimed that, at least for golf tournaments, no evidence showed a drop in fan attendance when corporations self-servingly changed the name of an event (Schlossberg, 1991b).

BACKGROUND SIGNAGE

Sponsors know that one major advantage to sponsorship is the background signage deals that come with the package. The sponsor's name plastered throughout the event—either integrated as part of the event's logo, or alone, as part of a billboard-like banner or sign—turns the live viewer into a captive consumer. Background signage also creates a captive TV audience by integrating the name of the sponsor with the television coverage. In fact, trends in sponsorship signage—strategic placement and micro placement—are designed to increase the television exposure—the number of impressions.

Strategic placement of on-site signage maximizes the television exposure the signs receive. College bowl games are a good example. College bowl sites are loaded with banners carrying the sponsor's name and logo, often placed in high-visibility locations. During the 1993 Weiser Lock Copper Bowl, for example, a Weiser Lock banner appeared behind the goal posts, directly under the bleachers, so that whenever a player kicked a field goal or extra point, all eyes (and TV cameras) looked directly at the banner.

A prime location for a corporate logo during such a game is, however, on the field itself. Especially valuable is placement where most of the action takes place (near the middle of the field) or where the most exciting action takes place (the end zones). Especially for logos on the 50-yard line, the corporate presence can be enormous. The big white block letters "WEISER LOCK" stretched almost 25 yards onto *both* sides of the field of the Weiser Lock Copper Bowl. Logos in the end zone, like the Mobil Cotton Bowl logo, receive the added benefit of showing up in sports broadcast highlights (because, presumably, most football highlights take place in the end zone).

Sports stadiums are becoming very sophisticated in offering strategic on-site signage that maximizes television exposure. At Candlestick Park, if a baseball slugger hits one "in the gap," then television highlights will show huge "The Gap" lettering, sponsored by the clothing retailer, placed on the outfield wall. Similarly, rotating signs behind home plate force the TV camera to center on the advertiser's message during an exciting at-bat. When new stadiums are built, the drive for sponsorship is considered in the stadiums' design. One writer for *Advertising Age* called Chicago's Comiskey Park and Baltimore's Oriole Park "the newest, most advertising friendly baseball stadiums in the U.S." (Winski, 1992, p. S2).

Besides strategic placement, microplacement of the sponsor's logo—putting the logo on anything that will hold an ad, no matter how small—is another way to expose the message to the live and televised captive audiences. Sponsors have gotten quite creative with this placement strategy. Again, starting with the college bowls, the corporate sponsor's name may appear on player uniforms: "Mobil Cotton Bowl" is sewn on the shoulders of players, for example. In the IBM OS/2 Fiesta Bowl, the vests worn by the people who hold the down markers, normally a bright orange color for easy spotting, featured a big, square IBM OS/2 symbol, gaining many TV impressions. But the bowls do not have a monopoly on microplacement. Major boxing matches may feature the sponsor's name on one or more of the boxing ring posts (Jensen, 1993a). And, in the sponsored equivalent to the microcommercial in cross promotion, tickets to the event usually will very prominently feature the name of the sponsor, with one long-term benefit being that when Paul McCartney's fans put the used ticket in their scrapbook or on their bulletin board, Visa's name goes with it.

PRODUCT PLACEMENT

Sometimes it is not enough for a sponsored event merely to feature the logo of a product or company; sometimes the sponsor requests that the product itself play a role in the event. Banners, logo-dyed football fields and promotional boxing ring posts are artificial. Product placement, in which an event participant actually uses the product during the event, can help give the sponsor an air of "natural" participation.

Product placement in sponsored events may be even more promotionally effective than product placement in film and television. For example, through sponsorship, product placement can occur in nonfictional sponsored events. In such cases, sponsorship counteracts the "fictionalized" problems of film and TV product placement, as well as the "contrived" problems of celebrity endorsements in paid advertising. One disadvantage for the product placer in movies is that when Clint Eastwood's character picks up an AT&T phone in *In the Line of Fire,* it is not really Clint using the phone, it is the character. Likewise, when Michael Jordan is eating a Big Mac in a McDonald's commercial, everyone recognizes the commercial form, and everyone knows that Jordan is eating the Big Mac specifically because he is getting paid to.

Product placement in many sponsored events presents the best of both commercialistic worlds. When Bob Vila, in the syndicated program *Home Again,* sponsored by Sears, Roebuck and Co., uses Craftsman tools, it is not a character Bob Vila is playing that is using the tools, it is *Bob Vila,* the real person in a real tool-using situation. It is not during a paid commercial that he is using the tools, it is during *his show.* The same sort of logic worked when Elton John drank a Diet Coke during his August 1992 concerts, sponsored by Coca-Cola ("Advertising Everywhere!" 1992); or when bottles of Evian water are handed to Olympic athletes as they go on camera for an interview (Lipman, 1992a).

Products are also being placed in more high-culture sponsored events, like theatrical plays. In this case, the sponsor becomes directly a *part* of the cultural event, strengthening even further the association between the sponsor and the elite referent system. Old General Foods commercials were shown in a scene set in the 1950s in the tour of *Elvis: A Musical Celebration,* sponsored by Maxwell House (Grimm, 1992b).

Such product placement has two implications. First, the advertising function is naturalized. It becomes a necessary *symbolic* part of the event, as well as a necessary economic part. The sponsor serves a function: It quenches Elton's thirst, and helps Bob fix the faucet. Second, to foreshadow an argument in this chapter's conclusion, it elevates the nature of endorsements. When Maxwell House can sneak into a play, even artists can become shills for corporations. In invades yet another previously commercial-free space.

PAID COMMERCIALS DURING THE EVENT

All of these logos and product placements are fine, but the sponsors also want to make absolutely sure that people get the message. Traditional spot advertising, then, is not ignored by sponsors during sponsored events. Often, as part of the contract, sponsors will receive ad slots during the televised coverage or in other media of the event, like the event's printed program. So, for example, about 8 minutes into the 1993 Poulan/Weed Eater Bowl, viewers were exposed to two 15-second spots for Poulan products, including the Weed Eater; other spots were sprinkled throughout the broadcast. During especially long events, sponsors will try to blitz the commercial time, doing their best to block out the competition. NBC's 1992 Summer Olympics broadcast featured Coca-Cola—by far the most visible advertiser—buying 92 spots or almost 68 minutes of airtime at a cost of $46 million (Mandese, 1992e). With the amount of money involved, sponsors have become very smart about using these spots to emphasize the connection between the sponsored and the sponsor.

The underwriting messages on PBS exemplify these strategies. In 1984, the FCC allowed more leeway as to the nature of promotional sponsorship messages on PBS (Schiller, 1989); and the FCC liberalized the rules even further in 1994 (E. Jensen, 1994). Today, sponsors can include 15-second spots before and after a sponsored program and can use many of the same commercials and spokespeople as on commercial television (E. Jensen, 1994). PBS underwriters have thus gotten quite creative in solidifying the link between sponsor and sponsored, and grabbing viewers' attention. One company, Public Broadcast Marketing, even specializes in creating promotional messages for the PBS environment (Jacobson & Mazur, 1995).

For example, in strengthening its image as a philanthropic giver, Toyota, an underwriter of PBS's *Where in the World Is Carmen Sandiego?*, showed two spots, one before the program and one after. In the preprogram spot, a Toyota pickup brings a TV set. In the post-program spot, a Toyota takes the TV set away. Both versions feature a child narrator who says, "This program was brought to you by [pause] Toyota." The message to kids is that Toyota literally supplies this show. Visual and verbal elements reinforce this message, both before and after the program. According to the spot, Toyota generates *Carmen Sandiego*.

The commercials for sponsors during the college bowls also seek to solidify symbolic connections between the money provider and the desired event. A commercial for CarQuest Auto Parts, shown during the CarQuest Bowl, begins with a football highlight. Then the commercial cuts to a guy pumping iron, with more football shots intercut with scenes of auto repair. The announcer says, "Making it to the pros takes a certain level of excellence, the experience to get the job right . . . a special brand of confidence, and for professionally trained technicians, that confidence is CarQuest." Becoming a professional football player is placed on the same level as an oil change.

Also, in commercial television, one benefit a sponsor may collect when placing several spots during a televised event is the promotional tag. These tags come at the start of a program, or at the top of the hour of a long program. Often, the broadcaster throws these tags in as gravy to reward the loyal spot buyer or sponsor. So at one point, for example, after a commercial break, an announcer for ABC's broadcast of the CompUSA Florida Citrus Bowl declares, "ABC's Sports Coverage of the 1994 CompUSA Florida Citrus Bowl, brought to you by CompUSA. With over 5,000 computer products, CompUSA is the computer superstore . . . " The bowl's sponsor thus receives three mentions from an authoritative, network announcer in one sentence. The equation that event = sponsor is yet again established.

COSPONSORING PARTS OF THE EVENT

Finally, the degree to which the level of promotion in sponsorship activity has increased is shown by the dissection of potentially sponsorable *parts* of the event. Although exclusive sponsorship is a concern for many promoters, what event planners have established is that if one sponsor of an event is good, several sponsors of that same event are even better. And, the event planners may reason, there may be dozens of sponsors of an event but we can still offer individual sponsors exclusivity. How? Because there is only *one* sponsor of the kickoff, or *one* sponsor of the first call to the bullpen or *one* sponsor of the play of the game. The drive toward sponsorship has led the sponsored to fragment themselves, to develop different levels of the event to be sponsored or to stress the different parts of the sponsored event.

Pro sports provide a great example of the fragmented nature of multisponsored events. Professional baseball parks have begun to thrive on multisponsored games. *Any* possible facet of the game, or of the sports experience, can be sponsorable. At Comiskey Park, for example, anyone strolling around the concession stands in the ballpark might stumble across the "Swatch Watch/Henry Kay Jewelers speed pitch booth"; when an error occurs during a game, the fans become aware of it through "Miller Lite Official Scoring"; to entertain the fans between innings, Colonial Iron Kids bread presents "Great Plays From Around the League"; when a double play occurs, it is a "Dove Bar Double Play." All told, the White Sox had 300 sponsors in 1992 (Winski, 1992).

The Olympics illustrate the fragmented nature of sponsorship as well. Once the Olympics institutionalized sponsorship, it became a very complicated process. Comiskey Park sponsorship, compared to the Olympics, is Amateur Hour. Olympics' sponsorship may be at least *seven* layers deep. Marketers can be sponsors of (a) the International Olympic Committee; (b) the United States Olympic Committee; (c) the city committee (like 1996's Atlanta Committee for the Olympic Games), which gives sponsorship rights to a specific year's games; (d) the host city itself;[6] (e) a country's individual teams (like Fuji Photo Film USA's team sponsorship of the U.S. Track and Field Team for the 1992 Olympics); (f) the network broadcast of the Olympic Games; or even, more and more, (g) individual Olympic participants.

Predictably, these levels conflict. Sponsors are concerned with exclusivity. Sponsors look out for number one. Here "number one" means that they want to be the *only* marketer associated with a sponsored event. But event coordinators, once sponsorship becomes institutionalized, go for the gold with as many sponsors as possible. The size of the Olympics exacerbates the dilemma, with so many different groups vying for sponsorship. The dilemma of multilayered sponsorship has manifested itself especially in two related controversies: the concern over "ambush marketing" and the 1992 Dream Team conflict.

Ambush marketers "are companies that promote around an event, attempting to gain recognition as and benefits of sponsorship without being an official sponsor" (quoted in Schlossberg, 1991, p. 18). In other words, ambushers are those that try to use the sponsored as referent systems—hoping the symbolism of the sponsored rubs off on the company or product—without a monetary commitment to the event organizers. The Olympics have been especially vulnerable to ambushers, given the different levels involved. The fact that marketers can negotiate with the broadcaster of the Olympics—separate from official Olympics bodies—to place advertisements during the events' broadcast encourages ambushing. Sometimes the networks have granted especially large advertisers the use of a "composite" logo, featuring a recombination of the networks' logo with the Olympic logo. This strengthens the symbolic benefit to ambushers (Mandese & Fahey, 1992).

Sponsors who pay millions of dollars for the official right to be linked with the Olympics become angry when competitors take a much cheaper route by just buying broadcast time, often with great symbolic effectiveness. During the 1988 Calgary Winter Games, for example, when the Olympics named General Motors as the official automobile sponsor, Chrysler quickly bought as much airtime as possible for the Games, countering GM's exclusivity in that category (Manning, 1987). Logically enough, the problem of ambushers started to become annoying to sponsors during the 1984 Games, the year that the commercialization of the Olympics really started its spiral upwards (Mandese & Fahey, 1992).

Increasingly, sensing the anger of sponsors over consumer confusion (and oversaturation) about Olympic sponsorship, committees work to eliminate or at least undermine ambushers. One strategy involves "shaming" the ambushers, revealing to key publics that such companies are getting symbolic benefit without financial contribution (to the Olympic Committees, anyway). The ambush protection surrounding the 1996 games sounds like the police warnings from *America's Most Wanted*. As stated in documents from the Atlanta committee, "avenues for ambush marketing . . . will be aggressively and relentlessly closed off. . . . A campaign [will begin] to immediately expose, identify and publicly embarrass those guilty, [and] a dedicated task force [will be] assigned to continuous surveillance" (Ruffenach, 1992, p. B1).

Another strategy against ambushes involves making it easier for marketers to gain multilevel sponsorship, increasing their visibility and connection to the Games, but at a price. A package developed by the Atlanta Committee offers the following: For $40 million each, 7 times the Barcelona average, corporate sponsors would receive sponsorship of both the 1994 and 1996 U.S. Olympic teams, sponsorship of the U.S. Olympic Committee and rights to the 1996 Atlanta Games (Ruffenach, 1992). As the amount of money sponsors pay to the Olympics reach Herculean levels, however, one wonders about the influence such mega-sponsors could have on the Games.

The marketing of the 1992 Dream Team, the United States' quasi-professional entry in the basketball competition, likewise wallowed in the Olympic sponsorship quagmire. The Dream Team foreshadowed the promotional glories and dilemmas that future Olympics will experience. How does one market an Olympic team filled with stars while juggling Olympic sponsorship with the previously existing endorsement deals of the individual athletes? The usual Olympic sponsorships (IOC, USOC) invaded the basketball competition. In addition, the team organization, USA Basketball, became a very hot sponsorship commodity once it announced that the top stars from the NBA, stars in both an athletic and marketing sense, would participate. Team sponsors, including McDonald's and Visa, spent around $1 million each for team sponsorship (Grimm, 1992a) and a combined $40 million in media advertising in the months preceding the events. In addition, USA Basketball also cranked out licensing material, like T-shirts, at an unprecedented level for an Olympic team (Liese, 1992).

Coordinating the Olympic sponsors with the individual players' deals was more of a nightmare than a dream. As a writer for *Marketing Week* describes the initial sponsorship mess,

> Charles Barkley endorses Gillette Sports Stick. That voided using Barkley's likeness on any Schick-sponsored USAB program. Magic Johnson pitches Pepsi and owns a stake in a Washington, D.C. bottler. That precludes any cameo in a Gatorade spot. Six of the 10 players are contracted to wear Nike sneakers, devaluing the USAB link for Converse, the official footwear sponsor. (Grimm, 1992, p. 29)

Michael Jordan, the most marketed of the Dream Teamers, was even threatened with being dropped from the team because of his grumblings about sponsorship conflicts with previous contracts (Grimm, 1992a).

The most visible conflict in levels of sponsorship of the Dream Team occurred in the days before the final medal ceremonies. Reebok, a U.S. Olympic Committee sponsor, demanded that all medal-winning athletes wear a Reebok uniform during the ceremonies. U.S. athletes signed off on this demand in their "Code of Conduct"—as if refusing to promote Reebok was a violation of athletic ethics. Players who had contracts with other footgear, such as Michael Jordan with Nike and Karl Malone with L.A. Gear, publicly refused to wear the competitor's clothes, at least at first (Levin, 1992b). As Charles Barkley described his motivations, "Us Nike guys are loyal to Nike because they pay us a lot of money. I have two million reasons not to wear Reebok" ("Advertising Everywhere!" 1992, p. 754). Eventually, the conflicted athletes agreed to wear the Reebok uniforms, but with the logo discreetly covered.

Both the ambush concern and the Dream Team controversy expose the grip sponsorship has upon the Olympics, and the pettiness of sponsorship. Sponsors are selfish. They want definite promotional value for their money. Reebok will contribute to the "social good" only as long as Nike is prevented from contributing. In the Olympics, the Cold War has passed the baton to the Cola Wars. Sponsorship and the marketing benefits of the Olympic image are woven into that event's fabric.

Observation Five:
Sponsorship Offers External Promotion

Despite the pervasive promotion during an event that sponsorship offers, it is not enough. For many sponsors, the promotion that occurs outside the event is at least equally as important as that occurring during the event. Some of this external promotion is free. A possible attraction of sponsorship is that sponsors get more than their money's worth. Also, like the promotion during the event, one major goal of external promotion is to increase the symbolic link between the sponsor and the sponsored in consumers' minds. External promotion can "inoculate" the audience to this link before the event happens.

FREE MEDIA COVERAGE

One big benefit of merging the name of the sponsor into the name of the event is the free press coverage that the sponsor receives. Such promotionally beneficial coverage happens before the event takes place and after it is over. News stories about the event—about the bowl game, about the traveling theatrical group—often will name the sponsor. The amount of free publicity sponsored events can receive can be enormous. When John Hancock paid $1.6 million to sponsor the John Hancock Bowl, the company estimated that it received more than $5 million worth of free publicity, with nearly 8,000 newspaper stories mentioning the sponsor (McCarthy, 1991). Although the amount of sponsor-mentioning coverage is quite extensive (given the sports-emphasis of media), nevertheless the true extent of the publicity depends upon the name of the bowl and the policy of the news vehicles covering the event.

Some news media will routinely include the name of the sponsor (The USF&G Sugar Bowl) even if they have the option of labeling the bowl without the sponsor (The Sugar Bowl). *USA Today,* for example, listed the *full* names of the 1993 bowls, including the sponsor, in their "Today's Line" section of the paper that lists all the bowl games. This might provide evidence for Bagdikian's (1992) implication that large chain newspapers (like Gannett's *USA Today*) are much more deferential toward advertisers than independent or smaller chain papers. Newspapers that are more sponsor-receptive may also print the logos of the bowl, including their sponsor-integrated nature, in stories or statistical comparisons of the teams. Most newspapers seem to mention the sponsor at least on the first reference (De Lisser, 1994). Other publications have a policy against giving bowl sponsors free publicity. *TV Guide* did not list the full names of the bowls, preferring to list the bowls under their original, nonsponsored names. That periodical even refused to list the sponsor in such bowls as the CarQuest Bowl, referring to the bowl instead in its TV listings as "College Bowl Game." This policy may point to the fact that the circulation-dependent *TV Guide* receives only 30% of its income from advertising revenue ("Top 300 Magazines," 1995). Yet sponsored events may receive free publicity in other television listings. If the mega *TV Guide* will not list the sponsor, more specialized program guides like those produced by PBS member stations or A&E will often include the sponsor's name with their listing of the name of the event.

Electronic media will also deliver the sponsor-bowl connection, as the coverage of the bowls on the advertiser-hungry networks show. ABC, covering the scores of other networks' bowls during halftime in the CompUSA Florida Citrus Bowl, used a graphic of the logo and the name of each bowl and included the sponsor's name in both.

Often, whether the publication has a policy against sponsor publicity or not, featuring the sponsor's name in a story may be difficult for a newspaper to avoid. Action photos from the game in the next day's paper can likewise feature the pervasive sponsor logos. One AP photo of a tackle from the 1994 Mobil Cotton Bowl serendipitously featured Mobil's logo on a uniform, for example.

What sponsors *really* hope for is that their names will appear favorably in headlines, a hope that is often realized. For example, the CarQuest Bowl extended an invitation to the University of Virginia football team after the Danny Ford-coached Arkansas team knocked off LSU. The front page of the *Richmond [VA] Times-Dispatch* the next day featured a very prominent headline, "U.Va. Takes a Ford Ride to CarQuest." The jump headline for the rest of this story on the next page read, "Ford Carries Cavaliers to CarQuest Bid." Research has indicated that when John Hancock insisted that the John Hancock Sun Bowl be changed to just the John Hancock Bowl, the amount of free publicity the sponsor received jumped by almost 50% (McCarthy, 1991).

If news coverage of the sponsored event seems like a small benefit, consider these elements. From a credibility point of view, when the news media plug the sponsor's connection to the sponsored, it is not a self-serving source that is promoting the connection. It is neither the funder nor the funded. It is the "objective" media that are showing the logo or integrating the name of the sponsor in a headline. Another credibility factor involves where the plug is found. Sponsorship is one of the few ways that advertising can sneak onto the front pages of newspapers. The *Roanoke [VA] Times & World-News,* in covering Virginia Tech's 1993 trip to the Independence Bowl, featured a color picture of the team getting its picture taken on the 50-yard line, with a big Poulan/Weed Eater logo poking through in the background. This picture dominated the front page, above the fold, that day. Poulan/Weed Eater was more prominently displayed that day than the president, the economy, foreign affairs or any human tragedy or triumph.

ADVERTISING FOR THE SPONSORED EVENT

Sponsors often will not rely simply on free (and sometimes uncontrollable) media to supply pre-event publicity—including their connection to the event. The events often will be publicized by advertising paid for by the sponsors, received by the sponsors as part of the sponsorship deal or provided by the network or television channel carrying the event on television. Such pre-event publicity introduces the audience to the symbolic ties between the funder and the funded.

Such advertising may solidify the connection between the sponsor and the sponsored to such a degree that it is often difficult to tell which one the ad is focusing on. A commercial airing on WTBS for the 1993 Outback Steakhouse Gator Bowl, featuring "supermodel" Rachel Hunter, stressed an Australian theme that was more symbolically beneficial to the sponsor than to the bowl. Another commercial for the Builder's Square Alamo Bowl has a voice-over of a pretend football game that describes a player getting "hammered" and "fans going wild," while showing hammers and ceiling fans. It easily could have stood alone as an autonomous Builder's Square ad.

Like cross-promotional deals with motion pictures, advertising for sponsored events often grants access to human referent systems that traditional advertising would not have. Mick Jagger would never appear in a Budweiser commercial. But he *did* appear in TV commercials for the 1994 Voodoo Lounge tour, commercials that also prominently mentioned Budweiser. As the tag line of the commercial hyped, "There's only one band that is rock and roll, and there's only one beer that can bring it to you" (Miller, 1994). And there's only one way to get symbolic access to Mick Jagger: sponsorship.

LICENSING AND MERCHANDISING

One final way sponsors use to promote their link to desirable events is through the proliferation of merchandising that results from the event. Much of the event merchandise will include the name of the sponsor. In such cases, the name of the sponsor often is permanently fixed with the event. People collect merchandise from sponsored events and keep the merchandise in their homes, perhaps in display cases. They also wear licensed clothing; they then become walking billboards for the sponsor.

At the various Olympic Games millions of Olympic pins, usually featuring the five rings *and* the name of a sponsor, are given away (and then feverishly bartered). Budweiser has a pin incorporating its name with "USA" and the Olympic rings (Fannin, 1988). T-shirts featuring the bowl game matchups are sold in participating school bookstores, university towns and surrounding communities, as well as at host city retail outlets and at the game itself. In Indianapolis in 1993, for example, one could have bought at the local Target store an "Officially Licensed" Poulan/Weed Eater Independence Bowl T-Shirt (featuring Virginia Tech vs. Indiana University, located about 50 miles from Indianapolis). This shirt featured the name of the sponsor at the top of the shirt *and* at the bottom (in the bowl logo). Sponsoring race cars may bring toy deals, which then become microcommercials. One such example is toy company Racing Champions Inc.'s manufacture of a "McDonald's Racing Team" set. This set included a heavily logo-ed McDonald's toy Nascar and a little pit crew with little golden arches on their little backs. Even programs on PBS can produce sponsor-promoting merchandise. Videotapes of the children's program *Ghostwriter*, underwritten by Nike and available for purchase in department stores, feature a Nike logo on the back of the tape. Inserted in the box is a Nike book mark. While a sponsor for *Where in the World Is Carmen Sandiego*, Holiday Inn offered activity books, games and trading cards flaunting their sponsorship (Goerne, 1992).

Merchandising, then, is not simply the domain of the commercialized event, like the Hollywood blockbuster or comic books. It can be another way for sponsors to guarantee their promotional return on not-for-profit events.

Observation Six: Sponsorship Subverts Democracy

Of all the different phenomena discussed in this book—place-based advertising, zapless ads, cross promotion—sponsorship is perhaps the one strategy that most affects culture. Sponsorship often uses as its referent system things that are not (supposed to be) commercialized. Sponsorship involves charities, schools, the arts and amateur sports. Yet, as noted throughout this book, advertising transforms referent systems, even "high-culture" referent systems. This holds true for sponsorship.

Much of what is becoming sponsored is a vital part of our society's democratic functioning. Much of what is becoming sponsored could contribute to a democratic notion of a public sphere. As Aufderheide (1991) explains, "The public is a social concept and as such needs social spaces in which to exist, to learn about the public interest, to debate it and to act" (p. 169). The public sphere is a place where various constituencies can state their cases, where the issues of society are highlighted. It is a location that must grant access to different viewpoints, and it must not let one or two viewpoints dominate. Social institutions like schools, public media and the arts have the potential to contribute to a public sphere.

However, commercial promoters grab, through sponsorship, exactly these elements of society (schools, public media and art). When this happens, the promoters' economic and symbolic control fundamentally alters the integrity of even these less-than-perfect elements of a public sphere. Advertisers, promoters and marketers could affect these institutions to the point where the term *public sphere* has no real meaning. With pervasive sponsorship, any notion of a public sphere really becomes a commercial sphere. When sponsorship touches the public sphere, commercial interests often become the dominant constituency. The big problem with this, besides the monolithic nature of a one-voiced democracy, is that often what sponsors want is not what a democracy needs. A democracy needs its citizenry to have equal access to a diversity of voices. Advertisers, via sponsorship, want to sell and to have a polished corporate image. Society cannot trust that when these two goals conflict, the democratic need will win. As a whole, the democratic need does not win. There is much evidence that sponsorship may lead to antidemocratic tendencies. This antidemocratic transformation takes several forms, including the types of messages that are sponsored (agenda setting), the type of audiences who benefit from sponsorship (a privileged audience) and the leveling that occurs between the sponsor and sponsored (a simultaneous elevating and devaluing effect).

AGENDA SETTING

Sponsors may become indignant at the insinuation that they influence the ideas of what they sponsor. Often, sponsors will claim that they "don't interfere with the artists," that they avoid the operational, everyday control of the sponsored activity. Sometimes, of course, they do not stay away. But, for the moment, let us assume that this is true. Let us assume that sponsors do not interfere, operationally, with the sponsored. Even in this case, sponsors still have a tremendous impact upon the sponsored, maybe even an unintended impact. Even if it were true that sponsors rarely interfere with the daily artistic decisions of the sponsored activity, their funding role, at the very least, grants them tremendous influence over the prominence and circulation of ideas. Sponsors can establish agendas. By placing their dollars in some activities and not others, sponsors help to determine which activities—and which activities' ideas—survive and prosper. They choose which projects to sponsor and which projects not to sponsor. This, then, influences what ideas circulate in a democratic space.

Such agenda-setting influence would potentially not affect the public sphere, however, if the agenda setters encouraged a variety of perspectives, funding a plurality of ideas. But this is not so. More likely, corporate sponsors fund one point of view: the conservative. They tend to support messages that somehow embrace or even maintain the status quo. Why do corporate funders lean toward conservative messages? One reason has to do with the general rule of promotion: Avoid the controversial or the experimental (Lubell, 1990; Schiller, 1989). Sponsors, like all advertisers, want pliant audiences. They do not want audiences too worked up, especially over political matters.

Frequently, then, when sponsors look for the sponsorable, they look for art or athletics that is *de*politicized. Here, then, *conservative* means the sponsoring of events that stress the generic human condition: broad issues of love, hate, death and timeless conditions that occur in all social and historical circumstances. As Schiller (1989) describes it, corporate sponsorship often funds events that stress "the social neutrality of art and its alleged universalistic essence" (p. 95). A production of Shakespeare's *Much Ado About Nothing* would find corporate funding much easier than the 1993 documentary about the intellectual activist Noam Chomsky, *Manufacturing Consent*. Why did Michelob choose to sponsor a Genesis rock tour? "They're not controversial," according to a Michelob spokesperson (Savan, 1994, p. 286).

The apolitical bias of sponsors is also shown by the type of content developed by advertisers who get involved in television production. Television Program Partners, a consortium of major television advertisers including AT&T and McDonald's, began its production career by producing award shows so bland and politically safe that even the trade journal *Advertising Age* chided them ("Safe (and Dull) at TPP," 1994).

In the rare case of a sponsorship of a quasi-political event with somewhat leftist leanings, often the sponsor indicates that such events are as far as they will go. Reebok's late-1980s sponsorship of "Human Rights Now!"—benefiting Amnesty International—occurred because Amnesty International, according to a Reebok executive, "had never done anything aligned to any constituency" (Schwartz, 1988, p. 49).

Such an attitude could explain why sports sponsorship, especially of the Olympics (the oldest of sponsorable events), is so popular: The ideas conveyed are those of competition, excellence and "the thrill of victory and the agony of defeat." Such themes are universal to all people, nonthreatening and easily contextualized within a focus on the individual athlete or team spirit. In college bowl games, no one is supposed to engage in a political argument. People simply cheer or boo the team. The only moments of controversy occur when the refs make a bad call. Nobody gets mad at the sponsor for that.

The conservative ideology of promotion goes beyond this at times, though. Spot advertising frequently contains pro-business messages. Because businesses pay for spot ads, and are often the target of spot ads, spot ads often celebrate business. The same may be true of sponsored messages that have explicitly political elements to them. Sometimes corporate sponsors actively seek political ideas. In such cases, the event or program will usually display an active conservative ideology, because such an ideology (free marketplace, less government) is conducive to the interests of corporate America.

For instance, sometimes sponsored events will promote the interests of a specific corporation (i.e., the sponsor)—often promoting conservatism or a strong pro-business emphasis as part of the deal. Sequent Computer Systems sponsored a program on CNBC called *Technology Edge* that, by interviewing corporate executives, discussed how business can integrate technology (Cuneo, 1993). PBS aired the series *The Prize: The Epic Quest for Oil, Money and Power,* sponsored by oil investor Paine Webber, and apparently the series was much more defending than disparaging of the industry powers. Similarly, Chevron sponsored the PBS *Living Against the Odds,* a special focusing on environmental risk assessment. This special included the statement, "we have to stop pointing the finger at industry for every environmental hazard" (the above two examples are from "PBS Rejects Another Oscar-Winning Documentary," 1994, p. 21).

Other sponsored items are more generally politically conservative. Mobil Oil sponsored a documentary airing on PBS called *Hollywood's Favorite Heavy,* arguing that movies displayed an antibusiness bias through their depiction of villainous corporate executives; Mobil Oil also sponsors William F. Buckley's *Firing Line* and has donated money to Reed Irvine's *Accuracy in Media,* the conservative newsletter ("The Right-Wing Agenda: Buying Media Clout," 1992). Prudential Securities underwrites *Wall Street Week* ("PBS Rejects Another Oscar-Winning Documentary, 1994).

If such events and programs are sponsored because of their political ideology, other potential cultural activities are not. Artists or others who coordinate sponsored events understand the ideological preferences of corporate sponsors, and as such may self-censor their work to maximize their sponsorship potential (Lubell, 1990; Schiller, 1989; Shaw, 1990; Wicklein, 1989). An executive with the Metropolitan Museum of Art in New York admitted that shows have been canceled because of their inability to draw corporate sponsorship, and that "which shows are likely to be funded by corporations and which are not" is an important criterion for selection (Lubell, 1990, p. 112). A fund-raiser for a PBS station disclosed that, "We now work more closely with the creative department at the station to keep them from producing 'unfundable' projects" ("The Private Life of Public Broadcasting," 1994). Although *unfundable* can mean a variety of things, given the ideological leanings of corporate America it is not unreasonable to think that the politics of the potential project are a factor.

CREATING A PRIVILEGED AUDIENCE

Some argue that sponsorship is healthy for a democracy. One argument for sponsorship from this perspective is its "popularization" function. Without sponsorship, its defenders claim, many events would not exist or would not receive the wide media exposure that they garner through corporate funding. Sponsorship, according to this perspective, helps to democratize society through the dissemination of sponsored events.

Yet in one sense, sponsorship does just the opposite. Instead of equalizing people through access to events and ideas, it limits access to the events. Sponsorship limits the equality of access to ideas in at least two ways. One is in the demographic purity that sponsorship seeks. Schiller has argued that sponsorship, because of its promotional incentives, tends to produce events that ignore or even actively exclude particularly small or undesirable audiences for advertisers (cited in Sebastian, 1992, p. B1). As noted earlier, desirable audiences are often so valuable a part of the sponsorship that the sponsors seek out audience mailing lists. Undesirable audiences do not receive as much attention. If an audience does not have a sufficient amount of disposable income and a propensity to give that income to marketers, then chances are slim that sponsors would be interested in funding a cultural event designed to appeal to that audience. These undesirable audiences, then, are not given a voice through cultural events to the same degree that the affluent are or the marketable 20-somethings are. Cultural festivals based upon ethnicity rather than marketability may find they have to redefine their demographic appeal if they are to survive.

Sponsorship fosters a privileged audience in another way. When a corporation agrees to sponsor an event, almost without exception the sponsor expects to receive special access to the event. This special access may be in the form of banks of free tickets—often located in prime viewing areas like the front row or even backstage or during prime times like opening night. Sometimes, even, particularly elite audiences are given private showings. The special access may also be in the form of prime space on the site of the event for courtesy tents.

Especially in the first case, those who are associated with the sponsor or need to be schmoozed by the sponsor become a privileged group. Sponsors and their clients get, literally, the best seats in the house. Sometimes, it is this perk of sponsorship that is the most important to sponsors. An American Express executive described that company's attitude toward sponsorship. "The problem is in educating [the sponsored] in the sense that we're not so much interested in 'American Express Presents,' because that's not a demonstratable loyalty builder. We want to get customer's access to the first seats, the best seats and backstage" (Levin, 1993a, p. 4). The company 3M primarily saw its Olympic sponsorship as a retail promotion: Through its sponsorship, 3M could send 1,900 dealers of its products to the 1988 Calgary Games ("3M's Global Hope," 1988). This element of sponsorship is so pervasive that it prompted one British writer to note about the issue in his country that, "the general impact of sponsorship is to encourage the growth of a new form of elitism into the artistic life of the country" (Shaw, 1990, p. 379).

ELEVATING THE SPONSOR, DEVALUING THE SPONSORED

A final effect of sponsorship has to do with its implications for the "leveling" of meaning systems. Sponsorship simultaneously brings up the social position of the promoter while at the same time bringing down the social position of the sponsored event. It levels elements in society, making it difficult to prioritize and evaluate different symbolic domains.

Sponsorship is designed to elevate the sponsor. Sponsors want to connect themselves with the socially good, so they sponsor charities, plays, art exhibits, school materials, concerts, public media or amateur sports hoping that the audience, and society, will associate the sponsor with these cultural entities. The sponsors stress the depth and the breadth of the sponsored-sponsor linkage to insure this association. To guarantee depth of association, sponsors stress how they were necessary for the generation of this cultural event. Sponsors trumpet that a sponsored event is "Brought to you by . . . " They work to get Phil Collins to appear in their sponsored ads. They make sure that the name of the sponsor is very visible, indeed intrusive, while the event is on. They also stress the breadth of the linkages. The whole point of the previous sections on the ubiquitous promotion during sponsored events and on external promotion was to show the range of the strategic linkages. Sponsorship as a whole serves to raise the social status not only of individual marketers, but of marketing, advertising and promotion in general. Sponsorship says, "Look how many things we contribute to the social good." Sponsorship does not say as much about the limits of what they provide, the economic strings attached and the effect that their skewed funding has on culture.

The public relations impact of sponsorship combined with the overall good image of manufacturers presented in conventional advertising hits society with a one-two punch of image management. In traditional commercials, advertisers are presented as problem solvers. "You're Not Socially Accepted?? Must Be Your Bad Skin! Buy Clearasil and Solve Both Your Popularity *And* Your Pus Problems!!" As an earlier chapter noted, advertising serves as cheerleaders for consumption. Sponsorship adds to the rah-rah. It joins with product advertising to give big businesses a relentlessly positive message. It says, "Not only do we solve your problems, we also provide you with good things! And no one is forcing us to do that! It's philanthropy!"

The association with high culture also helps corporations in another very real way. It gives them an extra degree of clout for influencing public policy. We noted earlier that one reason corporations might sponsor high-art events is the access this grants sponsors to social decision makers and opinion leaders. Sponsorship increases the ability to schmooze. Occasionally, though, corporations can use their sponsorship activities even more blatantly. They can use their sponsorship for explicit political leverage. If a governmental body is doing something the corporations do not like, the corporations' contributions to the arts may give them additional influence they would not otherwise have. They can use sponsorship as a social threat. They can say to policy makers, "Do what we want, or else we will remove our sponsorship from these desired events." Such was the case with Philip Morris in 1994. When the New York City Council was considering antismoking legislation, Philip Morris strong-armed the arts organizations it sponsors to lobby for Philip Morris before the Council. As a *New York Times* reporter noted about the tobacco conglomerate, "In the arts world, offending Philip Morris is the equivalent of crossing the National Endowment for the Arts" (Goldberger, 1994, p. C14).

While elevating the corporate, sponsorship simultaneously devalues what it sponsors. This is true for advertising generally, of course. Advertising subordinates its referent systems. By implication, advertising turns love, respect, companionship and other referent systems into utilitarian systems: They are useful for selling. Similarly, sponsorship turns cultural events into advertising vehicles. The sporting event, the play, the concert and the public television program become subordinate to promotion because, in the sponsor's mind and in the symbolism of the event, they exist to promote. It is not Art for Art's Sake as much as Art for Ad's Sake. In the public's eye, art is yanked from its own separate and theoretically autonomous domain and squarely placed in the commercial.

In addition to the public debasing that occurs when a cultural event is turned into a commercial, art and other cultural entities are also devalued in their own self-image. I discussed at the beginning of the chapter how organizations seeking sponsorship have had to redefine themselves as marketing organizations. They offer business a way to reach audiences and an image that corporations may exploit. This creates a promotional-utilitarian mentality. They may begin to think, "we, the artists, must maximize our selling appeal." Also, one effect may be that these organizations devote so many resources to finding and pleasing sponsors—resources of people and ideas—that they cannot devote these resources to their original purpose, communicating the artistic (Beck, 1990).

With the obvious connections between the corporate and the cultural through sponsorship's promotional techniques, and the subordination to which cultural institutions submit, the image of the arts as commercial property may become solidified in the public arena as the promotional imperative becomes more pervasive and more obvious. This imperative ultimately affects the content of the event itself, even beyond the agenda-setting influence. Every time the commercial intrudes on the cultural, the integrity of the public sphere is weakened because of the obvious encroachment of corporate promotion. Art becomes less valued, less credible and less engaging. Art begins to equal other commercial entities. Art equals the sitcom; art equals the 15-second spot.

Such devaluing occurs in the arts when not one member of an arts organization speaks to news organizations for attribution about Philip

Morris and its use of the arts as a lobbying tactic (Quindlen, 1994). Such devaluing occurs in health organizations when the National Breast Cancer Coalition receives sponsored assistance from *Playboy* magazine for a series of awareness advertisements. The ad was predictably headlined, "You've probably been a breast man since day one" (Roan, 1994, p. E1). This devaluing process happens every time the Royal Shakespeare Company allows a corporate sponsor's name to be larger on the logo than its own (Lister, 1993); or Guinness can get its image in an Elpidu Georgiou painting (Lees, 1992); or Barbara Mandrell's album is titled *No Nonsense,* the same name as her pantyhose-making sponsor ("Advertising Everywhere!" 1992); or a Ford is placed on display outside the Corcoran Gallery of Art in Washington, D.C.; or a Smithsonian exhibit includes no critical statements about the sponsor's institution ("Bossy Sponsors," 1994); or Coca-Cola sponsors an exhibit at the Royal Ontario Museum entitled "Santa—The Real Thing," featuring old Christmas-time Coke ads (Jacobson & Mazur, 1995, p. 102).

Even if the ideas are not so obviously influenced, the public itself will treat ideas in the cultural sphere less seriously, will see these ideas as less autonomous. As sponsors experience a "halo effect" from their symbolic linkage with the good and desirable, it is logical to believe that, conversely, the sponsored experience a "horns effect."

The Faustian implication of the metaphor may, in fact, be an apt one.

Notes

1. In "real life," of course, corporations have rarely been involved in purely philanthropic giving, without any expectation of promotional return. In this country, many chief philanthropic organizations, like the Rockefeller Foundation, were founded in part as public relations vehicles to turn around the negative image of the captains of capitalism during the Progressive Reform Movement. For example, John D. Rockefeller, who was labeled as one of the most hated men of his generation, was also very PR conscious. His 1914 hiring of the "father of public relations," Ivy Lee, illustrates his image orientation. The idea for the Rockefeller Foundation, created in 1913 after several years of fermentation, came not long after *McClure's* magazine published Ida Tarbell's "The History of the Standard Oil Company," a devastating piece of muckraking journalism.

2. The unobtrusive nature of sponsorship is not always successful in "hiding" the commercial imperative, however. In 1991, the FTC prevented Pinkerton's Red Man chewing tobacco from "displaying its name, logo, color or design during televised events" that it sponsored (Colford, 1991, p. 58). Although the issue of banning all tobacco sponsorship was raised at this time as well, the issue is made complicated by the fact that

the FTC has little authority over cigarette advertising ever since a mid-1960s Congressional ruling took such authority away (Jamieson & Campbell, 1992, p. 249).

3. Although sponsorship activity has increased both in the United States and in Great Britain since the 1980s, Roy Shaw, the Secretary General of the Arts Council in Great Britain from 1975 to 1983, is quick to note that, "It is worth recalling that sponsorship was an idea copied from American experience" (Shaw, 1990, p. 376).

4. The increased reliance on underwriters by PBS may make that outlet nearly as cluttered as commercial television, however. In a trade journal article headlined "Clutter Comes to Public TV" (Miles, 1994) the author explored the idea that too many underwriter messages have cluttered public television, especially at the local level.

5. If the intention of Philip Morris was to prevent criticism of its targeting of African Americans in cigarette ads by corporate sponsorship, it failed miserably in 1990 with its release of Uptown cigarettes. This campaign was so explicitly aimed at African American males that it caused a well-organized uproar and led to organized resistance among Harlem residents.

6. For the 1996 Olympic Games in Atlanta, for example, Visa has worked on a deal that would give the credit card company access to airport kiosks, sponsorship of a media center and logo space on the cover of a tourist guidebook. An Atlanta Olympic Committee executive said that this sort of sponsorship could go even further: "I could see Broad Street some day becoming Coca-Cola Boulevard" (Bayor, 1993, p. 53).

7

COMMERCIALS, CONTROL
AND THE COMPUTER REVOLUTION

A frequently discussed trend of modern life in 1993 and 1994 was the arrival of the interactive media revolution. Computers are changing everything, according to many news reports and specials, including our relationship to our media. We will have access to much more information than we ever had before, and it will be right at our fingertips. Computers will allow us to order only the information and entertainment that we want, when we want it. We will interact at a deeper and more significant level with our media producers and distributors, to allow us to shape our media content to our individualized tastes. Computers will allow us to improve the fidelity of our media, because digitized entertainment can be refined to the pixel level.

Computers may indeed lead to some sort of revolution in media content. Another type of revolution that computers could spark, however, is a revolution in advertising. Advertisers see this revolution approaching, and it makes them nervous. They are not yet quite sure how to react. Advertisers have developed a love/hate relationship with the fast-approaching computer revolution of their profession. As one major manufacturing executive summarized advertising's attitude toward the computerized future, "The advertising business may be heading for trouble—or it may be heading for a new age of glory" (Artzt, 1994, p. 24). Like many recent issues in advertising, advertiser nervousness comes down to the issue of control.

On the one hand, advertisers love computers because they offer increased control over market information and consumer desires. They love computers because they increase advertisers' ability to manipulate the symbols in advertising and match up these symbols for specific consumer markets. Advertisers can therefore control the selling messages to a much finer degree than before. The arrival of computerized *database marketing* has added the leverage to the internal, symbolic control over their messages that advertisers desire.

On the other hand, advertisers are concerned about their external, economic control over computers, interactive technology and new forms of information and entertainment. If computers will encourage all media to be subscription-based, all "pay-per" bits of content, how will they disseminate their selling messages? If there are no more "free" media, how do they justify their financial and symbolic encroachment? Will computerized media not need advertising as a source of funding? What will be the role of advertising on the Information Superhighway? What will be the role of advertising in an age of interactive TV? How will advertisers ensure that these developments will be properly "advertising friendly?"

The issue of the internal control of advertising messages using database marketing and the issue of external control over media messages in interactive media, combined, may lead to an advertising revolution. They both could change—and currently are changing—how advertising does business. But things are currently very dynamic and still quite ambiguous. It is too early to tell if there will be a fundamental and irreversible revolution. Nor is it clear, if there is a revolution, how upsetting to the promotional status quo the revolution will be. If there is a fundamental revolution in advertising, who will end up being in charge and who will end up being in chains?

Two things are sure. If advertisers sense that computers offer them more control than they had before, then they will exploit these digitized opportunities to the hilt. If advertisers sense that computers offer less control than they had before, then they will do everything they can to turn that around. Both possibilities are evident in modern advertising. This chapter will discuss each of these possibilities. The first section will discuss the impact of database marketing upon advertising's internal symbolic control. The second half of the chapter will explore the reaction of advertising to the Internet and other computerized interactive systems. It will also highlight advertising's attempt to ingrain itself into the Internet and advertising's use of the net to capture consumers.

Database Marketing and the Refinement of Internal Symbolic Control

Database marketing is the use of customer information—including names, addresses, phone numbers correlated with demographic and lifestyle information—to create specifically targeted selling messages. Database marketing is the most common term for the practice, but it is called other names as well, including relationship marketing, personal marketing, one-to-one marketing and targeted marketing (Berry, 1994).

The technique involves several steps. The first is the gathering of customer information. This information often comes from the customers themselves. Marketers receive such information through direct sales like telemarketing, home shopping or catalogues or through surveys. Then the information may be correlated with information from other databases, such as media subscription lists, credit records or public records like lists of drivers' licenses (which states have often sold to for-profit organizations). Data analysts then construct small clusters of consumer groups. Finally, marketers use the clustered information to create targeted ad appeals sent directly to specific consumers, drawn from the database, whom the marketers feel will most closely match the appeal (Berry, 1994).

THE GROWTH IN DATABASE MARKETING

The practice and theory of database marketing are not new, but before the universal use of computerized analysis, database marketing tended to be marginalized on the outskirts of promotion. Catalogue companies, book and record clubs and other mail-order and direct-sales firms were usually the first marketers to routinely keep banks of specific customer information. Marketers have stored databases on customers at least since the beginning of this century. Some of the largest mail-order firms had databases on as many as six million customers by 1915 (Strasser, 1989). Before computers made database analysis cost-efficient, however, firms might routinely purge their files of customer information simply because they did not know what to do with it ("Emery 'Discovers' Database," 1984).

This is no longer the case. Advertisers often know exactly what to do with information on specific consumers and know how to get that information. One survey of advertising agencies found that by 1992 approximately 61% of the agencies claimed that half of their clients maintained databases on customers. This was an increase from 48% in 1990 (Levin, 1992a). A marketing expert described the trend as "one of the most important marketing developments of the 1990s" (Berry, 1994, p. 58). Several factors have led to the popularization of database marketing.

The development of high-speed computer hardware and statistical computer software has been crucial to the adoption of the technique. Such computer developments can now analyze and distribute to other systems billions of bits of information in a fraction of the time it took earlier. Computers have also been crucial in collecting information from customers. Interactive kiosks, like the iStation found in music stores, often encourage customers to punch in information about themselves that the kiosk then stores for marketers to retrieve later (Cuneo, 1994). A key quality of such interactive kiosks that advertisers look for is *writability,* or the ability of the system to record the activity and the information that the participant volunteers ("Learning to Speak the Interactive Speak," 1994, p. S19).

Advertising's frustration with traditional media has also been a factor. A viewer's ability to ignore or zap a mass-produced sales message has pushed advertising to try more targeted approaches. Such an approach, advertisers hope, will cause the individual consumer to pause when exposed to a message that seems created just for him or her. If advertisers remove the "mass" image from a mass-produced advertisement, perhaps the consumer will not be able to discard it. As one marketing consultant concludes about the messages produced by database marketing, "It deals with you in the same personalized way as a mom-and-pop grocery store, where they knew customers by name and stocked what they wanted" (Berry, 1994, p. 58-59). Marketers bank on the assumption that it is hard to ignore mom and pop. Maybe even rude.

Advertising's increasing disdain for traditional media has also encouraged database marketing in another way. Media organizations may be increasingly willing to help advertisers build on and refine their databases to preserve advertising's interest in them. Many media organizations maintain valuable lists of subscribers, often accompanied by demographic information. They may also be willing to share that list with advertisers and even help them to exploit the marketing potential of that list. Through such services, media organizations hope to keep advertisers in the media fold. When a newspaper in Washington uses its database of readers, correlates it with dog owner information and then uses its delivery system to promote a sale at a local pet shop, the newspaper hopes that the pet shop will remain loyal to the newspaper and continue to place more traditional ads in the paper (Benenson, 1992). Some newspapers may view a desirable circulation list as a revenue source in and of itself. The *Cedar Rapids Gazette* even created a separate company, Gazette Database Marketing, to explore the marketing of its database to direct-mail and custom marketing companies (Fisher, 1993a).

Magazines and other media can similarly generate revenue from their customer lists. In 1993, Conde Nast Publications used its circulation information with other database information to compile demographic, psychographic and lifestyle information for the 11 million subscribers of its 13 magazines. The organization would use the information to help advertisers with targeted promotions and direct mailings. The utilization of databases by media organizations is likely to continue. One magazine executive argues about the trend that, "By the time we get into the latter part of the '90s, any publisher will have to be proficient in database marketing if they want to remain competitive" (Donaton, 1993e, p. 27).

The growth in direct response marketing such as direct mail, telemarketing and home shopping also has encouraged database growth. Direct marketing, because the customer is contacted personally, lends itself to the building of consumer databases. Direct mail, especially, has grown in marketing importance. In 1994, spending on direct mail advertising was more than $29 billion. The increase in this marketing sector from 1993 was 8.7%, more than newspapers, magazines and network television (Coen, 1995). Reasons for the growth include the targeting to narrow audiences that direct mailing allows and the creation or refinement of databases. Each time a consumer purchases an item from direct response marketing, another bit of information is added to the marketer's database and could be used to shape a future sales effect targeted at that consumer.

Two issues with database marketing warrant discussion. The first involves the implications of the refinement of the ultratargeted ad for individual consumers, and how that might increase commodity fetishism. Privacy and new media technologies are relevant here. Second, database marketing may increase other trends discussed in this book—place-based advertising, camouflaged ads, cross promotion and sponsorship—through its facilitation of integrated marketing.

DATABASE MARKETING, PRIVACY AND COMMODITY FETISHISM

In the 1967 spy spoof *The President's Analyst,* the one organization in the movie presented as all-powerful and all-seeing is not the CIA or FBI, but rather The Phone Company. The company can watch and listen to anyone in the country in this movie, including James Coburn's psychoanalytic protagonist. The Phone Company engages in this voyeuristic activity, in part, to find out as much as possible about potential consumer resistance to their planned projects. The Phone Company watches us, in other words, to improve its ability to sell.

The film might be closer to reality today than it was in the 1960s. Commercial companies seek to construct databases that include the most minute details about our consumption habits. They want to do this to control the effectiveness of their sales messages. The more information they have about the audience of their sales message, the more they can manipulate the symbols in these messages. Sophisticated databases are powerful tools for the internal symbolic control of advertisements.

What makes this especially frightening is that for commercial companies to have the most information about what we do buy, and thus to increase their ability to predict what we will buy, they must also try to get access to other information, like our financial status (or what we can afford to buy) and our leisure interests. As such, database marketing has been criticized in several venues as an attack on the privacy of citizens. Legislative bodies, especially state legislators, have proposed laws to limit the access to information by marketers, or at least fully disclose to consumers when such information may be used for marketing purposes. Virginia, for example, has a law that requires merchants to reveal when they intend to sell private information to a third party. This law also requires that marketers give consumers the option to request that their personal information not be included in such a database (Colford, 1993c).

There are a couple of problems with legislative protection from database marketers, however. One problem is that not enough such laws are passed, nor are they substantial enough when they are passed. As a writer for *Business Week* observed, "when politicians balance industry's interest in reaching markets against the customer's right to privacy, marketing usually wins" (Lewyn, 1994, p. 60).

Another problem with privacy legislation is that it usually guards against one marketer, who has compiled a database with consumer information, selling the database to another marketer. The laws protect against third-party participation. The laws do not often address the use of the database by the original company, however. If the original company is large enough, with enough marketable subsidiaries, then it really does not have to sell the database to external firms to maximize the exploitation of the information. A large enough commercial company does not need a third party. With the growth of media conglomerates, large manufacturers and multitiered advertising agencies, there may be plenty of opportunities within the parent company. The mining of the database can take place in-house.

Blockbuster Entertainment is a good potential example. As of 1994, Blockbuster Video had nearly 4,000 video rental stores nationwide, and its video rental information makes it a prime source of database marketing (Zbar, 1994c). Blockbuster's video rental master database contains 40 million names, which it integrates with the two million transactions it processes from the individual stores (Berry, 1994; Zbar, 1994a). Blockbuster has claimed that it will never release its database to external firms. It does not need to. Blockbuster certainly can exploit its database on its own. One example just touches the surface: The company sent a direct mail promotion to the children in its database— and, presumably, anyone who had rented a children's video (Zbar, 1994a). Likewise, the organization has used in-store kiosks that inform customers about movies that they *may* like to rent based upon their previous rentals (Zbar, 1994c). But even if Blockbuster were to hit the ceiling on its own use of the database, then potentially its sibling entertainment companies, Paramount and Viacom, would have an interest in people's movie habits. Paramount's motion picture and television production companies, and Viacom's cable networks Nickelodeon, MTV and VH-1 could greatly benefit from a list of 10 million people and the entertainment they prefer. The publisher Simon & Schuster, also part of the Viacom/Paramount/Blockbuster mix, could similarly exploit the information. The Discovery Zone, a children's play center subsidiary, might also find use for the databased children and parents (Berry, 1994). With the growth of such firms, the selling of databases to external firms may simply be unnecessary.

Whether a firm with a database uses it internally or sells it for external use, the ultimate point is often to shape a selling message for a narrow market. With more information at their disposal about the characteristics of individual people, advertisers can potentially even shape the message for an individual. This is where an idea explored in an earlier chapter—the fetishism of commodities—becomes relevant.

The reader may recall that the fetishism of commodities refers to the extent to which advertising celebrates consumption. Advertising presents consumption as the solution to problems and encourages people to think of commodities only in terms of consumption. Because advertising is the main source of product information, its emphasis on the consumption side of products may be influencing our evaluations of commodities. We may romanticize a product specifically because of what ads tell us the product can do for us. Buying the product will give us romance, or peer respect, or whatever. We also may romanticize products generally because advertising serves as a massive public relations system for consumption. Other ways of seeing the product—such as the social costs of producing the product—are not socially discussed as often as consumption is in advertising.

One problem with this argument is that we are exposed to many ads that simply do not appeal to our interests. Many ads are not effective for particular people. An ad may symbolically imply, "Buy this product to help you achieve social value X." Because we might not really desire this particular social value, the ad may not work on us. Because we see the particular appeal as uninteresting or silly, the ad may turn us off. Or because of the other referent systems in the ads (like the characteristics of the actors, the setting in which the ad takes place or the language of the ad), the ad may not work for us. For us, this ad does not really fetishize the commodity. It still emphasizes consumption, to be sure. The particular consumption emphasized, though, does not happen to appeal to us as individuals. Because it does not appeal to us as individuals, it might enhance our critical evaluation of this particular ad or even advertising in general. As we approach the ad as nonaddressed "other," we maintain a symbolic distance from the ad that allows us to evaluate it more critically than ads that do strike a chord with us. We may be more likely to see the rhetorical techniques and ideological implications of advertising when we do not personally identify with the ad.

Advertisers often use database marketing to prevent exactly this sort of nonidentification from occurring. Advertising rhetoric founded upon database marketing research may decrease ineffective or inefficient appeals in advertising, and therefore increase the degree to which advertising successfully engages us. Database analysis augments the marketer's ability to control the symbolic manipulations in advertising for particular people. Database marketing, then, may also increase advertising's ability to fetishize commodities successfully.

The whole point of database marketing is to create niched ads for small groups, perhaps even individual consumers. One goal of database analysis is "drilling down," in which as many demographic and personality variables are combined and refined as possible to come up with precise and pure audiences for particular products (Berry, 1994, p. 61). A database might reveal that a consumer is a male, lives in a college town, has a credit card and likes cyber-punk science fiction novels with strong female protagonists. There are marketers out there ready to sell niched products for that combination and ready to create ads that would most appeal to that ultraspecialized market. The referent systems that their research tells them would most appeal to that market fill the ad; the ad is then sent directly to the drilled-down name. The database-created ad increases the chances that the ad will appeal to that person and that no troublesome critical distance will get in the way.

Database marketers, in fact, have shown little hesitation to go for narrowed audiences who may be particularly vulnerable to certain advertising messages. Kay-Bee Toys, for example, sent a specially created "magalogue" (half magazine, half catalogue) to 10 million households with children between 4 and 14 *and* who lived within a 10-minute drive of a Kay-Bee Toy store (Kim, 1993a). Casinos and cigarette companies have also used database techniques to reach targeted markets that they know are heavy gamblers and smokers. American Express has experimented with "relational billing," where the company inserts a discount or coupon in the credit card bill that matches last month's purchase. This may encourage even more spending based upon the card holder's consumption history (the above three examples are from Berry, 1994). One company sells a database of those in dire economic straits to quick-cash (but high-fee) companies (Jacobson & Mazur, 1995).

Although traditional advertisers may be nervous about new interactive media, as the next section will discuss, the possibilities of interactivity excite database marketers. One version of the communications future involves the *digital switch,* or a computerized coordinating device. We will have a digital switch in our home that will connect our phone, computer, bank, video store, cable and network television, stereo, library, home shopping and music store together in one system (Elmer-Dewitt, 1993). We could then order from *all* these entities on a subscription basis, and even combine them. Companies are scrambling to become "full service networks" (FSNs) to exploit the synergistic possibilities of such a media system. Time Warner's test of a prototype FSN began in December 1994 in Orlando (Florida), offering (to only five households at first) movies, videogames and interactive shopping on demand (Donaton, 1994b).

Such interactive communication systems have the potential to balloon databases. This is a primary danger, for democracy and personal privacy, of such an interactive system. With traditional broadcast and basic cable TV, we cannot alter what we receive, but we do have complete anonymity. No one knows if we are watching *Mr. Rogers' Neighborhood, Masterpiece Theater, Baywatch,* or *Geraldo.* No one knows unless we tell them. With interactive TV, as proposed, we are always telling them. It will be, in all likelihood, a "pay-per" system, where media companies bill us for what we specifically order. The normally mass-distributed *broad*cast system will become an individually distributed *narrow*cast. We might get exactly the programming we want, but we lose our anonymity. The sender of the message is now aware of the viewing behavior of the receiver. The loss of anonymity occurs with any subscription-based medium. This is why newspapers and magazines can exploit their circulation lists as database information, but network television cannot. With interactive network television, they could.

It is precisely the database possibilities of interactive entertainment that database marketers like. Potentially, every time we order a program, sports event or movie, that will be recorded in a database. Interactive TV operators might also know the mix of programs that we order, the days and times we watch these programs and the order in which we watch them.

All of this new mammoth amount of information could be used to "drill down" even deeper than before. They may have our entertainment preference profiles calculated very exactly. Marketers will be anxious to create sales messages based upon these calculations. We as individuals potentially will receive television commercials that are different from anyone else's commercials on the planet. The idea of one, monolithic "brand" may even disappear. Instead, the brand image, and referent systems that go with that brand image, will be different depending upon what the ultrarefined database tells marketers about our preferences, demographics and lifestyle. "Adaptive branding" is one name for this concept ("Learning to Speak the Interactive Speak," 1994, p. S18). One excited marketing consultant called it the "virtual brand." As he describes the virtual brand, and the role of database marketing in this idea,

> New media will be capable of understanding an individual's existing product context and social circumstances before a message is delivered. This advance knowledge will allow advertisers to customize messages to a specific consumer based on what he [sic] owns, likes, and hopes to become. (Susman, 1994, p. 18)

In this quotation, "product context" and "social circumstances" refer to the advertisers' knowledge about which referent systems and appeals would most manipulate the potential consumer. With an entirely subscription-based media system, the information is potentially available about what the most successful referent systems would be for us as individuals. Based upon database analysis, we would receive a branded image of Pepsi that no one else would receive.

The interactive capabilities could also be extended to the advertisements themselves, providing even more information. We could participate in "dialogue marketing" with advertisers, where they could entice us to ask specifically for more information about the virtual brand. It will not really be a dialogue, though. It will be a conversation with very close-minded and self-centered individuals. They will listen and respond when we ask about something *they* want to talk about. When we ask them about consumption information, they are all ears. When we ask them for more information about a product's characteristics, they will respond enthusiastically. This is because, when we ask them for such information, we are telling them specifically when a sales pitch and referent system is working. This would give advertisers even more information to add to their database about us. Advertisers would also love this scenario for another reason. Because home shopping capabilities will also be part of the system, we have instant consumer gratification opportunities. We could instantly "act" on the commercial's promises. We could instantly act upon the fetishes of the commodity our dialogue has enhanced. The word *act*, in this case, refers to the behavior most preferred by advertisers. We could instantly *buy*.

In discussing advertising's use of referent systems that speak to our innermost desires, Williamson (1978) had the following to say: "Advertisements are selling us something else besides consumer goods: in providing us with a structure in which we, and those goods, are interchangeable, they are selling us ourselves" (p. 13). This much-quoted statement is even more true with the rise of database marketing. With databases allowing the potential creation of an advertisement so individualized that only one person will receive it, ads will quite literally be "selling us ourselves." We might see commodities more rigidly than ever because the ad is so targeted to us and our desires. A consumer orientation toward self-image, social-problem solving and life in general may be overwhelmingly presented in this discourse. The hegemony of the commodity fetish may be solidified through database maneuvers.

James Coburn's nosy Phone Company may soon be behind the curve.

DATABASE MARKETING AND INTEGRATED MARKETING

Advertising industry buzzwords have filled this book. Here is another one to be added to the mix: Integrated marketing campaign or communication (IMC). Integrated marketing can be defined in several ways, but the term often connotes the coordination of different promotional techniques by one company (see Nowak & Phelps, 1994, for a discussion of integrated marketing and its different definitions). In integrated marketing, traditional media advertising (electronic and print), direct sales (mail or telemarketing), sales promotion (couponing), public relations and the new techniques discussed in this book (sponsorship, cross promotion, etc.) are manipulated and matched with a long-term strategy or marketing goal in mind. Sometimes integrated marketing is designed to accentuate a unified corporate "voice" to consistently communicate the same brand appeal, the same referent systems, for a product or corporation. Other times the term may simply mean increasing the degrees to which the different promotional activities communicate with each other for increased efficiency (Nowak & Phelps, 1994).

Marketers thus use IMC to maximize the total control they have over their promotional activities. The activities of place-based ads, camouflaged ads, cross promotion and sponsorship, in and of themselves, have a great deal of potential to be socially influential when done effectively. This book has attempted to make that argument. For large companies with the ability to do more than one of these activities, IMC can increase the totality of social influence that the company may experience with these techniques. IMC allows the marketing whole to be greater than the sum of the promotional parts. If the social influence of Coca-Cola is a bit frightening because it sponsors 900 events and institutions a year, imagine this influence when the company engages in cross-promotional activity (which it does), anti-zapping TV commercials (which it does) and place-based activity (which it does), *all* coordinated for one purpose. IMC increases the control large advertisers may have. As with other new strategies discussed here, companies often look to IMC when they sense a loss of control over the effectiveness of traditional advertising media approaches (Nowak & Phelps, 1994).

And a large piece of the IMC coordination puzzle is database marketing. Database marketing allows the blending of the different strategies to be smoother. It gives marketers information about how best to reach particular audiences with the mix of traditional ads, coupons, sponsorship, cross promotion or whatever. The information provided by databases, including where the information was compiled, helps marketers to determine which efforts worked and which efforts worked together. It is logical, then, that Nowak and Phelps (1994) argue that IMC often accompanies a greater use of consumer databases by the implementing company.

Database marketing also encourages the use of four other trends discussed previously: place-based advertising, camouflaged ads, cross promotion and sponsorship. These trends, in turn, often help to contribute to the database.

With place-based media, advertisers are often more attracted to the strategy when it uses advertising-supported interactive kiosks. By 1994, there were at least 750 different ad-supported, place-based kiosks in operation throughout the United States (Zbar, 1994b). Such place-based operations are often able to secure consumer information as the curious interact with the place-based interactive device. The Chicago White Sox used kiosks with a trivia-game hook at Comisky Park to develop a database of potential season-ticket purchasers (Zbar, 1994b).

Camouflaged ads could be made fundamental to an interactive, database system. Advertising might become integrated into programs so that opportunities to request more information about a product we see on the screen would increase, even during a noncommercial program. And we might be more willing to make this request if such content is influenced by a marketer's database information about us. A database might show when consumers are likely to tolerate such things as product placement or infomercials. In an interactive episode of *Seinfeld,* for example, when Jerry reaches for his Wayfarer sunglasses, we could pause the program, ask for more information about the brand and even place an order. As one executive described the possibilities, "the inter-relationship of advertising and programming increases because customer tastes and preferences are known in advance. Programming and advertising become interchangeable, as consumers are living inside a perpetual marketing event" (Susman, 1994, p. 18). This writer is referring mostly to increased access to information in ads, but the flip side also applies: increased marketing opportunities in programs. Database marketing, combined with content interactivity and instant purchasing, could therefore lead to an increased control of the external, programming content of media by advertisers. Advertisers might offer programmers a piece of the sales pie that results from interactive camouflaged ads.

Database marketing also facilitates cross-promotional activity. Corporations may be more likely to join when they discover, on their separate databases, many of the same names. It would make the matching of shared demographics that much easier. Marketers may even individualize the cross promotion: It becomes a virtual cross promotion, like a virtual brand. If a person likes a particular product and is a desirable market, other marketers might create more personalized, "adaptive" cross promotion for that person. Someone on an interactive system who requests on demand *Forrest Gump* and NFL football, may find Forrest on his or her system hawking NFL jerseys.

Sponsorship has also been integrated with customer databases. As discussed in Chapter 6, one function of sponsorship is to develop databases of desirable consumers. Especially for elite audiences, a cultural event's list of patrons or season ticket holders would be of great value to upper-scale marketers. Events seeking sponsorship could even attract funding through the value of their database.

The point of this discussion is that database marketing in all likelihood will increase the phenomena discussed in this book, as well as the control these phenomena offer advertisers and marketers. It offers the ability to control the symbolic effectiveness of sales messages by more precisely matching that message to an audience's desires and vulnerabilities. If ads become narrowly targeted demagoguery—instead of just mass-distributed demagoguery—then the effectiveness of these ads will increase. As it is now, we can often create a critical distance between ourselves and advertising discourse when we see ads aimed at others or that simply do not appeal to us. What will happen to our ability to evaluate advertising critically in the age of database marketing and interactivity? What will happen when nearly every ad to which we are exposed, every cross promotion, every camouflaged ad, has been created especially for us?

Billboards Along the Information Superhighway: The Reification of Advertising

If one looks at the programming of early television, pre-1952 or so, it was a pretty exciting medium. On 1948 prime-time television, for example, one found very diverse programming, arguably much more diverse than on network television today. That 1948 season included programs such as *Photographic Horizons,* which explored the nature of photography. *America's Town Meeting on the Air* was a roundtable discussion that explored such subjects as "Are We Too Hysterical About Communism?" *We, the People* would often feature interviews with leaders in public-service organizations. Dramatic teleplays were shown on *Studio One. Meet the Press* was on prime time. Reading was promoted in *Teenage Book Club* and *Author Meets the Critics*. Not to romanticize the "high-culture" content, one might also have found plenty of boxing and wrestling on television that year. Comedy, children's programs, game shows and musical variety could also be found on prime time (for a complete schedule, see Brooks & Marsh, 1992). These programs could often be found right next to the high-art programs. It was a delightful patchwork of programming.

Why was early TV such a mish-mash of different genres? Several reasons could be pointed out, including the low cost of many of these programs, their ease of broadcast and the fact that many programs were drawn from radio. The biggest reason may be, however, that the leveling effect of commercialism had not yet taken hold. It took a few years for sponsorship and, later, spot advertising to firmly grip television programming criteria. Television had not yet refined the most efficient ways to deliver audiences to advertisers. It did not take long, however. By the end of the 1950s, the diversity was gone—or at least commercially circumscribed. Dramatic teleplays were mostly replaced by Westerns; public affairs shows were mostly replaced by sitcoms. The debate program *Court of Current Issues* was supplanted by the crime drama *The Court of Last Resort*. George Gallup's *America Speaks* gave way to Garry Moore's *I've Got a Secret*.

The Internet in the early 1990s may be the closest recent equivalent to network television in the late 1940s. The Internet is a connection of computer networks that allows the networks to function as one system on a linked computer. Like 1948 television, the numbers of users are still relatively small. In 1994, there were 3.3 million households on-line with either the Internet or a commercial service like Prodigy or America On-Line. One estimate states, however, that 10.5 million households will be on-line by 1998 (Aho, 1994).

For those with access to the Internet, its offerings seem practically overwhelming and are growing literally every day. The Internet is like a wild informational frontier for the early nineties. "Alt" newsgroups offer unmoderated discussion and postings about topics ranging from Trotsky socialism to locksmithing to out-of-body experiences. Gopher and other tunneling software offers access to reference information, including library sources. Mosaic and Netscape allow users to maneuver the multimedia "locations" on the World Wide Web that just about anyone can create. Some locations are *home pages,* which act as a table of contents for other location links. Such home pages can lead to Internet locations that offer graphics, photographs, video, sounds, music and text for local computers to download or may show the way to other home pages with more multimedia options. For those who have access to university systems or large libraries, the Internet is virtually free to its users. Granted, access is still limited and intimidating to many people. Also, there is much silliness on the Internet and much that is vulgar. The diversity and openness of the system are astounding, however. It is television in 1948, but with seemingly unlimited channels.

And this makes advertisers nervous. Advertisers are concerned about the lack of control they have over computer networks and other new communications options. As with broadcasting in its infancy, advertisers are concerned about the fact that the new systems have not been socialized into an advertising mind-set. As it is now, the Internet provides another way for people to escape advertising.

A much-discussed 1994 speech to the American Association of Advertising Agencies by Procter & Gamble's CEO, Edwin L. Artzt, is indicative of this concern. The concern comes down to an anxiety about a loss of advertiser control over new computerized and interactive media. Artzt at one point made this explicit in his speech. "We've got to borrow a page from our own history [sponsorship of early broadcasting], and start getting control of the new environment" (Artzt, 1994, p. 42). The Procter & Gamble executive went on to warn that the lack of control could directly affect the issue advertisers most care about, sales. He advocated not simply creating ads that would fit in with computerized and interactive media, but that would actively take control of it. The blunt nature of the discourse is telling: "We run the risk of simply adapting to these changing technologies, but if we don't influence them—and if we don't harness them—loyalty to our brands could suffer in the long run" (p. 24). One must keep in mind that this is not some loose cannon talking about "harnessing" new media. It is the top executive of the largest advertiser in the United States.

Such a warning receives notice. Advertisers are looking for ways to economically control the new media options. Four months after Artzt's speech, the American Association of Advertising Agencies and the Association of National Advertisers formed a task force to look into creating a reality for Artzt's vision of control. This task force, the Coalition for Advertising-Supported Information & Entertainment, is designed to create "an environment where advertising revenue is the key funding source for the large majority of information and entertainment sources in the evolving world of media" ("New-Media Summit Called," 1994, p. 8).

The paranoia that advertising feels about its potential loss of economic control over the new media may have some legitimacy in the case of the Internet. In many ways, the Internet has been antagonistic toward advertising and commercial promotion. Some early advertisers on the Internet have been burned, or more precisely, *flamed*. Anyone who posts a promotionally driven announcement about a commercial service or product on many usenet or listserv discussion groups is likely to be flamed. Users often verbally attack these unsolicited commercial messages with a vengeance, sometimes flooding the marketer's e-mail with nasty notes. In addition, some World Wide Web home pages are downright subversive to advertising and corporate interests. There are blacklists of abusive Internet advertisers available on the net, for example. One location on the Internet contains a text that is headlined, "Screwing Over Your Local McDonald's." An editorial in *Advertising Age* acknowledged the negative image the Internet had for some marketers. As it observed, "marketers exposed to tales of a cyberspace community peopled by academics and intellectuals who delight in shooting electronic 'flames' at any and all ad messages might instead view the 'net as advertising hell" ("Flamers on the Internet," 1994, p. 24).

It is incorrect, however, to think that advertisers are not moving toward the Internet and the use of computer services as a promotional tool. The above editorial acknowledges this. In a subtle anti-intellectual slam against the early, ad-hostile users of the Internet, *Advertising Age* noted that, "It is becoming more and more a mass medium whose real-world users are accustomed to having their information subsidized by advertisers" ("Flamers on the Internet," p. 24). The $54,000 median income of these "real-world" users is very attractive to advertisers (Verity, 1994). Some advertising agencies, like Chiat/Day, have created divisions called "Emerging Media" for such efforts (Cleland, 1994). Other companies are designed solely for marketing on the Internet (Cleland, 1995). *Advertising Age* devotes a section of every issue to "Interactive Marketing." In 1991, there were around 9,000 registered commercial domains on the Internet; by 1994 there were more than 21,000 (Verity, 1994). Advertisers and advertising agencies look for ways to increase the commercialization of the Internet and increase their economic—or at least symbolic—control over Internet services. Although there are a variety of ways that commercialization could influence the Internet, two possible influences are especially significant: the sponsorship of computer services and the creation of marketer Internet locations and home pages.

As with noncomputerized activities, marketers often hope to link with things that people value. Sponsorship is one version of this association. Computer services are no different. Advertisers want to link their names to the on-line computer services that people use and find valuable.

Commercial services like Prodigy, America On-Line and CompuServe have been especially receptive to computerized sponsorship. Prodigy has perhaps been the most aggressive for-profit computer networking service to solicit ads. When the service first started, it featured ad messages across the bottom 20% of the screen. In 1994, however, it subdued the advertising intrusion with smaller ads that more closely matched the content of the computer screen (Donaton, 1994a).

Sponsorship and advertising are also becoming more common on the Internet. One Internet location visited by approximately 120,000 surfers a day is the "What's New" page, created by the National Center for Supercomputing Applications. The site offers links to new locations that those surfing the Internet can explore. Originally advertising-free, this domain became advertiser sponsored in 1994 (Cleland, 1994). One of the first links now encountered on the What's New page is the week's sponsor. The day this discussion was written, for example, the sponsor was CBS. "Come visit and play the *Road to the Final Four Sweepstakes,*" read one line. A large multicolored bar with the CBS logo dominated the page and acted as a viewer-friendly link to CBS's home page. Place your cursor on the bar, click your mouse and off you go to CBS-land. Once there, instead of participating in CBS's basketball celebration, you could visit the "Late Show With David Letterman" computerized page or "Find Out *What's On CBS*" by exploring that link.

CBS thus receives a dual benefit from sponsoring the What's New page. First, CBS receives publicity every time someone visits What's New. A user cannot miss the CBS presence there. Second, the What's New page facilitates, through Internet links, a computer user's visit to the CBS advertising home page. All one has to do is touch the CBS logo.

Other Internet services are sponsored as well. The Internet version of the *New York Times* is available to surfers free, but also features advertising. When the e-newspaper first started, one could scroll to the bottom of the *Times'* home page and click on the Advil, AT&T and American Management Association logo-oriented links featured there to e-travel to their home pages. Above these ads is a command from the *Times* telling one to "Click our advertisers' logos for valuable information, special offers, and sweepstakes." Besides this, once one started reading the high-tech version of the Old Gray Lady, one found ads on virtual page 5 for the three marketers that refer back to their links on the *Times'* home page.

In this way, advertisers hope to inculcate computer users to their presence on the Internet and perhaps influence economically the environment and development of the Internet. They use sponsored materials to publicize their companies and to encourage users to visit their own electronic domains where more aggressive selling can take place.

But even with an increased visibility on the Internet, there are a few difficulties in control that advertisers are seeking to overcome. Using a World Wide Web home page as an advertising vehicle, on the surface, has both a strong advantage and disadvantage. The obvious advantage is that, once the page is created, it is very inexpensive for the marketer. Advertisers do not pay the Internet to carry their advertising locations, as they would television or newspapers. The issue of user control, however, is problematic. With advertising domains on the Internet, the degree of autonomy and control by the user is greater than even the most sophisticated remote control could offer TV viewers. Even if marketers can blanket Internet services with links to their home pages, people still must actively choose to visit these pages. People can easily choose not to click on an advertiser's home page link. Then the user would never see the selling message the advertiser has created. As opposed to TV advertising that comes to viewers whether they like it or not, the user has to go to an advertiser's home page.

This is a dilemma. How can the advertiser encourage the user to seek it out? One way around this is to make the advertisers' home pages so engaging and seductive that people will voluntarily go to them. Advertisers are learning how to do this. What the Internet and other interactive systems allow is the creation of a virtual, but completely structured, advertising place. The advertising "location" may become literally a location (at least in etherspace). Advertisers have turned the Internet into a medium for virtual place-based advertising. In this virtual place everything is fun, upbeat and conducive to the selling message. Advertisers hope that their computerized spaces will cause people to linger, to increase the attractiveness of the company and the product, and perhaps even to spur instant buying through computerized home shopping.

So, for example, you can participate in virtual Tupperware parties over the Internet (Verity, 1994). You might also visit a full-color, noisy virtual bar. In this bar, you can hear pick-up lines ("What's your sign?" asks one woman patron), you can play the jukebox and you can read the graffiti on the bathroom walls. But the only drinks you can "order" (virtually) are DeKuyper's. Click on a bottle above the bar and on the screen appears a Peachtree Peach Schnapps bottle, with a sales pitch and recipe. (I visited this location on St. Patrick's Day, so the particular recipe I found was for the Fuzzy Leprechaun.) Signs on the tavern's wall are for DeKuyper's products. Why does DeKuyper so dominate? It is because you've visited the DeKuyper's Dot Com bar. It is DeKuyper's home page—an electronic space where your eyes can drink in DeKuyper images.

One of the most interesting advertising links created in 1994 is the MCI Gramercy Press location. Originally, the Gramercy Press campaign was a series of serialized TV ads that dramatized the adjustments of a faux publisher, Gramercy Press, adapting to network MCI business, a computer system. In the TV version of the ads, the campaign introduces us to such Gramercy Press employees as Darlene the receptionist and Ellen the editor.

The MCI home page complemented and greatly extended the TV campaign. It added a depth to the campaign that simply could not have existed before computers. On-line, you could *visit* Gramercy Press. As the home page stated, "You're about to embark on a fascinating tour of the premises of Gramercy Press." It became a way to wander the halls, to visit the characters (you could visit Darlene Davis in the reception area) and to find out more about them. Through the various links of the Gramercy Press location, you could overhear gossip about those at Gramercy. You could read about Darlene's secret career ambitions, find out more about her background (she has an M.A. in Medieval Literature) and her hobbies. You could see the floor plans for the Gramercy Press offices to understand the spatial nature of their office politics. With each of these office visits, however, the characters would plug the benefits of network MCI business.

Most astounding of all, the home page even allowed Gramercy Press to act as a real publishing house, albeit electronic publishing. Visitors could submit stories and poems to MCI via their Gramercy Press Internet site. It then claimed to publish selected ones electronically on their links for later visitors to read and critique.

Advertisers often personify their products in their ads. By associating products with human referent systems, the products themselves often become human-like. This is part of the fetishism of commodities. Advertising reifies products—in ads, products frequently possess human qualities and encourage consumers to see them as real.

With Internet home pages such as MCI's Gramercy Press, the product is not so much reified as the campaign is. It becomes a fetishism of campaign as well as commodity. With Gramercy Press, the computer advertising and TV advertising were symbiotic: They built upon each other. The TV version created the interest and the friendliness of the campaign. The computer version added depth and a behind-the-scenes feel to the campaign. Gramercy Press, in other words, came alive on the Internet. You could visit the people you saw on TV. You could talk to them in their offices. The TV version of the campaign told viewers that Gramercy Press was a publishing house. The computer version made this a reality. You could be published by Gramercy Press.

Such a computerized strategy serves to deepen the symbols of and identification with the campaign. Darlene becomes more of a real person. But she is not a real person. She is a referent system in an ad. With the Internet advertising site, the distinctions between a real and virtual place and a human being and a referent system become blurred. The Internet has become a way for advertising to increase its commercial reality. Those who visit Gramercy Press on-line may view the TV campaign differently than before. The persuasive power of the MCI referent system may be increased because of the symbolic depth offered by the electronic space. After we visit the Gramercy Press Internet location, it is no longer a strange actress selling us MCI products, it is our friend Darlene whom we have visited.

Commercial and advertising locations will probably never force their noncommercial equivalents off the Internet. At least not literally force them out. The flashy, seductive virtual places created by advertisers, however—a fun bar, an intriguing work place, a party—could symbolically marginalize the noncommercial. These for-profit marketing home pages look really good. They are amazingly attractive. It was noted earlier that advertising through the use of Internet sites is cheaper than traditional advertising because the "media time" is free. The cost of conceiving, developing, constructing and maintaining a commercial home page, though, is not free. It can cost anywhere from $10,000 to $200,000 (Cleland, 1995). For that kind of money, advertisers expect, and are delivered, flash. They want plenty of multicolored eye candy, fun interactivity and stereophonic sounds. They want the next level of the DeKuyper bar; the next, even more humanly detailed Gramercy Press. Other nonprofessionally designed home pages may offer more substance and more valuable resources, but they do not look as good, and they could begin to pale in comparison. They draw fewer visitors to their locations. The flash of the commercial may begin to dominate, by the sheer blinding brilliance of the flash, what is on the Internet.

Where have we heard this before? Where have we seen another wild frontier medium "civilized" and flattened by the influence of commercial forces? The history of television, with its legacy as a medium with wasted potential, may provide the answer.

8

CONCLUSION

ADVERTISING during the last decade of the 20th century has taken some very well-defined forms for very well-defined reasons. The imperative of control that drives advertising and the contextual problems that modern advertising has faced and is still facing have pushed advertisers into new venues and strategies. These serve to solidify advertising's social credibility and influence, but the venues and strategies also are often not democratically sound.

The new strategies offer different versions of control for advertising. Place-based media reach desirable markets in their different gathering places and take away the markets' ability to control the message. Place-based helps to create a captive audience. Zap-less ads offer ways to recapture the control that traditional media previously offered advertising before remote controls, VCRs and premium cable channels. They re-empower the promotion message in television, newspapers and magazines. Cross promotion increases the reach that marketers may have through promotional partnerships. It allows advertisers to amplify their voices through teamwork. Sponsorship grants marketers control over cultural events, so that the events become one big advertising vehicle. Database marketing increases the effectiveness of feedback mechanisms from consumer behavior to marketer, potentially fetishizing the commodity symbols in campaigns to a greater degree than before. Advertising on the Internet socializes a new form of communication to the idea of promotion.

These phenomena are different manifestations of the same context: the flux in control that advertising has experienced. Advertising's reaction to this flux has not been to downshift to a new, lower level of social and cultural influence than the industry experienced in the past, but rather to go into overdrive. Advertising is headed in a very frightening direction. It is a direction that puts promotional discourse on a collision course with a democratic society. The new tactics provide advertising with a vehicle that has increased power, mileage, speed, off-road abilities and a siren.

It may be useful at this point to summarize the implications of advertising's search for control through its new promotional tactics. These trends do not bode well for the ideals of participatory citizenship.

The Antidemocratic Trends of New Advertising

A summary of the antidemocratic direction of new advertising would include many of the following.

New advertising is ubiquitous. The new strategies blanket our lives with advertising. Billions of impressions are the goal. Place-based advertising locates the promotional message in social locations such as schools, doctor's offices and movie theaters. Traditional media content becomes advertising in camouflaged ads. Cross promotion situates the selling message in places such as Pizza Hut and McDonald's. Operatic events, theatrical plays and amateur sports become locations for promotion via sponsorship. The cigarette brand Winston appears on TV despite a federal ban on cigarette advertising on television. Viewers see it on a local TV station's report on the Winston Cup automobile race. The Internet becomes an Adnet with advertising home pages that perhaps have signaled the beginning of advertising's dominance over the new technology. The new advertising technique surrounds society with promotional messages. Such ubiquity affects nonpromotional messages. Even if a message in one of these places is not advertising based, it must be compared to the flashy, entertainment-oriented advertising content.

New advertising is microscopic. With new promotional techniques, anything can be turned into an ad. Product placement turns movies and television programs into ads. Cross promotion thrives on the micro-commercial. Toys, soap boxes, food, credit cards or whatever item a promotional partner has to offer can be "advertisement-ized." Sponsorship, especially in sports, places the sponsor's name on just about anything in the sponsored event. The corporate logo can appear on the field, on the equipment, on the players and on the support staff. A useful Internet home page is now a carrier of advertising through sponsorship. Whenever we see these items, their promotional function shines through—sometimes above all other possible meanings. Advertising's ubiquity and microscopic nature supply it with a voice louder than just about any other single voice in this society.

New advertising limits the diversity of public messages. Some ways advertising limits diversity are small. A video game's volume is turned down in arcades that have installed a place-based system. The word *shit* is edited out of the video version of a movie to placate an angry product placer. Other ways are more significant. Channel One presents its nonadvertising content in an MTV style that is very friendly to the promotional spots and includes many "commodity-friendly" stories inspired by corporate press releases. Teachers may feel they have to beef up the entertainment quota to keep up. Whole cable channels are taken up by home shopping and infomercials. Product placement and cross promotion provide funding for certain types of movies but not others. A CBS network special for *Batman Returns* is nearly completely populated by Time Warner commercials. Cultural events with particular messages receive sponsorship, but events with other messages do not. The Smithsonian does not mention the dangers of pesticide in an exhibit on insects sponsored by Orkin (Savan, 1994). Desirable audiences receive sponsored events; other nonmarketable groups do not. Advertisers are brainstorming ways to encourage new media to be economically dependent upon advertising. The advertising dollar often allows advertising to control public messages for its own promotional interests. Even without that direct financial influence, advertisers may have symbolic impact upon institutions. Noncommercial voices often must try to match the volume and style of the commercial message in order to be heard.

New advertising may turn anything into a referent system for use in an ad. Advertising draws attention to itself and enhances its own credibility and likability by increasing the number of symbolic systems it exploits. Place-based advertising is not simply an ad-supported medium in a social place; it is also the use of the place (the school, the doctor's office) as a way to increase the credibility of the advertising message. Television advertising turns to the written word to boost its authority. Bookended ads turn ads for other products into ads for their product. Barbie's pal Skipper eats at Pizza Hut. Camouflaged ads can grab the symbolic authority of any genre of television, sometimes in such a seamless way that viewers see no makeup. Cross promotion increases the symbolic power of one product by using it as a referent system for another product. Sponsors on PBS desperately desire the association with Ken Burns and Big Bird. Both cross promotion and sponsorship allow advertisers access to Hollywood and rock-and-roll stars they would not otherwise have. Database marketing increases the marketers' ability to know with more precision what referent systems we like.

New advertising devalues other institutions. What is a result of advertising's use of such diverse referent systems? It often devalues the original institution, cultural event or social icon. School is no longer a place where advertising does not influence. Channel One has seen to that. The real news program that resembles "Movie News" is treated with suspicion by those who guess the true nature of Disney's camouflaged strategy. Joan Lunden's news authority does not seem quite the same after watching her pitch on a "Vaseline Intensive Care Update." People forget whether they heard something on an infomercial or a nonadvertising talk show. The Olympics seem a little less special now that there are official cameras and official soft drinks. Woodstock goes from a symbol of free love to a symbol of corporate love. Not-for-profit organizations devote much of their time and effort to keeping their sponsors happy. The National Breast Cancer Coalition uses a sexually provocative ad sponsored by the misogynist *Playboy*. The *New York Times* asks that you "Click our advertisers' logos" in its electronic Internet version. Media organizations sell their customers' names, addresses and personal information to maintain advertisers' interest in media.

New advertising can be deceptive or misleading. Much of new advertising is designed to deceive the consumer. It may be unclear to students whether the school endorses the selling messages on Channel One or in the corporate-sponsored video. The appearance of McDonald's in *Bye Bye Love*—was this an artistic decision or a commercial decision? Is *The Danny Bonaduce Show* a real Letterman-esque talk show or an infomercial for a memory program? Viewers may not be sure when the *Star Trek: The Next Generation* episode ended and the Hallmark commercial began. *Hot Pix* claimed to give us "the best" in entertainment, but then talked only about Blockbuster's cross-promotional partners. Sponsors use the noncommercial image of cultural events as a commercial. Direct mail addressed to us appears at our home, but we are not sure why we received it. Advertising home pages on the Internet offer a detailed personal biography for a likeable, but made-up, company receptionist.

New advertising is being normalized. The prevalence of nearly every tactic discussed in this book is increasing. For some of them, like place-based and sponsorship, the increase is evident in the growing amount of money spent on the activity by marketers. For nearly all of them, the increase is evident by *Advertising Age* or another trade journal devoting special sections to the activity or quoting an advertising executive as saying, "This trend is one of the hot trends of the next decade." The increase is evident by the key role that database marketing plays in the coordination of the trends and the rise of integrated marketing communications. And the increase is evident by the disturbing extent to which people accept the practices; it is evident by the degree to which debates are redefined and narrowed. Has being exposed to advertising in schools, in the movies, on television programs, on Barbie, in high school football games and on the Internet normalized advertising's pervasiveness for us? It seems to me that much less booing now goes on when movie theaters show blatant commercials than a few years ago. Not too long ago it would have been an issue of social discussion whether to allow an Olympic athlete to flaunt a manufacturer's logo visibly on his or her outfit. Now the controversy is *which* manufacturer should go on the outfit. The controversy is not whether to open the Olympics to sponsorship or not, but whether to open the Olympics' host city's street names to sponsorship. People will watch home shopping channels even when they do not intend to buy anything.

So now we must ask the question, "What can be done about this?" Can anything be done to stem the tide of advertising's powerful social position? I vary in my personal answer between overwhelming pessimism and the flash of optimism. The task that faces a democratic society—if it is to live up to that name—is somehow to counterbalance the above effects resulting from promotional enterprise. Advertising is an overwhelmingly powerful social vehicle; what avenues can be built to slow this vehicle down? Several routes may be chosen to do this. All have potential value, but all also have potential drawbacks.

Tactics for Counterbalancing Advertising's Antidemocratic Trends

Different scholars and social critics who have grappled with advertising's power have suggested the following avenues for resisting advertising's grip on society and culture.

The Legal Avenue. Critics of advertising have advocated placing further legal restrictions on advertising's symbolic and economic influence. Ivan Preston (1994), the author of *The Tangled Web They Weave: Truth, Falsity & Advertisers,* has explored the possibilities for legal restrictions on the use of symbols in ads. His focus is specifically on the issue of factual falsity, but it has implications for advertising's use of referent systems as well. Preston argues that advertisers should be held legally accountable not just for their explicit factual claims, but for their implied claims as well. He proposes requiring that advertisers be prepared to justify the implied claims of their ads, not only for the truth of the content but also for using the claims as a *valid* reason for buying the product. Preston points to other countries' legal restrictions on advertising for support. For example, Finland banned a McDonald's commercial that told the story of a depressed little boy, moving to a new town, who was cheered up by the new town's McDonald's. The court found that the commercial "falsely leads people to believe that a Big Mac can replace friends and ease loneliness" (Preston, 1994, p. 154).

Other critics (Bagdikian, 1992; Baker, 1994; Mazzocco, 1994) have advocated legal options for limiting advertising's economic power over media. Bagdikian (1992), for example, has argued for a progressive tax on advertising, so that if a company spends more than a certain percentage of its total budget on advertising, taxes on advertising increase. Baker (1994) has refined this idea. With newspapers, he advocates the "Tax-Advertising/Subsidize Readers Proposal," which would generate revenue from the taxation of advertising and then redirect that revenue into newspapers with a lower percentage of advertising revenue. The plan would potentially increase the influence of readers and decrease the influence of advertisers. With broadcasting, an advertising tax could help move funds from commercial media to public media, and without sponsorship strings attached. As far as advertising's specific control over media content, Baker also argues for increased laws about informing the public when advertisers have paid for such publicity as product placement and when press releases influence news stories. With broadcast media, increased restrictions on advertising influence might also help, especially by implementing laws that would restrict advertisers' advance knowledge of, and access to, particular programs. Baker also explores the possibilities of limiting advertising placement in media, perhaps creating an "advertising block" where ads are lumped together to avoid the influence of any one advertiser over a particular program.

Federal and state bodies have flirted with such restrictions, especially taxes on advertising, usually as a way to raise government revenues. Bagdikian (1992) and Baker (1994), however, acknowledge that such proposals have their drawbacks, including the difficulty of getting such laws passed. Advertisers are powerful lobbyists. When rumors floated around the industry in January 1995 that President Clinton might propose a tax on advertising to help cut the federal deficit, the advertising powers-that-be formed the Advertising Tax Coalition to lobby against it (Teinowitz, 1995). As of this writing, the tax proposal has not materialized.

The Media Avenue. Much has been made throughout this book of the degree of control that advertising has over traditional media. Indeed, advertising has much control over the content of television, newspapers, magazines and other advertising-supported media. It even has influence over *non*-ad supported media, like movies. But advertising does not have complete control. The mass media are huge, cranking out content every day. In addition, as we become a more mediated world, the media cover media-related topics more. This includes advertising. Some anomalies are bound to appear simply by the sheer volume of content. Some critical stories are bound to be part of the mix. Other reasons encourage content critical of advertising in mainstream media. Media are human endeavors. Humans sometimes break rules, even rules not in their best economic interest. This goes for humans who work in the media, too. There is also a small economic incentive for critical stories about advertising and promotion. Media also have to attract audiences, and sometimes media decision makers may feel that a program or article critical of advertisers will attract these audiences.

For these reasons, the mainstream media may occasionally be a source of advertising criticism. Many of the facts and ideas in this book were drawn from news stories in the *New York Times,* the *Los Angeles Times,* even *Sports Illustrated* and the *Wall Street Journal.* On television, programs like *Saturday Night Live, The Simpsons,* and the sharp-edged *TV Nation* ridicule advertising, often revealing the absurdity of advertisers' symbolic manipulations. The criticism is usually limited (forget socialist critiques) and is not found as often as celebrations of advertising, but it is nevertheless there.

In addition to traditional media, often much more critical messages are levied against advertisers in alternative media. Recent books, including Michael F. Jacobson and Laurie Ann Mazur's *Marketing Madness: A Survival Guide for a Consumer Society* (1995), help focus attention on promotion excesses and what might be done about them. Publications such as *The Progressive, Extra!,* and *Adbusters Quarterly* frequently publish very pointed and detailed critiques of media and advertising. *Extra!,* a magazine of leftist media criticism, has published articles critically exploring such advertising topics as Channel One (Murray, 1991) and public television sponsors ("The Private Life of Public Broadcasting," 1994). Although their circulation is low and they may be difficult to find in some small communities, such publications nevertheless offer more in-depth critiques against commercial abuses than do mainstream media.

The Organized Avenue. There are movements specifically organized against the hegemony of advertising growth and control. Among its other goals, *Adbusters Quarterly: The Journal of the Mental Environment,* published in British Columbia by the Adbusters Media Foundation, is designed to distribute tools of resistance against advertising's pervasiveness. For example, the magazine offers stickers that readers can subversively place in highly advertised locations to highlight the degree of commercialization or industrialization there. One sticker, to be placed near Channel One monitors, reads "Ad Free Zone: Our School"; another sticker, targeted for McDonald's, features the word *Grease,* with the two *es* shaped like McDonald's Golden Arches. One issue presented a "Whittle Update" that included such tips as "Write anti-

Whittle letters to your principal and school board," and "Answer classroom questions using jingles from the sponsors" ("Whittle Update," 1993).

Likewise, the Center for the Study of Commercialism, located in Washington, D.C., is a watchdog group keeping a critical eye on the powers in mass advertising and promotion. Founded in 1990, the Center is directed by Michael Jacobson and has as its goals to "on the one hand, try to cut down on this commercialism pressure and, on the other hand, encourage people to get involved in building a better society" ("Jacobson: Battling 'Excess of Marketing,' " 1991).

Occasionally, such protestors of advertising's direction are effective enough to become at least a public annoyance to advertisers. Absolut Vodka threatened *Adbusters* with a lawsuit after the magazine published parody ads of their Absolut campaign. One faux ad, for example, titled "ABSOLUT NONSENSE," contained copy that read, "Any suggestion that our advertising campaign has contributed to alcoholism, drunk driving or wife beating is absolut nonsense. No one pays any attention to advertising." In response to Absolut's threats about the fake ad, *Adbusters* distributed a press release with the headline, "Absolut Vodka Tries to Censor Magazine" (Lasn & Schmalz, 1992, p. 2). This incident received coverage in the leading trade journal for the industry, *Advertising Age* (B. Brown, 1992).

The not-for-profit Center for the Study of Commercialism and other consumer groups similarly led a very visible, if legally unsuccessful, campaign against product placement that received coverage in both the popular and trade presses (Colford & Magiera, 1991; Elliott, 1992). Although ultimately denied by the Federal Trade Commission (FTC), the Center petitioned the FTC to require on-screen disclosures when paid product placements appeared in a motion picture. Specific promotional projects may bring pointed criticism from groups. Channel One, for example, was targeted for attack by such groups as Action for Children's Television and the National Parent-Teacher Association (Kleinfield, 1989). In 1991, Louis W. Sullivan, then the Secretary of Health and Human Services, suggested to sports fans that they boycott sporting events sponsored by tobacco companies (Hilts, 1991). Activism such as this, especially with its promotional and political savvy, helps to provide a small counterbalance to the commercial wave.

But the other side has billions of dollars at its disposal and at least as much promotional and political experience. Even when such counter-hegemonic organizations have the economic clout and the promotional know-how to turn advertising's own tools against it, they are frequently not successful. Network affiliates, for example, denied *Adbusters* commercial time in Boston when that organization attempted to place several "anti-TV commercials" on the air (B. Brown, 1992).

The Boycott Avenue. Other organizations have attempted to influence advertisers through publicized and coordinated boycotts of their products. If protestors enacted such boycotts to limit the symbolic and economic power of advertising, with clear communication to the advertiser as to the purpose of the boycott, then such efforts might be valuable. These activities might send clear signals to advertisers that citizens become angry when advertising crosses the democratic line. The National Education Association, for example, investigated the possibility of withdrawing investments of teachers' pension plan monies from corporations that advertised on Channel One. This was a significant threat. In 1994, such pension plans had approximately $525 million invested in McDonald's. The NEA considered the proposal as a way to remove advertising influence, via Channel One, from schools (Mandese, 1994b).

Unfortunately, the most visible boycotts against advertisers have not worked in this way. The most visible boycotts have been, if anything, destructive to democratic society. This is because many boycotts against advertisers, paradoxically, serve to increase the social influence of advertisers. Conservative media critics—such as Donald Wildmon of the American Family Association—often target advertisers of TV programs that they find objectionable. They boycott (or threaten to boycott) the advertiser's product unless the advertiser removes its commercials from that program. Essentially, they coerce advertisers into asserting their economic control over media content. If the boycott is successful, it has increased the power of advertising over media. To stop the boycott, advertisers may withdraw funding from a program, which may send a message to the media that such programs are not wanted. A successful boycott of this kind teaches the media another lesson about the power of advertising.

Another reason that such boycotts are antidemocratic is their goal. The purpose of these boycotts is often to subtract ideas from public forums, rather than to add to them. Such boycotts serve the purpose of removing content diversity from the media. These boycotts do little to add to the range of media messages; instead they further mainstream the messages to encourage the least objectionable programming. Sometimes, in fact, such conservative organizations do not threaten boycotts only for violent or sexually explicit programs, but for programs that they simply disagree with. In 1982, for example, Wildmon wrote letters to advertisers complaining about the NBC telefilm, *Sister, Sister*. Wildmon warned advertisers against the program, calling it "Anti-Christian." The made-for-TV movie, about the lives of three African American sisters, was written by Maya Angelou (Montgomery, 1989).

The Education Avenue. This avenue is one to which I strongly subscribe. At Virginia Tech, I teach a "Media in Society" course that deals with the power of advertising. I would like to think the course helps to open some eyes, including my own. This book would not have been written if I did not feel that increased knowledge about and critical thinking toward advertising would, at least to a small degree, help decrease advertising's influence. Such educational efforts, I hope, help citizens understand the economic incentives of media, the social influence of advertising, the ideological boundaries of media and their rhetorical techniques. Most colleges offer classes in Media Literacy or Media and Society.

In elementary and high schools, however, the United States is behind the learning curve. Other countries, like Canada, Great Britain and Australia, offer courses in media literacy much sooner in the curriculum than the United States (Mazzocco, 1994). One difficulty in this country is the fight over "traditional curriculum" (i.e., reading, writing and arithmetic) versus "alternative curriculum" that would include courses that explore such issues as the economic incentives of media. Media literacy courses at the elementary school level are important, however, given the degree to which marketers directly target children. In the United States such organizations as Strategies for Media Literacy, located in San Francisco, have helped advance the visibility of media literacy in K-12 education.

The Local Avenue. Mazzocco (1994) has argued for the development of local community "media councils" to organize protests, letter-writing campaigns and educational efforts to decrease the power of corporate media and advertising influence. Although such councils may have little influence in the national arena, locally they may be able to "demand more time for community issues and concerns than is presently being offered by the local newspapers, cable systems and radio or television stations that are supposed to be 'serving' the community" (p. 146). Local media councils may encourage more participation at the local level, more access to media organizations and more reflection about the role of media and promotion in our lives.

The Personal Resistance Avenue. I noted above that there seems to be less booing when commercials are shown before movies in the theater. A good friend of mine still boos, though, with relish! Internet flaming of advertising still occurs. People still become irritated with advertising. Students have marched out of school in protest over Channel One, and community leaders have painted over offensive billboards (Jacobson & Mazur, 1995). People frequently have the ability to see when ads try to manipulate them as well as when an advertisement is being deceptive. This ties in with many of the avenues discussed above. Increased knowledge of advertising's activities as learned through the media or through education, for example, may sensitize individuals to advertising's wrongdoings and may prompt calls to action.

In one sense, advertising lends itself to such critical viewing and, therefore, to small personal acts of protest. Because advertising often uses implied arguments rather than explicit arguments, advertising may lend itself to alternative, or even oppositional, interpretations of its message. As noted earlier, ads that do not specifically target us may be viewed with a distance and therefore with a critical eye. Many other ads are simply poorly constructed, and their attempts at manipulation are obvious.

Unfortunately, R. Goldman (1992) argues that especially competent advertising has developed ways to co-opt alternative interpretations of their messages and even prevent them from occurring. As he observes,

> More than any other mass media form, ads are shaped to accomplish "preferred" interpretations. Advertisers employ rationalized formats to delimit fields of possible meanings, privileging certain interpretations over others. Ad formats consist of framing procedures which select our (and, hence, exclude as well) ways of seeing. (p. 79)

Advertising would not spend the amount of money it does if it did not feel that it could often influence people. Advertisers have spent millions to refine and expand the selling process. R. Goldman's quote addresses the result of that work. Also, because so much of the economic influence of advertising happens "behind the scenes," even the most critical viewer may be unaware of advertising's full effect upon a particular program or article. A final problem with a purely individual-receiver solution is that advertising's influences are often structural in nature. To solve advertising's economic abuses would require a structural solution (like the legal solution presented above) rather than a perceptual one.

For creative human beings, however, criticism and resistance of advertising are possible. The above avenues are designed to enhance that resistance. To what degree will these resistant avenues win out against the power of advertising? Time will tell, of course, but it appears that the promotional trends discussed here are not part of an unfortunate historical bubble but part of a longer trend. I do not believe that they will go away on their own. Advertising has become an octopus, reaching out to as many different sectors of society and culture as it can. Some sectors are being strangled by the tentacles. Slapping the tentacles away will be extremely difficult; cutting the tentacles off, at least in the current promotional zeitgeist, may be nearly impossible. But given the democratic cost of the tentacles' reach, the attempt is worth the effort.

REFERENCES

Acts of contrition. (1991, January). *Harper's Magazine,* p. 40.

Ad time giveaways. (1993, July 12). *Advertising Age,* p. 16.

Advertising everywhere! (1992, December). *Consumer Reports,* pp. 752-755.

Aho, D. (1994, July 25). Industry outlook is cautiously optimistic. *Advertising Age,* p. 23.

Alaimo, D. (1992, November 9). Sell-through's future tied to tie-ins. *Supermarket News,* p. 23.

Alter, J. (1989, May 22). The era of the big blur. *Newsweek,* pp. 73, 75, 76.

Artzt, E. L. (1994, May 23). P&G's Artzt: TV advertising in danger. *Advertising Age,* pp. 24, 40, 42.

Aufderheide, P. (1991). Public television and the public sphere. *Critical Studies in Mass Communication, 8*(2), 168-183.

Baker, C. E. (1994). *Advertising and a democratic press.* Princeton, NJ: Princeton University Press.

Bagdikian, B. H. (1992). *The media monopoly* (4th ed). Boston: Beacon.

Bailey, D. (1992, June 8). What's so special. *Mediaweek,* pp. 18-20.

Banks, A. (1987, January). Clutter in the era of control. *Marketing and Media Decisions,* pp. 51-52.

Banks, A. (1992, November 30). How to assess new place-based media. *Advertising Age,* p. 36.

Barker, R. (1991, April 22). Tubular marketing, dude. *Business Week,* p. 105.

Barnouw, E. (1966). *A tower in Babel: A history of broadcasting in the United States to 1933.* New York: Oxford University Press.

Barnouw, E. (1970). *The image empire: A history of broadcasting in the United States from 1953.* New York: Oxford University Press.

Barnouw, E. (1978). *The sponsor: Notes on a modern potentate.* New York: Oxford University Press.

Barry, A. M. (1989). Advertising in the classroom: The controversy over *Channel One. Journal of Visual Literacy, 9*(2), 35-65.

Bates, S. (1989, October 16). First, this message. *The New Republic,* pp. 16, 18.

Bayor, L. (1990, July 23). Atlanta schools' phones get ads. *Advertising Age,* p. 17.

Bayor, L. (1993, January 18). '96 Olympics city signs Visa to controversial deal. *Advertising Age,* pp. 1, 53.

Beck, A. (1990). But where can we find a Heineken?: Commercial sponsorship of the arts on Merseyside. *The Political Quarterly, 61*(4), 393-401.

Bell, D. (1973). *The coming of post-industrial society.* New York: Basic Books.

Benenson, L. (1992, May 4). The data chase. *Adweek,* pp. 6-7.

Beniger, J. R. (1986). *The control revolution: Technological and economic origins of the information society.* Cambridge, MA: Harvard University Press.

The Berkeley Pop Culture Project. (1991). *The whole pop catalog.* New York: Avon.

Berry, J. (1994, September 5). Database marketing. *Business Week,* pp. 56-62.

Big ads back on Super Bowl. (1993, January 18). *Advertising Age,* pp. 1, 52.

Bogart, L. (1994, March/April). Who pays for the media? *Journal of Advertising Research,* pp. 11-18.

Bossy sponsors. (1994, April 30). *The Economist,* p. 98.

Bowes, E. (1992, December 14). Coffee couple's story to percolate in book. *Advertising Age,* p. 6.

Bretl, D. J., & Cantor, J. (1988). The portrayal of men and women in U.S. television commercials: A recent content analysis and trends over 15 years. *Sex Roles, 18*(9/10), 595-609.

Brodie, J., & Robins, J. M. (1993, May 24). TV's year of living cautiously. *Variety,* pp. 1, 65.

Brodinsky, B. (1993, March). How "new" will the "new" Whittle American school be?: A case study in privatization. *Phi Delta Kappan,* pp. 540-543, 546, 547.

Brooks, T., & Marsh, E. (1992). *The complete directory to prime time network TV shows: 1946-present.* New York: Ballantine.

Brown, B. (1992, July 27). Magazine's parody makes marketer Absolut-ely mad. *Advertising Age,* p. 3.

Brown, K. (1990, June 11). Marketing through flop or fame. *Adweek,* pp. 1, 6.

Brown, K. (1991, October 7). Promotions may be studio's ticket. *Adweek,* p. 6.

Brown, P. B. (1992, September 1). Eternally yours, Barbie. *Financial World,* p. 36.

Browning, E. S. (1992, April 1). Disney gets many helping hands to sell the new Euro Disney. *Wall Street Journal,* p. B4.

Brunelli, R. (1993, August 16). The big event gets bigger. *Mediaweek,* p. 9.

Brunelli, R., & Kiley, D. (1992, July 13). Clutter bomb. *Adweek,* pp. 1, 5.

Bryant, A. (1993, March 30). With product placements winning fans, a comedy network tailors some broadcasts for sponsors. *New York Times,* p. D23.

Buchanan, R. (1992, August 10). Higher, faster, farther. *Adweek*, pp. 20-21.

Buckeye ad bucks? (1991, June 10). *Advertising Age*, p. 50.

Burgi, M. (1992, August 23). Comedy Central, NBC smile over new pact. *Mediaweek*, p. 3.

Busch, A. M. (1994, August 22-September 4). "Killers" doesn't go better with Coke. *Variety*, pp. 7, 8.

Cable penetration reaches 65% of all television homes. (1993, February 22). *Advertising Age*, p. C4.

Call it classic-aid. (1992, March 30). *Advertising Age*, p. 50.

Channel One's education plan. (1992, August 17). *Adweek*, p. 24.

Cleland, K. (1994, December 12). Chiat goes from virtual to interactive. *Advertising Age*, p. 22.

Cleland, K. (1995, February 13). Three 20-somethings and the Web. *Advertising Age*, p. 20.

Clutter suffers zap attacks. (1992, March 30). *Advertising Age*, p. 38.

Coen, R. J. (1994, May 2). Ad gain of 5.2% in '93 marks downturn's end. *Advertising Age*, p. 4.

Coen, R. J. (1995, May 8). More gains foreseen for '95 ad spending. *Advertising Age*, p. 36.

Colastosti, C. (1993, June). Going private. *The Progressive*, pp. 29-31.

Colford, S. W. (1990, December 3). Lawsuit drills Fox, Cato. *Advertising Age*, pp. 3, 57.

Colford, S. W. (1991, November 11). Tobacco sponsorships hit by FTC. *Advertising Age*, p. 58.

Colford, S. W. (1992, April 6). Cable losing grip on infomercials. *Advertising Age*, p. S6.

Colford, S. W. (1993a, January 25). Transition team report: Don't change the FTC. *Advertising Age*, pp. 1, 43.

Colford, S. W. (1993b, February 8). Admen beware, zapper is here. *Advertising Age*, p. 12.

Colford, S. W. (1993c, February 15). States take the lead from Congress on privacy. *Advertising Age*, p. 36.

Colford, S. W., & Magiera, M. (1991, June 10). Products in movies: How big a deal? *Advertising Age*, p. 12.

Coming to your ATM screen: Ads. (1993, June 14). *Advertising Age*, p. 47.

Cook, G. (1992). *The discourse of advertising*. New York: Routledge & Kegan Paul.

Cooper, J. (1993, May 24). Infomercials welcomed back into ad fold. *Broadcasting & Cable*, p. 69.

Cortez, J. P. (1992a, February 3). Kmart happy with holidays. *Advertising Age*, p. 28.

Cortez, J. P. (1992b, March 30). Ads become sitcoms. *Advertising Age*, p. 2.

Cortez, J. P. (1992c, March 30). Marketing execs itch to fill the right niche. *Advertising Age*, pp. S2, S3, S40.

Cortez, J. P. (1992d, May 18). Ads head for bathroom. *Advertising Age*, p. 24.

Cortez, J. P. (1992e, August 17). Media pioneers try to corral on-the-go consumers. *Advertising Age*, p. 25.

Cortez, J. P. (1992f, October 12). Growing pains can't stop the new kid on the ad block. *Advertising Age*, pp. S28, S30.

Cortez, J. P. (1993, May 10). Taco Bell logs odd hours to lure Xers in new ads. *Advertising Age*, pp. 3, 46.

Cray, D. (1990, September 3). Not in the same boat: Firm sets sails to sell ads. *Adweek*, p. 4.

Crumley B., & Wentz, L. (1992, March 30). Tie-ins add magic to Euro Disney. *Advertising Age*, p. 33.

Cuneo, A. Z. (1993, September 29). Sequent seeks new edge via TV show. *Advertising Age*, p. 31.

Cuneo, A. Z. (1994, August 29). With an "i" toward music lovers. *Advertising Age*, p. 18.

Curran, J. (1991). Mass media and democracy: A reappraisal. In J. Curran & M. Gurevitch (Eds.), *Mass media in society* (pp. 82-117). New York: Routledge & Kegan Paul.

Daly, S. (1992, July 31). Batlash. *Entertainment Weekly*, pp. 32-35.

Danna, S. R. (1992). Conventional and alternative advertising media: Two views, two purposes. In S. R. Danna (Ed.), *Advertising and popular culture: Studies in variety and versatility* (pp. 3-21). Bowling Green, OH: Bowling Green State University Popular Press.

Davidson, M. (1992). *The consumerist manifesto: Advertising in postmodern times*. New York: Routledge & Kegan Paul.

Davis, R. A. (1993a, January 25). Shoppers, see the special on aisle 11's floor. *Advertising Age*, p. 8.

Davis, R. A. (1993b, April 5). Konica turns on to AMC. *Advertising Age*, p. 31.

De Lisser, E. (1994, April 13). Newspapers avoid naming names. *Wall Street Journal*, p. B1.

DeNitto, E. (1994a, July 25). Citrus exits Limbaugh, NOW sees still more ad villains. *Advertising Age*, p. 1.

DeNitto, E. (1994b, August 8). Make peace, make love, make money. *Advertising Age*, pp. 13, 14.

Donaton, S. (1991, April 29). "Journal" goes to high school for new readers. *Advertising Age*, p. 15.

Donaton, S. (1992a, March 9). Advertorials "are like a drug." *Advertising Age*, p. S16.

Donaton, S. (1992b, March 23). McDonald's adds publishing to menu. *Advertising Age*, pp. 1, 45.

Donaton, S. (1992c, August 17). Whittle wrestles to control his four-headed Hydra. *Advertising Age*, pp. 32-33.

Donaton, S. (1993a, January 11). Six Flags woos nat'l advertisers. *Advertising Age*, p. 13.

Donaton, S. (1993b, February 1). The media wakes up to Generation X. *Advertising Age*, pp. 16-17.

Donaton, S. (1993c, February 22). Flaws ax Checkout Channel. *Advertising Age*, pp. 2, 42.

Donaton, S. (1993d, March 1). Newsstand operator plans place-based network. *Advertising Age*, p. 37.

Donaton, S. (1993e, June 7). Publishers find gold in databases. *Advertising Age*, p. 27.

Donaton, S. (1993f, August 2). QVC ups the ante, and its image. *Advertising Age*, pp. 1, 26.

Donaton, S. (1994a, September 26). Prodigy to scrap "intrusive" ads in redesign. *Advertising Age*, p. 14.

Donaton, S. (1994b, December 19). Time Warner Orlando net intriguing, limited. *Advertising Age*, p. 37.

Donaton, S., & Fitzgerald, K. (1990, May 14). New media concepts grow. *Advertising Age*, p. 4.

Ducoffe, R. H., & Smith, S. J. (1993). Mergers and acquisitions among advertising agencies. In A. Alexander, J. Owers, & R. Carveth (Eds.), *Media economics: Theory and practice* (pp. 309-330). Hillsdale, NJ: Lawrence Erlbaum.

Dyer, G. (1982). *Advertising as communication*. London: Methuen.

Elliott, S. (1991, August 2). Bud Bowl's preseason has begun. *New York Times*, p. D5.

Elliott, S. (1992, September 2). Product placement is under new attack. *New York Times*, p. D4.

Elliott, S. (1993, May 3). The media business. *New York Times*, p. 8.

Elmer-Dewitt, P. (1993, April 12). Take a trip into the future on the electronic super-highway. *Time*, pp. 50-58.

Emery "discovers" database. (1984, October 25). *Advertising Age,* p. 6.

Engelhardt, T. (1986). The shortcake strategy. In T. Gitlin (Ed.), *Watching television* (pp. 68-110). New York: Pantheon.

Entertainment marketing. (1992, November 2). *Adweek,* p. 57.

Ewen, S. (1976). *Captains of consciousness: Advertising and the social roots of the consumer culture.* New York: McGraw-Hill.

Ewen, S. (1988). *All consuming images: The politics of style in contemporary culture.* New York: Basic Books.

Fahey, A. (1990, June 18). Advertising media crowd into aisles. *Advertising Age,* p. 18.

Fahey, A. (1991a, March 25). $75M World Cup plan gives global exposure. *Advertising Age,* pp. 3, 45.

Fahey, A. (1991b, April 22). Turner's new gamble. *Advertising Age,* pp. 3, 44.

Fahey, A., & Hume, S. (1991a, February 18). Marketers team in time of trouble. *Advertising Age,* p. 36.

Fahey, A., & Hume, S. (1991b, June 17). Turner, BK huddle. *Advertising Age,* pp. 2, 48.

Fannin, R. (1988, September). Gold rings or smoke rings. *Marketing & Media Decisions,* pp. 64-67, 70.

Fanning, D. (1989, April 17). The return of "the sponsor." *Forbes,* p. 136.

Farhi, P. (1992, February 23). Hard news or soft sell? *Washington Post,* pp. H1, H4.

Farhi, P. (1993, June 8). Trucker TV hits a dead end but promises to roll again. *Washington Post,* p. D1.

Farhi, P. (1994, July 5). Disney blurs the line between ballyhoo and broadcasting. *Washington Post,* p. E1, E2.

Fawcett, A. W. (1993, July 12). Free TV "ad plugs" are on the rise. *Advertising Age,* p. 21.

Fisher, C. (1991, February 18). Wal-Mart's way. *Advertising Age,* pp. 3, 48.

Fisher, C. (1992, August 10). "USA Today" Sky Radio preparing for takeoff. *Advertising Age,* p. 26.

Fisher, C. (1993a, April 26). Databases fill the need in targeted counterattack. *Advertising Age,* p. S12.

Fisher, C. (1993b, April 26). Help wanted: Newspapers call to arms in fight over classifieds. *Advertising Age,* pp. S1-S2.

Fitzgerald, K. (1993, May 24). Kmart to test in-store TV channel. *Advertising Age,* p. 8.

Fitzgerald, K. (1994a, August 29). Hallmark cast for new role. *Advertising Age,* p. 12.

Fitzgerald, K. (1994b, October 17). Brands wed marketing plans. *Advertising Age,* p. 30.

Flamers on the Internet. (1994, May 2). *Advertising Age,* p. 24.

Fletcher, J. E. (1993). The syndication marketplace. In A. Alexander, J. Owers, & R. Carveth (Eds.), *Media economics: Theory and practice* (pp. 283-307). Hillsdale, NJ: Lawrence Erlbaum.

Fox, S. (1984). *The mirror makers: A history of American advertising and its creators.* New York: William Morrow.

Fraser, N. (1993). Rethinking the public sphere: A contribution to the critique of actually existing democracy. In B. Robbins (Ed.), *The phantom public sphere* (pp. 1-32). Minneapolis: University of Minnesota Press.

Garfield, B. (1992, November 9). It's amazing!!! So call now!!! *Advertising Age,* p. 44.

Garfield, B. (1993, July 26). One more cup of coffee for that perky couple. *Advertising Age,* p. 40.

Gitlin, T. (1985). *Inside prime time.* New York: Pantheon.

Gellene, D. (1989, January 29). Forever young. *Los Angeles Times,* pp. D1, D4.

Gelman, M. (1984, May 17). Fewer sponsors—But greater impact. *Advertising Age*, p. M6.

Gerbner, G., Gross, L., Morgan, M., & Signorielli, N. (1986). Living with television: The dynamics of the cultivation process. In J. Bryant & D. Zillmann (Eds.), *Perspectives on media effects* (pp. 17-40). Hillsdale, NJ: Lawrence Erlbaum.

Goerne, C. (1992, May 11). Funding losses, competition force PBS to pitch itself as a "marketing company." *Marketing News*, pp. 1, 16.

Golding, P., & Murdock, G. (1991). Culture, communications, and political economy. In J. Curran & M. Gurevitch (Eds.), *Mass media and society* (pp. 15-32). London: Edward Arnold.

Goldberger, P. (1994, October 5). Philip Morris calls in I.O.U.'s in the arts. *New York Times*, pp. A1, C14.

Goldman, K. (1992, November 3). Network targets drivers at truck stop. *Wall Street Journal*, pp. B1, B6.

Goldman, K. (1994a, April 28). Three place-based TV supplies tune in. *Wall Street Journal*, p. B6.

Goldman, K. (1994b, October 5). Grey looks back to the future with plans for TV production. *Wall Street Journal*, p. B9.

Goldman, K. (1995, March 6). You will soon see too much of Casper, Pocahontas, Batman. *Wall Street Journal*, pp. B1, B7.

Goldman, R. (1992). *Reading ads socially*. New York: Routledge & Kegan Paul.

Greenberg, B. S., & Brand, J. E. (1993). Television news and advertising in schools: The "Channel One" controversy. *Journal of Communication, 43*(1), 143-151.

Grimm, M. (1992a, April 6). The Dream Team magnet. *Adweek's Marketing Week*, pp. 28-29.

Grimm, M. (1992b, August 24). Chrysler, MCI back new tours. *Brandweek*, p. 9.

Grimm, M. (1992c, August 24). Pizza Hut, Disney team for tie-in. *Brandweek*, p. 32.

Grimm, M. (1992d, September 7). McTed offensive and fries to stay. *Brandweek*, pp. 12-13, 16.

Grimm, M. (1992e, November 2). Kevin dances with Ronald in Noel promo. *Brandweek*, p. 2.

Grimm, M. (1993, September 20). Pizza Hut cooks up dino promo. *Brandweek*, p. 12.

Habermas, J. (1989). *The structural transformation of the public sphere*. Cambridge, UK: Polity.

Hallin, D. (1992). Sound bite news: Television coverage of elections, 1968-1988. *Journal of Communication, 42*(2), 5-24.

Hallmark, J. R., Mangum, A., & Worthington, D. (1993, November). *Program length commercials: The persuasive effect of "infomercials."* Paper presented at the meeting of the Speech Communication Association, Miami Beach, FL.

Hammer, J. (1991, May 27). Pages and pages of pain. *Newsweek*, pp. 39, 41.

Hart, A. (1991). *Understanding the media: A practical guide*. New York: Routledge & Kegan Paul.

Harty, S. (1989, December-1990, January). U.S. corporations: Still pitching after all these years. *Educational Leadership, 47*(4), 77-78.

Hayakawa, S. I. (1972). *Language in thought and action*. New York: Harcourt, Brace, Jovanovich.

Hilts, P. J. (1991, April 11). Sullivan would end tie of sports and tobacco. *New York Times*, p. B13.

Hinsberg, P. (1992, March 30). Infomercials shift onto mainstream airwaves. *Adweek*, p. 2.

Horovitz, B. (1990, September 22). Sun, surf, sand—and ads. *Los Angeles Times,* pp. D1, D4.

Horovitz, B. (1994, January 4). The sponsorship game. *Los Angeles Times,* D1, D6.

Horton, C., & Serafin, R. (1992, March 16). Volvo fine-tuning infomercial. *Advertising Age,* p. 2.

How to avoid being zapped. (1984, April 30). *Broadcasting,* p. 130.

Hume, S. (1992a, March 23). Sponsorships up 18%. *Advertising Age,* p. 4.

Hume, S. (1992b, June 1). Blockbuster means more than video. *Advertising Age,* p. 4.

Hume, S. (1992c, June 1). Marketers rally around school sponsorships. *Advertising Age,* p. 32.

Infomercial network launched. (1991, September 30). *Marketing News,* p. 21.

Jacobson: Battling "excess of marketing." (1991, June 10). *Advertising Age,* p. 12.

Jacobson, M. F., & Mazur, L. A. (1995). *Marketing madness: A survival guide for a consumer society.* Boulder, CO: Westview.

Jamieson, K. H., & Campbell, K. K. (1992). *The interplay of influence: Mass media and their publics in news, advertising, politics* (3rd ed.). Belmont, CA: Wadsworth.

Jensen, E. (1994, June 1). PBS may ease rules as way to increase corporate support. *Wall Street Journal,* pp. A3, A9.

Jensen, J. (1993a, May 31). KFC joins Foreman for his boxing finale. *Advertising Age,* p. 46.

Jensen, J. (1993b, August 30). NFL, star players work as team for sponsors' ads. *Advertising Age,* p. 4.

Jensen, J. (1993c, December 6). High school "Olympics" seek big-time sponsors. *Advertising Age,* pp. 1, 40.

Jensen, J. (1994a, February 7). Smith sets out to score integrated marketing deals. *Advertising Age,* pp. 3, 51.

Jensen, J. (1994b, July 4). Bill Holford, Mighty Ducks. *Advertising Age,* p. S-28.

Jensen, J. (1994c, October 24). NFL plans rush to Hollywood. *Advertising Age,* p. 16.

Jensen, J. (1995, January 23). Chrysler enlisting partners for sports. *Advertising Age,* p. 3.

Jhally, S. (1987). *The codes of advertising: Fetishism and the political economy of meaning in the consumer society.* New York: Routledge & Kegan Paul.

Johnson, B. (1992a, May 4). Bank hypes new ad medium: Itself. *Advertising Age,* p. 18.

Johnson, B. (1992b, September 14). What's next? A brew-haha? *Advertising Age,* p. 4.

Johnson B., & Mandese, J. (1992, February 3). Nestle, ABC strike Taster's Choice deal. *Advertising Age,* p. 3.

Judson, S. H. (1994, April 3). Maestro, hand me a sales brochure. *New York Times,* p. F11.

Just don't try to lubricate your skis with the stuff. (1992, February 3). *Adweek,* p. 16.

Kauchak Smith, T. (1993, May 24). Top-rated shows mean less now. *Advertising Age,* p. S10.

Kellner, D. (1990). Advertising and consumer culture. In J. Downing, A. Mohammadi, & A. Sreborny-Mohammadi (Eds.), *Questioning the media: A critical introduction* (pp. 242- 254). Newbury Park, CA: Sage.

Kelly, J. (1991, September 16). Out-of-home builds. *Advertising Age,* p. 28.

Kelly, K. J. (1994, August 8). Flops fail to derail place-based. *Advertising Age,* p. 12.

Kern-Foxworth, M. (1994). *Aunt Jemima, Uncle Ben, and Rastus: Blacks in advertising yesterday, today, and tomorrow.* Westport, CT: Greenwood.

Kilburn, D. (1991, February 25). Japanese VCRs cut out ads. *Advertising Age,* p. 2.

Kim, J. B. (1993a, February 15). Databases open doors for retailers. *Advertising Age,* p. 38.

Kim, J. B. (1993b, April 19). Step aside for the 500-channel elephant. *Advertising Age,* p. S2.

Kleinfield, N. R. (1989, March 19). In search of the next medium. *New York Times,* pp. F1, F7.

Kleinfield, N. R. (1991, May 19). What is Chris Whittle teaching our children? *New York Times Magazine*, pp. 32, 46, 49, 79.

Kubey, R. (1992). A critique of *No sense of place* and the homogenization theory of Joshua Meyrowitz. *Communication Theory, 2*(3), 259-270.

Kunkel, D. (1988). From a raised eyebrow to a turned back: The FCC and children's product-related programming. *Journal of Communication, 38*(4), 90-108.

Kostyra, R. (1984, March). Zapping—A modest proposal. *Marketing & Media Decisions,* pp. 94-96.

Kunkler, S. (1992, December 14). This is the place (-based). *Advertising Age,* p. 24.

Kurtz, H. (1993, April 18). Read all about it. *Washington Post Magazine,* pp. 8-11, 24-25.

Lasek, A. (1994, January 10). Infomercials help shape home fitness. *Advertising Age,* p. S-6.

Lasn, K., & Schmalz, B. (1992, Summer/Fall). Absolut debacle. *Adbusters Quarterly,* p. 2.

Lawrence, J. (1993, January 25). Travel agents to carry line of ad-backed videos. *Advertising Age,* p. 12.

Lawrence, J. (1994, March 14). Belted by ad messages. *Advertising Age,* p. 30.

Lawson, L. (1988). Advertisements masquerading as news in turn-of-the-century American periodicals. *American Journalism, 5*(2), 81-96.

Learning to speak the interactive speak. (1994, July 25). *Advertising Age,* pp. S18, S19.

Lee, M. A., & Solomon, N. (1991). *Unreliable sources: A guide to detecting bias in news media.* New York: Lyle Stuart.

Lees, C. (1992, May 24). Arts diary. *Sunday (London) Times,* pp. G6-G7.

Lefton, T. (1992a, August 17). GE clout comes to crowded card market. *Brandweek,* p. 3.

Lefton, T. (1992b, October 5). Mastercard's new wheels. *Brandweek,* pp. 17-20.

Lefton, T. (1993, August 23). "Hillbillies" partners hope to strike it rich. *Brandweek,* p. 2.

Leiss, W., Kline, S., & Jhally, S. (1990). *Social communication in advertising: Persons, products and images of well-being.* New York: Routledge & Kegan Paul.

Lev, M. (1990, April 24). Do people mind theater commercials? *New York Times,* p. D19.

Levin, G. (1992a, June 8). Database draws fevered interest. *Advertising Age,* p. 31.

Levin, G. (1992b, August 3). Endorsements cause dilemma for Dream Team. *Advertising Age,* pp. 1, 28.

Levin, G. (1992c, November 9). NBA is real pro in scoring sponsorships. *Advertising Age,* pp. 3, 41.

Levin, G. (1993a, March 15). AmEx, CAA huddle on event deals. *Advertising Age,* p. 4.

Levin, G. (1993b, May 24). Big marketers will reshape infomercials. *Advertising Age,* p. 46.

Levin, G. (1993c, June 21). Sponsors put pressure on for accountability. *Advertising Age,* pp. S1, S4.

Levin, G. (1994a, March 28). MasterCard grabs share with co-branded cards. *Advertising Age,* p. 3.

Levin, G. (1994b, August 15). Big brands hit infomercial circuit. *Advertising Age,* p. 25.

Levin, G., & Mandese, J. (1994, November 7). Joe O'Donnell betting on 24-hour infomercial net. *Advertising Age,* p. 64.

Lewyn, M. (1994, September 5). You can run, but it's tough to hide from marketers. *Business Week,* pp. 60-61.

Lieberman, D. (1992, February 22-28). Fake news. *TV Guide,* pp. 10-14, 16, 26.

Liese, J. (1992, May 25). Marketers aiming for Olympic slam-dunk. *Advertising Age,* pp. 1, 51.

Lipman, J. (1989, November 14). Comic books put ads in the picture. *Wall Street Journal*, pp. B1, B6.

Lipman, J. (1991, July 30). Hurt by ad downturn, more magazines use favorable articles to woo sponsors. *Wall Street Journal*, pp. B1, B6.

Lipman, J. (1992a, February 11). Product plugs dot Olympic landscape. *Wall Street Journal*, p. B2.

Lipman, J. (1992b, May 11). ABC tests "place-based media" at Penney. *Wall Street Journal*, p. B6.

Lister, D. (1993, March 24). When the corporate customer cracks the whip. *The Independent*, p. 14.

Loro, L. (1992, December 7). Bell to roll out "sitcommercial." *Advertising Age*, p. 47.

Lovdal, L. T. (1989). Sex role messages in television commercials: An update. *Sex Roles*, 21(11/12), 715-724.

Lubell, E. (1990, April 25). Corporations and art: They mean business! *Variety*, pp. 112, 118.

Lublin, J. S. (1990, October 1). More charities reach for corporate sponsorship. *Wall Street Journal*, pp. B1, B4.

Lucas, J. A. (1992). *Future of the Olympic Games*. Champaign, IL: Human Kinetics Publishers.

Magazines set ad page record in '94. (1995, January 18). *Advertising Age*, p. 2.

Magiera, M. (1990a, October 8). Studio ad bans aid in-theater media. *Advertising Age*, p. 72.

Magiera, M. (1990b, October 15). Disney plugs up new film. *Advertising Age*, p. 8.

Magiera, M. (1991, March 25). Flintstones tie-ins set for summer. *Advertising Age*, p. 49.

Magiera, M. (1992a, April 13). Jake works out for marketing. *Advertising Age*, p. 16.

Magiera, M. (1992b, May 4). Hollywood zeros in. *Advertising Age*, p. 18.

Magiera, M. (1992c, June 1). "Batman Returns"—Licensees cheer. *Advertising Age*, pp. 1, 29.

Magiera, M. (1992d, September 14). Movie success goes beyond box office. *Advertising Age*, p. 20.

Magiera, M. (1993a, February 8). Kids, or young adult? Tie-ins can be PG-13. *Advertising Age*, p. S14.

Magiera, M. (1993b, December 13). On-screen ads unspool new tactics. *Advertising Age*, p. 10.

Magiera, M. (1994, March 28). Disney units energize "Ducks," "Lion." *Advertising Age*, p. 13.

Maisel, R. (1973). The decline of the mass media. *Public Opinion Quarterly*, 37(2), 159-170.

Mandese, J. (1991a, June 3). CBS seeks repeat of promotional hit. *Advertising Age*, p. 4.

Mandese, J. (1991b, September 23). Fight looms over TV clutter. *Advertising Age*, p. 1, 42.

Mandese, J. (1992a, May 4). TV clutter: Who has the most, who's hurt the worst. *Advertising Age*, p. 18.

Mandese, J. (1992b, June 1). ABC is exposed as clutter culprit in BBDO study. *Advertising Age*, p. 40.

Mandese, J. (1992c, July 20). "Blossom" promotion flowers at NBC, Target. *Advertising Age*, p. 4.

Mandese, J. (1992d, August 3). E!, UA link for in-theater ads. *Advertising Age*, p. 29.

Mandese, J. (1992e, August 10). GE helps NBC score Olympic ad sellout. *Advertising Age*, pp. 1, 36.

Mandese, J. (1992f, August 17). CBS gives lesson in reaching college kids. *Advertising Age*, p. 38.

Mandese, J. (1992h, September 7). Advertisers vote for "Murphy Brown." *Advertising Age,* pp. 3, 36.

Mandese, J. (1992i, November 30). CBS, cable network link to plug same show. *Advertising Age,* p. 8.

Mandese, J. (1992j, December 21). TV's next wave. *Advertising Age,* pp. 3, 28.

Mandese, J. (1993a, January 4). Nets put casts to work on TV ads. *Advertising Age,* pp. 3, 35.

Mandese, J. (1993b, January 18). Stations change their thinking on infomercials. *Advertising Age,* p. 39.

Mandese, J. (1993c, March 1). Big 3 start thinking big. *Advertising Age,* pp. 1, 46.

Mandese, J. (1993d, March 1). Blockbuster, CBS team up. *Advertising Age,* p. 8.

Mandese, J. (1993e, April 26). Big advertisers link to fund TV shows. *Advertising Age,* p. 2.

Mandese, J. (1993f, July 19). NBC and Kellogg co-star. *Advertising Age,* pp. 1, 32.

Mandese, J. (1993g, September 6). "Home Improvement" wins $ race. *Advertising Age,* pp. 3, 26.

Mandese, J. (1993h, September 13). New way to fund a TV show. *Advertising Age,* p. 60.

Mandese, J. (1993i, September 20). Nancy Shalek has a big idea. *Advertising Age,* pp. 22, 24, 46.

Mandese, J. (1993j, October 4). Not ad, not show—It's blurmercial. *Advertising Age,* p. 16.

Mandese, J. (1993k, November 15). Measuring place-based media. *Advertising Age,* p. 33.

Mandese, J. (1993l, November 22). Glut of rival brands worsens ad clutter. *Advertising Age,* p. 28.

Mandese, J. (1994a, July 4). Alan Cohen, NBC TV. *Advertising Age,* p. S-26.

Mandese, J. (1994b, July 11). Whittle suffers new woes as NEA targets sponsors. *Advertising Age,* p. 40.

Mandese, J. (1994c, September 5). NBC entertains new viewer hook. *Advertising Age,* p. 8.

Mandese, J. (1994d, September 19). "Seinfeld" rates soar. *Advertising Age,* pp. 1, 6.

Mandese, J., & Fahey, A. (1992, March 17). Sponsors lash Olympic ambushers. *Advertising Age,* pp. 3, 55.

Mann, C. (1992, April). Death in the afternoon. *Washington Journalism Review,* pp. 36-41.

Manning, R. (1987, December 28). The selling of the Olympics. *Newsweek,* pp. 40-41.

Marchand, R. (1985). *Advertising the American dream: Making way for modernity, 1920-1940.* Berkeley: University of California Press.

Martin, D. (1991, July 21). How did the subways get so full of such depressing ads? *New York Times,* p. E6.

Martin, G. L., & Mandese, J. (1993, October 4). Olympics may package sponsorship, ad deals. *Advertising Age,* p. 4.

Mattel planning Barbie expansion. (1991, February 8). *New York Times,* p. D3.

Mattelart, A. (1991). *Advertising international: The privatisation of public space.* New York: Routledge & Kegan Paul.

Mayer, M. (1991). *Whatever happened to Madison Avenue?* Boston: Little, Brown.

Mazzocco, D. W. (1994). *Networks of power: Corporate TV's threat to democracy.* Boston: South End.

McAllister, M. P. (1992). Recombinant television genres and *Doogie Howser, MD. Journal of Popular Film & Television, 20*(3), 61-69.

McAllister, M. P. (1993). "What did you advertise with the war, daddy?": Using the Persian Gulf War as a referent system in advertising. In R. E. Denton, Jr. (Ed.), *The media and the Persian Gulf War* (pp. 213-233). Westport, CT: Praeger.

McAvoy, K. (1994, December 19). Public broadcasters go on offensive. *Broadcasting & Cable*, pp. 48, 49.

McCarroll, T. (1992, March 30). Grocery-cart wars. *Time*, p. 49.

McCarthy, M. J. (1991, April 24). Keeping careful score on sports tie-ins. *Wall Street Journal*, pp. B1, B5.

McCullaugh, J. (1992a, June 6). More vid cos. walking down aisle. *Billboard*, pp. 52, 55.

McCullaugh, J. (1992b, July 11). Nestle sweetens "Wayne's World" promo picture with $5 rebate. *Billboard*, pp. 47, 51.

McManus, J. (1994, February 28). Did the shoe fit? *Mediaweek*, p. 12.

McNeely, M., & Marshall, S. (1992, January 13). Thumb wrestling. *Adweek*, pp. 18, 19.

McQuail, D. (1991). Mass media in the public interest: Towards a framework of norms for media performance. In J. Curran & M. Gurevitch (Eds.), *Mass media in society* (pp. 68-81). New York: Routledge & Kegan Paul.

Meehan, E. (1991). "Holy commodity fetish, Batman!": The political economy of a commercial intertext. In R. E. Pearson & W. Uricchio (Eds.), *The many lives of the Batman: Critical approaches to a superhero and his media* (pp. 47-65). New York: Routledge & Kegan Paul.

Merger plans for HCTV. (1992, November 17). *Wall Street Journal*, p. B10.

Meyrowitz, J. (1985). *No sense of place: The impact of electronic media on social behavior*. New York: Oxford University Press.

Michalowska, A. (1990, September 10). Benetton Barbie. *Advertising Age*, p. 83.

Miles, L. (1993, May 24). And now: Radio infomercials! *Mediaweek*, p. 2.

Miles, L. (1994, April 11). Clutter comes to public TV. *Mediaweek*, p. 10.

Miller, C. (1992, February 3). MTV "video capsule" features spots for music retailers, corporate sponsors. *Marketing News*, p. 5.

Miller, C. (1994, November 7). Stones strut their marketing stuff. *Marketing Week*, pp. 1, 18.

Miller, M. C. (1986). Deride and conquer. In T. Gitlin (Ed.), *Watching television* (pp. 183-228). New York: Pantheon.

Miller, M. C. (1990). End of story. In M. C. Miller (Ed.), *Seeing through movies* (pp. 186-246). New York: Pantheon.

Miller, R. (1989, December 11). No escaping ads. *Advertising Age*, p. 34.

Millman, J. (1991, February 4). High school hype. *Forbes*, p. 117.

Millman, N. (1992, November 26). Will the violent "Home Alone 2" and its product tie-ins become victims of their own commercialism? *Chicago Tribune*, p. B1.

Montgomery, K. C. (1989). *Target: Prime time*. New York: Oxford University Press.

More companies tune in to PBS. (1991, April 22). *Fortune*, p. 17.

Morreale, J., & Buzzard, K. (1992). The serialized mini-drama: A new trend in advertising. In S. R. Danna (Ed.), *Advertising and popular culture: Studies in variety and versatility* (pp. 94-102). Bowling Green, OH: Bowling Green State University Press.

Moshavi, S. D. (1993, March 22). Lifetime finds niche in advertiser co-production. *Broadcasting*, p. 42.

Motz, M. F. (1983). "I want to be a Barbie doll when I grow up": The cultural significance of the Barbie doll. In C. D. Geist & J. Nachbar (Eds.), *The popular culture reader* (3rd ed.) (pp. 122-136). Bowling Green, OH: Bowling Green University Popular Press.

MTV's Pittman gets "physical" with Six Flags. (1992, June 1). *Advertising Age*, p. 42.

Murdock, G. (1982). Large corporations and the control of communications industries. In M. Gurevitch, T. Bennett, J. Curran, & J. Woollacott (Eds.), *Culture, society and the media* (118-150). New York: Methuen.

Murphy, R. (1993, May 21). Losing pitcher. *Entertainment Weekly*, pp. 6-7.

Murray, J. (1991, September/October). TV in the classroom: News or Nikes? *Extra!*, p. 6.

Mussey, D. (1995, February 6). Benetton, German retailers squabble. *Advertising Age*, p. 46.

New-media summit called. (1994, September 26). *Advertising Age*, pp. 1, 8.

Nothing simpler than a movie tie-in. Not. (1991, September 16). *Adweek*, p. 12.

Nowak, G. J., & Phelps, J. (1994). Conceptualizing the integrated marketing communications' phenomenon: An examination of its impact on advertising practices and its implications for advertising research. *Journal of Current Issues and Research in Advertising, 16*(1), 49-66.

On the air at Channel One. (1992, June 22). *Adweek*, p. 9.

100 leading national advertisers. (1995, January 2). *Advertising Age*, p. 12.

Ourusoff, A., with Ozanian, M., Brown, P. B., & Starr, J. (1992, September 1-14). What's in a name? *Financial World*, pp. 32-37, 40, 45-49.

Paskowski, M., & Pfaff, F. (1986, February). A 15-second time bomb? *Marketing and Media Decisions*, pp. 36-37, 40.

PBS rejects another Oscar-winning documentary. (1994, July/August). *Extra!*, p. 21.

Penney prepares video network. (1992, August 24). *Brandweek*, p. 8.

Petersen, L. (1991, June 24). Promotions get better next time around. *Adweek*, p. 20.

Petersen, L. M. (1993, October 4). Demo derby. *Brandweek*, pp. 1, 6.

Pleased to be TV's Wal-Mart. (1993, July 12). *Advertising Age*, pp. 12, 14.

Postman, N. (1985). *Amusing ourselves to death: Public discourse in the age of show business*. New York: Penguin.

Postman, N., & Powers, S. (1992). *How to watch TV news*. New York: Penguin.

Pratkanis, A., & Aronson, E. (1991). *Age of propaganda: The everyday use and abuse of persuasion*. New York: Freeman.

Presbrey, F. (1968/1929). *The history and development of advertising*. New York: Greenwood.

Preston, I. L. (1994). *The tangled web they weave: Truth, falsity, and advertisers*. Madison: University of Wisconsin Press.

Prime-time network television viewing. (1991). In R. Abelman, *Instructor's manual for mass media VI* (p. 119). New York: Longman.

Prince, S. (1992). *Visions of empire: Political imagery in contemporary American film*. New York: Praeger.

Print. (1992, April 27). *Mediaweek*, p. 25.

The private life of public broadcasting. (1994, January/February). *Extra!*, p. 23.

Product placement brings movies, TV shows to life. (1992, September). *PR Services*, p. 48.

Quindlen, A. (1994, October 8). Quid pro quo. *New York Times*, p. 23.

Raffio, R. (1990, April 25). Events marketing: Art as advertising. *Variety*, pp. 112, 120.

Rickard, L. (1994a, June 20). Ads find premium spot at new gas pumps. *Advertising Age*, p. 10.

Rickard, L. (1994b, June 27). In-floor ads open door to higher sales. *Advertising Age*, p. 53.

The right-wing agenda: Buying media clout. (1992, June). *Extra!*, pp. 16-17.

Roan, S. (1994, April 31). Public good or private gain? *Los Angeles Times*, pp. E1, E4.

Robins, J. M. (1991, May 27). Fall skeds trade class for mass. *Variety*, pp. 1, 99.

Robins, J. M. (1992, May 11). Ad execs prescreen for disaster. *Variety*, pp. 59, 64.

Robins, J. M. (1994a, January 24-30). Mutter over clutter. *Variety*, pp. 1, 79.

Robins, J. M. (1994b, June 13-19). Admen label fall shows "Bland X." *Variety,* pp. 1, 42.

Robins, J. M. (1994c, August 8-14). Peace, love & ancillaries. *Variety,* pp. 1, 81.

Rudinow, J. (1989a). Channel One whittles away at education. *Educational Leadership,* 47(4), 70-73.

Rudinow, J. (1989b). My view remains the same: A response to Rukeyser. *Educational Leadership,* 47(4), 76.

Ruffenach, G. (1992, June 4). Olympic backers will pay Atlanta plenty for exclusivity and ambush protection. *Wall Street Journal,* pp. B1, B3.

Safe (and dull) at TPP. (1994, March 14). *Advertising Age,* p. 22.

Sanchez, J. (1989, August 23). Watch out corn flakes—Barbie takes on breakfast. *Los Angeles Times,* pp. VI1, VI12.

Sandomir, R. (1994, July 4). In World Cup, business just sees net. *New York Times,* pp. 35, 38.

Savan, L. (1994). *The sponsored life: Ads, TV, and American culture.* Philadelphia: Temple University Press.

Schiller, H. I. (1989). *Culture Inc.: The corporate takeover of public expression.* New York: Oxford University Press.

Schiller, H. I. (1993, July 12). Public way or private road? *The Nation,* pp. 64-66.

Schlossberg, H. (1991a, May 27). Olympic ambushers lie in wait for official sponsors. *Marketing News,* p. 18.

Schlossberg, H. (1991b, July 22). Fans favor corporate sponsors in tennis, golf. *Marketing News,* p. 19.

Schlossberg, H. (1991c, October 14). Health club TV targeting an audience that can't click back. *Marketing News,* pp. 1, 15.

Schlossberg, H. (1992, April 13). Cash-strapped groups dial AT&T to ring up corporate sponsorships. *Marketing News,* p. 7.

Schreiber, A. (1993, June 21). Generation X the next big event target. *Advertising Age,* p. S3.

Schudson, M. (1986). *Advertising, the uneasy persuasion.* New York: Basic Books.

Schwartz, J., with Hurt, H. (1988, September 26). Wing-tip rock and roll. *Newsweek,* pp. 48, 49.

Sebastian, P. (1992, February 19). Arts groups go after corporate sponsors with all the brashness of the Big Top. *Wall Street Journal,* pp. B1, B5.

Selnow, G. W., & Gilbert, R. R. (1993). *Society's impact on television: How the viewing public shapes television programming.* Westport, CT: Praeger.

Shaw, J. (1993, September 24). But can they spell potato? *Entertainment Weekly,* p. 12.

Shaw, R. (1990). An adjunct to the advertising business? *The Political Quarterly,* 61(4), 375-380.

Serafin, R., & Fahey, A. (1991, April 8). GM tries "documercial." *Advertising Age,* p. 58.

Sharkey, B. (1991, April 15). Barbie to Petra: You're no friend of mine. *Adweek,* p. 16.

Sharkey, B. (1994, August 28). The secret rules of ratings. *New York Times,* pp. B1, B29.

Sharkey, B., & Battaglio, S. (1992, May 18). This summer, it's one world under Coke. *Adweek's Marketing Week,* p. 4.

Shoemaker, P., & Reese, S. D. (1991). *Mediating the message: Theories of influences on mass media content.* New York: Longman.

Simons, J. (1985, June 6). Mattel's Barbie grows into marketer's dream. *Advertising Age,* p. 20.

Simkins, J. (1986). *Sponsorship 1986.* London: The Economist Publications.

Slate, L. (1993, January 24). The subtle side of TV marketing. *Los Angeles Times*, p. 77.

Sloan, P. (1992, July 6). Dan stays alive at Reebok. *Advertising Age*, p. 4.

Sloan, P. (1995, May 8). Brands are back. *Advertising Age*, pp. 1, 40.

Smythe, D. (1977). Communications: Blindspot of western Marxism. *Canadian Journal of Political and Social Theory, 1*(3), 1-27.

Spain, W. (1994, August 1). Blimps no longer just flights of fancy. *Advertising Age*, pp. 27, 28.

Spethmann, B. (1992, April 13). Whittle fine-tunes research. *Advertising Age*, p. 34.

Spethmann, B., & Benezra, K. (1994, November 21). Co-branded or be damned. *Brandweek*, pp. 21-24.

Steenhuysen, J. (1993, October 11). Custom publishing is catching on. *Advertising Age*, pp. S24, S25.

Stein, M. L. (1994, May 7). Dangling a $500 million ad budget. *Editor & Publisher*, pp. 13, 14.

Stern, C. (1993, May 24). The single-sponsor comes to cable. *Broadcasting & Cable*, p. 70.

Stern, C. (1994, December 19). FCC raises roof on TV ownership. *Broadcasting & Cable*, pp. 6, 8.

Stewart, D. (1989, December). In the cutthroat world of sales, child's play is serious business. *Smithsonian*, pp. 73-76, 78, 80-83.

Strasser, S. (1989). *Satisfaction guaranteed: The making of the American mass market*. New York: Pantheon.

Strauss G., & Reeves, L. D. (1992, September 8). A fine line becomes finer. *USA Today*, p. B6.

Students give passing grade to products advertised in class. (1991, April 29). *Marketing News*, p. 34.

Susman, A. (1994, August 8). New media and brand reformation. *Advertising Age*, p. 18.

Syedain, H. (1992, April 2). BBDO: A "place-based" approach for Frito-Lay. *Marketing*, p. 10.

Szathmary, R. R. (1992, May). Newspapers fight back: Read all about it! *Sales & Marketing Management*, pp. 57-62.

Teinowitz, I. (1992, May 11). United, McDonald's make skies friendlier and tastier for kids. *Advertising Age*, p. 70.

Teinowitz, I. (1995, January 30). Hanging in the balance. *Advertising Age*, pp. 1, 8.

3M's global hope. (1988, September). *Marketing and Media Decisions*, pp. 66, 67.

Timberg, B. (1982). The rhetoric of the camera in television soap opera. In H. Newcomb (Ed.), *Television: The critical view* (3rd ed.) (pp. 132-147). New York: Oxford University Press.

Top 300 magazines by gross revenues. (1995, January 2). *Advertising Age*, p. 15.

Turner checks out. (1993, March 1). *Advertising Age*, p. 16.

Turow, J. (1982). Unconventional programs on commercial television: An organizational perspective. In J. S. Ettema & D. C. Whitney (Eds.), *Individuals in mass media organizations: Creativity and constraint* (pp. 107-129). Beverly Hills: Sage.

Twentysomethings: Facts and feelings. (1995, February 6). *Advertising Age*, p. 27.

Tyrer, K. (1992, November 2). License to overkill. *Adweek*, pp. 48, 50, 52, 54.

Underwood, E. (1993a, March 22). Marketers, retailers line up to ride home shopping's highway. *Brandweek*, p. 8.

Underwood, E. (1993b, April 19). "Why I'm a home shopper." *Brandweek*, pp. 23-24, 26, 28.

Upshaw, L. (1990, December). Calling all clutterbusters. *Media and Marketing Decisions,* pp. 101-102.

U.S. agency brands ranked by gross income. (1995, January 2). *Advertising Age,* p. 13.

U.S. Bureau of the Census. (1994). *Statistical abstract of the United States 1994* (114th ed.). Washington, DC: U.S. Bureau of the Census.

Vadahra, D. (1993, August 16). My, how TV spots have changed! *Advertising Age,* p. 16.

Verity, J. W., with Hof, R. D. (1994, November 14). The Internet. *Business Week,* pp. 80-86, 88.

Wallenstein, A. (1995, May 8). Fox pumps up the clutter. *Advertising Age,* p. 42.

Ward, A. (1991, September 9). Zapping takes bit out of radio results. *Advertising Age,* p. 52.

Warner, F. (1994, October 17). Choose your partner. *Superbrands: An Adweek supplement,* pp. 16, 18, 20, 22.

Wasko, J., Phillips, M., & Purdie C. (1993). Hollywood meets Madison Avenue: The commercialization of US films. *Media, Culture and Society,* 15, 271-293.

Wentz, L. (1993, November 29). New coffee romance; same old problem. *Advertising Age,* p. 3.

Wernick, A. (1991). *Promotional culture: Advertising, ideology and symbolic expression.* Newbury Park, CA: Sage.

Whalen, J. (1993, December 6). Cigarette interest flags in racing. *Advertising Age,* p. 28.

What's hot. (1992, October 12). *Advertising Age,* p. S28.

What's not. (1992, October 12). *Advertising Age,* p. S28.

Whittle communications empire now gone. (1994, October 3). *Advertising Age,* p. 2.

Whittle update. (1993, Summer). Big noise. *Adbusters Quarterly* (Suppl. Summer), p. 18.

Wicklein, J. (1989, February 26). Time for a public broadcasting overhaul. *New York Times,* pp. H35, H41.

Wilke, M. (1995a, January 16). Liberal talk radio lacking sponsors. *Advertising Age,* p. 25.

Wilke, M. (1995b, February 6). Why Rold Gold "pretzel boy" leap looked so real. *Advertising Age,* p. 38.

Williamson, J. (1978). *Decoding advertisements: Ideology and meaning in advertising.* Boston: Marion Boyars.

Winski, J. M. (1992, August 24). "Impressionism" makes its mark on the national pastime. *Advertising Age,* pp. S2, S4.

Winters, P. (1993, July 5). Leonard Marsh: Snapple. *Advertising Age,* p. S21.

Winzenburg, S. (1993, February 22). Infomercials flowering on cable TV. *Advertising Age,* p. 18.

Wolff, J. (1991, January 7). Bringing it home. *Advertising Age,* pp. C34-C35.

World's top 50 advertising organizations. (1995, April 10). *Advertising Age,* p. S18.

Wussler, K. (1992, February 17). Alternative media. *Mediaweek,* p. 34.

Zapping zappers. (1994, September 19). *Advertising Age,* p. 22.

Zbar, J. D. (1994a, July 28). Blockbuster's database to fuel future expansion. *Advertising Age,* p. 26.

Zbar, J. D. (1994b, August 1). Comfort factor a problem, but databases, curiosity soar from high-traffic kiosks. *Advertising Age,* p. 30.

Zbar, J. D. (1994c, August 15). Blockbuster plays into new avenues. *Advertising Age,* p. 4.

INDEX

ABOUT THE AUTHOR

Matthew P. McAllister is Assistant Professor of Communication Studies at Virginia Polytechnic Institute and State University in Blacksburg, Virginia. He has published works on media criticism in *Journal of Communication, Journal of Popular Culture,* and *Journal of Popular Film and Television,* as well as several book chapters.